RONALD FIRBANK

RONALD FIRBANK

A Biography

MIRIAM J. BENKOVITZ

ALFRED · A · KNOPF

New York

1969

To the memory of my uncle

DR. S. M. BLOOMSTEIN

❧ *Foreword* ❧

To facilitate my preparation of *The Bibliography of Ronald Firbank* a few years ago, Thomas Firbank made available to me through his solicitors, Field Roscoe & Co., a number of unpublished papers—letters, literary manuscripts, and notebooks—left by Ronald Firbank. As I read them, I realized that, with the letters of Firbank in my possession and various holographs in the Henry W. and Albert A. Berg Collection of The New York Public Library, they presented the picture of a man with a far more complex personality than had hitherto been attributed to Ronald Firbank. They denuded him of a part of his amusing eccentricity, but he took on greater humanity. I determined then to write the biography of Ronald Firbank.

Thus this account depends largely on unpublished material. Any account of Firbank must start with Ifan Kyrle Fletcher's *Ronald Firbank*. The book contains not only Fletcher's admirable memoir but also personal reminiscences by Lord Berners, Vyvyan Holland, Augustus John, and Osbert Sitwell. Any critical discussion of Firbank's work must rely first on James Hafley's article in the *Arizona Quarterly* of summer 1956, "Ronald Firbank." But the manuscript material alters and enlarges all prior concepts of Firbank and his career.

The papers which I read at Field Roscoe's offices were dispersed by sale at auction in 1961. Happily I had read most of them earlier, and those which I had not I have since been allowed to see. For biographical purposes the most im-

portant papers are Firbank's letters, and of these the letters to
his mother, Lady Firbank, outweigh all others. These are the
property of a private collector who also owns as many as 450
postcards which Firbank sent to his sister, Heather Firbank.
Nothing is quoted from the postcards in this biography; all
quotations from Firbank's letters to his mother appeared first
in my book *The Bibliography of Ronald Firbank*. Some forty
letters to his sister are a part of the Fales Library, New York
University Libraries. The surviving holograph letters to Grant
Richards, Firbank's chief publisher, are mostly in my possession, but a few are the property of Alan Anderson of Edinburgh, The Lilly Library of Indiana University, and the
Library of University College London. Also at University
College London are copies of an additional thirty letters
which Firbank sent to Richards. Fortunately the text of the
other side of this correspondence exists in the copies of Grant
Richards's replies mounted in his firm's letter-books and preserved in the University of Illinois Library. Similarly, copies
of letters from Richards to Lady Firbank and others and from
George Wiggins, Richards's manager, to Ronald Firbank are
at the University of Illinois. Stuart Rose owns the letters
which Firbank wrote to him when Rose was connected with
Brentano's, Firbank's American publisher in his lifetime. An
invaluable exchange of letters between Carl Van Vechten and
Firbank is a part of the Berg Collection. A few other letters
from Firbank survive, but those are the major ones. As for his
literary manuscripts, typescripts, and notebooks, they are
scattered to the Berg Collection, private collections, the Fales
Library, and the libraries of three universities: Harvard,
Rochester, and Texas.

To all these, to the trustees of The New York Public Library, Astor, Lenox and Tilden Foundation, and to Thomas
Firbank I am grateful for their generosity in allowing me to

read and reread the Firbank materials. I am indebted also to the following for expert assistance: The Beinecke Rare Book and Manuscript Library (Yale University), Mrs. Charles Szladits of the Henry W. and Albert A. Berg Collection (The New York Public Library), the late Miss Nancy Cunard, Mr. Robert Murray Davis, the staff of the Fales Library (New York University Libraries), the Honorable Thomas G. D. Galbraith, the late Mr. Vyvyan Holland, Sir Shane Leslie, Mr. Jean Pozzi, Miss Jane Rollins, Miss Gladys Brownell and the staff of the Skidmore College Library, Mr. Jean Schlumberger, Mr. Graham Stainforth, Mr. Sewell Stokes, Mr. Graham Storey, the late Mr. Carl Van Vechten, and Mr. J. Steven Watson.

I wish also to acknowledge various kinds of help from The Reverend A. J. Adams, Mr. William Anderson, Mr. Ian Angus, Mr. Timoth d'Arch-Smith, Mr. Walter Armytage, Mr. Bart Auerbach, Mr. Brian Belk, Mr. R. C. Bird, Mr. G. P. Bowen, Miss Dorothy W. Bridgwater, Mr. P. Allen of the British Museum Newspaper Library, Father Burns, Mr. Ivor Burton, Father Wilfred Burton, Mr. J. Longden of the Café Royal, the University Registry of the University of Cambridge, Lord David Cecil, Mr. F. A. Chapman, Mr. Anatole Chujoy, Mr. R. E. Clifford, Mr. Alan Clodd, Mr. Collins of The Coopers, Miss Geraldine Counahan, *The Daily Telegraph and Morning Post*, Mr. L. I. Davidson, Father Stephen Dean, Mr. R. B. Downs, Mr. Basil Drennan, Mr. R. F. Drewery, the Most Reverend Joseph A. Durick, Mr. Joseph W. Egerer, Mr. J. M. Eyles, Mr. Frank Faraone, Monsignor Philip Flanagan, Mr. Ifan Kyrle Fletcher, Mr. George Ford, Mrs. Stanley Fuller, Mr. Donald C. Gallup, Monsignor Matino Giusti, Mr. Charles F. Gosnell, Mr. Patrick Gregory, Mr. Theodore Grieder, Mr. Philip Lyman and Miss Frances Steloff of Gotham Book Mart, Mr. Bruce Harkness, David Higham As-

sociates, Ltd., Mrs. Mary M. Hirth, Mr. and Mrs. Anthony
Hobson, Lord Horder, Mr. Herbert Howarth, Mrs. Mary
Hyde, Miss Julia Hysham, Mr. Frank Paluka of the Library
of the University of Iowa, Mr. Evan James, Mrs. Augustus
John, Mr. Laurence Josephs, Mr. Philip Kaplan, Miss Sonja
P. Karsen, Sir Geoffrey and Lady Keynes, Mr. Jean Lambert,
Mrs. Anne Wyndham Lewis, Miss Carolyn T. Lee, Mr. Mark
Lutz, Mr. Eric Maschwitz, Mr. Edmund Maloney, Mr. John
Masters, Mr. Walter Michel, Mr. A. T. Miller, Miss E. Alice
Moshier, Miss Winifred A. Myers, The New York Public Li-
brary, Mr. Nigel Nicolson, the University Registry of Ox-
ford University, Miss Kathleen B. Francis of the Library
of the University of Richmond, Routledge & Kegan Paul Ltd.,
The Reverend T. P. Rumsey, Mr. Anthony Rota, the late Mr.
Bertram Rota, Mr. Martin Secker, Father Brocard Sewell,
Miss Joan Siegfried, Mr. and Mrs. George F. Sims, Sir Osbert
Sitwell, Mr. Sacheverell Sitwell, Father Vincent Smith, Mr.
Joseph Solomon, Mr. Ralph E. McCoy of University Libraries,
Southern Illinois University, Mr. Francis W. Steer, Sterling
Memorial Library (Yale University), Mr. Walter Talevi,
Misses Barbara and Georgette Tallerman, Mr. Harold J.
Tanant, Miss Mary P. Waesche of The Tate Gallery, Mr. Alan
G. Thomas, Mr. John Thorn, *The Times Literary Supplement,*
Mrs. Carl Van Vechten, Mr. R. W. T. Vint, A. P. Watt &
Son, Mr. Donald Wing, Mr. Edwin Wolf 2nd, Miss Marjorie
G. Wynne.

A special acknowledgment is due to Bishop G. A. Chase,
who sent me names of Ronald Firbank's contemporaries at
Trinity Hall, Cambridge, and to those contemporaries who
replied to my inquiries about Firbank. They are Mr. W. H.
Adgey-Edgar, Mr. C. A. Chaplin, Mr. Sidney H. Haughton,
Mr. E. G. Hornidge, Mr. David Hughes and Dr. W. Hywel
Jones, who wrote in behalf of Mr. Hughes, Sir Eric Redeal,

The Reverend L. Whitcombe, and Mr. S. H. Woodhouse.

I want also to thank those people who remained nameless to me—taxi drivers, drivers of hired cars, hotel porters, chance passers-by, and the police—who so kindly helped me locate the numerous places in which Firbank lived, all of which I attempted to inspect insofar as the state of the world and my own limitations permitted.

Last of all I wish to record my gratitude to the late Mr. John D. Gordan, Sir Rupert Hart-Davis, and Mr. Herbert Weinstock, who invariably had wise solutions to the numerous problems with which I confronted them, and to Miss Mary E. Williams, who had the kindness and the stamina to read this book three times and to offer valuable comments at each reading.

Miriam J. Benkovitz

Saratoga Springs, New York

❧ *Illustrations* ❧

❧ *Note* ❧

Names or initials in parentheses in the footnotes indicate the owner of the letter, manuscript, or typescript cited. In the case of Ronald Firbank's letters to Grant Richards and George Wiggins, those belonging to the biographer have no ownership indicated; similarly, all letters addressed to her are in the biographer's possession, and the fact is not further stated here. All letters addressed to Sewell Stokes are in his possession, and those to Richard Buckle are assumed to be in Mr. Buckle's possession. In all other cases where no owner is shown, the letter or document is a part of a large collection, and the name of the owner may be found in the Foreword (p. viii). In a few instances the whereabouts of a letter is unknown; that fact is also stated in parentheses. This book was in press when, in December 1968, Sotheby & Co., London, offered for sale by auction holographs of eighteen of the thirty letters designated here as copies in the possession of the Library of University College London. The eighteen letters, hitherto known to exist only in copies, were purchased by E. L. Dieff Inc., New York, and in turn by the Humanities Research Center, the University of Texas.

A key to the initials and other short forms used in the footnotes follows.

MJB   the biographer, Miriam J. Benkovitz
Berg   The Henry W. and Albert A. Berg Collection, the New York Public Library

Fales   The Fales Library, the New York University
         Libraries
RF   Arthur Annesley Ronald Firbank
HJGF   Lady Harriette Jane Garrett Firbank, Ronald Fir-
         bank's mother
HF   Heather Firbank, Ronald Firbank's sister
GR   Grant Richards, Ronald Firbank's publisher
UCL   Library, University College London
CVV   Carl Van Vechten, Ronald Firbank's American
         sponsor

Part I
1886–1915

HE HAD GONE ABOUT HERE AND THERE, TINTING
HIS PERSONALITY AFTER THE FASHION OF A VENETIAN
GLASS. CERTAINLY HE HAD WANDERED. . . . HE HAD
BEEN INTO ARCADIA, EVEN, A PLACE WHERE ARTIFICIAL
TEMPERAMENTS SO SELDOM GET—THEIR
NEAREST APPROACH BEING, PERHAPS, A MATINÉE OF
A *Winter's Tale*. MANY, INDEED, THOUGHT HIM
INTERESTING. HE HAD GROPED SO. . . .

Vainglory, pp. 21–2.

❧ I ❧

Immediately after Ronald Firbank, age eighteen, returned from a summer holiday at Lac d'Annecy to Paris for the continuation of his language studies, he received a letter from his mother—Baba, he called her throughout her life—which began by thanking him for his own "dear letter." It went on:

> Yes darling "Baba" *does* & *ever will* sympathize with you. Your soulful ideas thrill me with pleasure & wonderment I read & *re*read all your writings over & over again . . . I do fear you take far too much out of yourself writing and thinking out all these plays and stories I am sure you cannot rest and sleep as you ought . . . every spare minute you should rest your Brain—With all your vivid imagination it must be forever at concert-pitch![1]

Implicit in that letter is the crux of Firbank's life, the ardent love which he and his mother had for each other. Their relationship determined his growth as a man and a writer.

No one in the history of English letters has been more dedicated to the literary vocation than Ronald Firbank. Nothing lessened his fervor. Until his ninth novel was published in 1924, he had got back not "one farthing piece" for all his work, and even then he received less than a thousand dol-

1. HJGF to RF, Chislehurst, September 25, 1904 (Berg).

lars.[2] Critical recognition of his novels was so scant that when
he had a thoroughly favorable notice in an American periodical, he carried the piece about with him and showed it to
anyone who would look.[3] Nevertheless, his earliest inclina-
tion was toward literature—in 1901 when his younger
brother, Bertie, spent 4s. 6d. on *Stalkie & Company,* he did so
with the idea of forming a library exactly like Ronald's[4]—
and his enduring dream was to be a writer. From time to time
Firbank professed an ambition for various careers such as
diplomacy, a parliamentary clerkship, or service at the Vatican; but he kept his dedication to writing.

   To justify it, to fulfill his dream, Firbank had first to face
his relationship with his mother; he had to adjust to it. Her
"passionate gentleness" was essential to him when at eighteen
he was still immature and groping. Because he was an artist
and vulnerable at every age to the sweetness as well as the
pain and cruelty of life, he needed the enveloping warmth of
Baba's love. It was a refuge. But it was also a frustration. Her
love for him and his dependence on her inhibited his comic
perception of the environment which she made. Yet her environment and the ritual of her life provided the materials of
his fiction. Only after he had maintained for a period of several years a compromise with his attachment to her could he
resolve in 1912 to exploit those materials, that is, to write and
publish a full-length novel. From that time, his whole life
went to developing the matter and manner of his fiction.

   That last statement exaggerates the integrity of Ronald

2. Cf. RF to CVV, Bordighera, [April 22, 1923], April 28, 1923, May 26,
1923; Rome, September 25, 1924; RF to HF, Rome, October 3, 1924.
3. Cf. Nancy Cunard to MJB, Mallorca, [1958]; Sewell Stokes: "A Recent
Genius," *Pilloried!* (London, [1928]), pp. 222–3; CVV: "Ronald Firbank,"
The Double Dealer, III (April 1922), 185–7.
4. Cf. Hubert Somerset Firbank to RF, Windsor, October 15, 1901 (Berg).

Firbank's life. The materials got first through observation of
Baba's circumstances were useless without intellectual focus
and artistic form. The intellectual focus came from the kind
of education and experience he had. It was a part of his growing up. The artistic form was another matter. Firbank shared
with other writers of the early twentieth century—Joyce,
Pound, Ford, Woolf, Eliot, all giants by comparison—the
struggle for a form by which he could convey the inner reality
of what he talked about. Firbank needed a means to impart at
one level his amusement and, at another, his dismay with the
human scene at a time of cultural and social upheaval of
cataclysmic proportions. He realized this form only after hesitant and complex artistic decisions. Furthermore, the attachment to his mother precluded simplicity or serenity. As long
as she lived she dominated his emotions. She shaped his perceptions and part of his taste. This control made frustrations
which were not literary ones. Indeed, the devotion between
mother and son created tensions for him which were limiting
or even crippling in their effect.

As might be expected, by comparison with his mother's, the
influence of his father, Joseph Thomas Firbank, was unimportant. Born in 1850, Joseph Thomas was the first son of another Joseph Firbank, whose expectations when he went to
work as a colliery "putter" at the age of seven amounted only
to life as a miner in the pits of Bishop Auckland, Durham.
But in his twenty-second year, having educated himself as best
he could in evening classes and progressed from the pits to
day labor on the new railway construction between Bishop
Auckland and Weardale, this elder Joseph saw opportunity
and seized it. In 1841 he secured a subcontract at a profitable
figure on the Woodhead Railway Tunnel. By 1845 he held another contract on a section of the Midland Railway, and in

1854 he began work in Newport on the Monmouthshire Railway and Canal Company. More contracts at greater profits as well as the sale of land bought with an eye to the requirements of the railways built a fortune.

Of course there was something more, something intensely personal, in Joseph Firbank's success. Work was his obsession. It may not have been his laborers', but he did everything possible to get the best out of them. He could jump into a ditch to show them how to use a pick; he served them oatmeal and barley water when the weather was warm or provided them with beef and beer in an affectionate gesture; but he also cursed them with a wide-ranging vocabulary. His faith was in work. Religion he left to those who needed it. Holidays interrupted his routine and disordered his habits of eating plain fare and getting to bed by eight and up by five. The machinery of construction and the practical solutions of grades and cuts were the only beauty Joseph saw.

He made the environment in which Thomas grew up. Joseph's wife, who had been Mrs. Sarah Black Fryatt, a widow when she married him, was a woman of strong character and considerable education. She died when Thomas was only four. When Joseph married again, he chose for his second wife a woman less his superior than the first Mrs. Firbank. In any case, this second wife, who bore five children in scarcely more than five years, had little time for Thomas. So Joseph, with his healthy respect for learning, sent his son to school, proudly allowing him to end his education at Cheltenham College. The boy's attendance there was a triumph over class origin. Although Cheltenham College was less than twenty-five years old when Thomas Firbank entered, it had already acquired respectability among England's public schools, and the Victorian public school was a sure step up the social ladder. Young Firbank was at Cheltenham, living in Newick House, from August 1864 until December 1866.[5]

Thomas was almost seventeen when he left Cheltenham. He had been schooled in the latest commercial methods there, but as soon as he had enjoyed a brief holiday, that is, in 1867, his father put him to work on the fifteen miles of railway construction between Radlett and the London terminus which was the predecessor of St. Pancras Station. Life for the boy was not easy. He was expected to keep his father's hours and to work at least as hard as the older Firbank. By degrees Thomas came to play a more important part in his father's business, but he was never his own man. Joseph Firbank kept a sharp eye on his son's activities. He was suspicious of pleasure or indulgence. Once when he found a hunter stabled with the cart horse, he said to Thomas, "Eh lad! That woarnt pull a load o' muck!" Joseph distrusted everything but hard work and strict attention to the job at hand; what he got "for nowt," he said, he valued "at nowt."

Thomas soon showed that, except in general appearance— a "short, rotund man, his head set low on a wide neck"—he resembled his father very little. Joseph's taste for simple, long-lasting clothes differed considerably from his son's foppishness. Thomas was fashionable and impeccable in his dress. With the help of Macassar oil, he reduced his crisp curls (also like Joseph's) to mere waves; and his mouth, better formed but weaker than his father's, he enhanced with a careful mustache. He had none of his father's resolve or boldness of vision. Indeed, he took pride in small accomplishments, and the older man's decisiveness was never more than half-hearted firmness in Thomas.[6] When at thirty-three he married Har-

5. L. I. Davidson, Librarian, The College, to MJB, Cheltenham, October 20, 1966.
6. Cf. Ifan Kyrle Fletcher: *Ronald Firbank A Memoir* (London, 1930), pp. 13–18; Frederick McDermott: *The Life and Work of Joseph Firbank, J.P., D.L.* (London, 1887).

riette Jane Garrett, a beautiful woman who was only a year
younger but some inches taller than he, Thomas willingly exchanged the autocracy of his father for that of his wife.

Miss Garrett was born in 1851, the fourth daughter of
James Perkins Garrett, Rector of Kellistown, County Carlow,
Ireland. Kellistown, six or eight miles southeast of the city of
Carlow on a little-traveled byroad, is today only a townland.
A few houses line the road, there is one shop, and the church
which the Reverend Garrett served is abandoned and dilapi-
dated. Standing behind a stone wall and a large iron gate at
the northwestern edge of Kellistown is the shell of the church,
which was made of gray stone partially covered with stucco.
Its tower is Norman square with Gothic modifications. The
churchyard is overgrown, and black flies buzz in the tall grass.
The graveyard, which is now filled with nettles, is marked
with several nineteenth-century versions of the Celtic cross;
legends on the gravestones have long been defaced by
weather. No doubt the Kellistown church is the victim of the
automobile and the ease with which churchgoers can hear a
sermon in Carlow and get back to Kellistown in time for
Sunday dinner. It was a more active and vigorous community
in Garrett's day, drawing its parishioners from the farmers
and cattlemen who professed Anglicanism in that part of the
county.

In any case, the Garretts had wider horizons than Kellistown's. The family was descended from Sir William Garrett,
Lord Mayor of London in 1555. Five of this family, all
brothers, had come to Ireland with Oliver Cromwell when he
landed at Dublin on August 15, 1649. Of these, two were
killed at the siege of Bunratty in the county of Clare and at
least one settled at Kilgarron or Janeville near Fenagh in
County Carlow. There by the Act of Settlement in the reign
of Charles II the Garretts secured two parcels of land, Bally-

gerrel or Garrett, amounting to about 567 acres, and Bally-walden, amounting to about 75 acres. Various Garretts were put to rest in the burial ground of the church at Fenagh with inscriptions attesting to their merits. One who died in 1759 is called the "charitable Thomas Garrett," and James, who died on July 17, 1818, is labeled as without "panegyric, since no eulogy would do justice to his merits." He was twice High Sheriff of County Carlow, and his son William, Harriette Jane's grandfather, held the same office in 1806; the year before, he had been appointed captain of the First Carlow Yeomanry Cavalry. Furthermore, the men in the family were university men. This grandfather, William, had matriculated at Trinity Hall, Cambridge; and Harriette Jane's father, when he was eighteen, had entered Trinity College, Dublin, to emerge five years later with a B.A. degree.[7] And they married their own kind, daughters of Irish landowners. The Reverend J. P. Garrett's wife, and thus Harriette Jane's mother, was Caroline Anne Elizabeth, daughter of Hugh Moore, Esq., of Eglantine House, County Down; her sister was Priscilla, Countess Annesley.[8] That was a connection in which the Garretts took pride. Harriette Jane, Mrs. Firbank, testified to that pride in many ways after her marriage but most obviously when she gave her second son, Arthur Annesley Ronald, almost the same name as an Annesley cousin.

Whatever Harriette Jane's connections and background, marriage with Thomas Firbank had its advantages. At her age, thirty-two, not to be married was disquieting. Youth was gone, and beauty was sure to fade. Opportunities in an isolated

7. Cf. John Ryan: *The History and Antiquities of the County of Carlow* (Dublin, 1883), pp. 364–5; Edward Walford: *The County Families of the United Kingdom* (London, 1860), p. 247; Geraldine Counahan, Trinity College, to MJB, Dublin, January 24, 1967.
8. Second wife of William Richard Annesley, third Earl (second creation, 1789).

Irish village were scant. To compound this difficulty, Harriette Jane Garrett was a Protestant in a county whose chief city, Carlow, is the seat of the Roman Catholic diocese of Kildare and Leighlin; she was a member of a minority, a fact which cut her off from much of the life of the county. It was also a fact which fed her frustrations. How she behaved as a girl and a young woman is unknown; but once she was Mrs. Firbank she became increasingly imperious. With the conviction that it "made things easy," she invariably "thought for" anyone who would let her.[9]

That she did so, however docile a man Thomas Firbank may have been, implies a marriage unsatisfactory in many ways. That conjecture is supported not by documentation but by hindsight, by the knowledge of what Mrs. Firbank made of her sons. No statement exists from either Thomas or Harriette Jane about the other or about their life together. In the absence of contrary proof, the Firbank family life, at least at first, takes on the conventional and sugary quality of popular Victorian fiction.

It was one of affluence, as Thomas's financial position made possible the pleasures and advantages of wealth. In the autumn of 1883 the bridal couple moved into a London residence at 40 Clarges Street. This was close to Piccadilly, long considered, with the possible exception of Park Lane, the finest residential street in London. Perhaps Clarges Street was nearer the wrong than the right end of Piccadilly, too remote from Constitution Hill, to be wholly fashionable. Still, the Firbanks were in the right neighborhood and at the same time in the center of the hustle and bustle of the great city; and if they craned a bit fom their upper windows, they had a view of the peaceful beauty of Green Park before a strip of it was

9. A. E. Hallett to RF, Kington Magna, Gillingham, Dorset, February 16, 1925 (Berg).

sacrificed to widen Piccadilly. At 40 Clarges Street they kept
a carriage and a fine pair of horses. There, at Mrs. Firbank's
urging, they began to collect *objets d'art*—English porcelains
including Derby, Bow, and Chelsea figures, a Bristol tea service originally the property of Lord Nelson, Dresden groups
and figures, Sèvres serving dishes, carved ivory statuettes, a
panel of Gobelin tapestry, a three-leaf screen with old
Beauvais tapestry—and fine old English and French furniture.[1] These were not mere museum pieces; they were used,
they were a part of the Firbanks' daily life. The screen stood
before the door to the butler's pantry, and the Sèvres serving
dishes came to the table. Louis XV tables were scattered
through the drawing room, which was illuminated with Louis
XV wall lights of ormolu chased with cherubs' heads and
scrolls, all reflected over and over in a carved and gilt Chippen-
dale mirror.

In this ambiance, though not at 40 Clarges Street, Ronald
Firbank spent his early childhood. He and his elder brother,
Joseph Sydney, were both born there, Joey on September 30,
1884, and Ronald (Arthur Annesley Ronald, always called
Artie by his family) on January 17, 1886. But at the end of
that June, at his residence, St. Julian's near Newport in
Monmouthshire, old Joseph died, leaving Thomas his chief
heir. After some litigation and the threat of more, Thomas
became the owner of extensive properties. Within the year he
had moved his growing family—by that time Mrs. Firbank
was pregnant with their third child, Hubert Somerset
(Bertie), born May 27, 1887—to The Coopers, Chislehurst,
Kent. The Firbanks had already made plans to leave London,
and Thomas had acquired Morden Lodge in Surrey. The

1. The entire collection was sold at auction by Messrs. Christie, Manson &
Woods on May 18–19, 1904. It brought something less than £9,000, with the
first day's sale amounting to exactly £3,952. 1s. The sales catalogue showing
prices is a part of the Berg Collection.

Coopers, however, was much grander. The estate consisted then of about a hundred acres. It is situated on a country road running east from Chislehurst past the old inn, The Tiger's Head, and the Rectory Cottages, where it becomes Hawkwood Lane, known in Firbank's time as Botany Bay Lane. The house itself, built in the eighteenth century, was backed against a brick wall which edged the lane; the front windows looked out over a gently sloping lawn planted with flowers, ancient cedars, and a tulip tree close by the house. The kitchen garden and the stables were on opposite sides of the lawn with the stables to the east, and beyond was a park of fine trees. To the east, also, was the right-of-way through the estate's fields; it was entered from the lane by a stile and, passing the end of a lime tree walk, looked off toward Orpington.[2] Within, the rooms were numerous and well proportioned, with Adam mantels and wainscoting on the main floor.

This place, which Mrs. Firbank referred to as "dear home" and once described as "looking a Paradise," was indeed an enchanting place in which to be a child. Without question it was where Firbank acquired his love of natural beauty. That he was aware of it quite young is apparent from a photograph, made when he was a small boy of perhaps six, showing him with a large nosegay on his lapel. His early compositions abound with the tulips and roses and violets in the garden at The Coopers, the birds in the trees, and the trees themselves. Inside the house was the elegance of the antique furniture and the collection of objects of *vertu*. The addition of a Worcester tea set or another ormolu clock was cause for a family council. Beauty surrounded Firbank. Naturally there were minor household disturbances. Sometimes the ice-making machine

2. Cf. E. A. Webb, G. W. Miller, and J. Beckwith: *The History of Chislehurst Its Church, Manors, and Parish* (London, 1899), pp. 210–11.

❧ II ❧

The reality was something else entirely. Most apparent under the lovely surface were two nagging problems. Joey might play cricket at a time when the athlete was king, but he was unruly and hard to manage, qualities which did not improve as he grew up. Baba always scolded and forgave him and then explained to Daddy what had happened, but soon it had to be done all over again. Artie—Ronald—was a frail boy. Osbert Sitwell maintains that when traveling in Egypt as a small child, Artie was "laid low with sunstroke" and was thereafter "delicate." Kyrle Fletcher, in his *Memoir,* declares that Artie suffered from a throat infection; Nancy Cunard says he had asthma.[1] Whatever the correct diagnosis, Artie's health was not good. He was finical about his food, he tired easily, and he caught cold with too much regularity.

Perhaps these things sharpened his perceptions. Certainly Artie understood the truth about the life of the Firbank family, that in actual fact it differed greatly from its storybook façade. His comprehension of that difference is obvious in his first novel, "Lila," which he wrote, according to his own word, in 1896, when he was only ten.[2]

Before then, the family's pattern had changed. In the early summer of 1895, at the insistence of his wife, Thomas Firbank had stood for Parliament; and on July 17, Herbert

1. Cf. Osbert Sitwell: "Ronald Firbank," *Noble Essences* (London, 1950) p. 71; Fletcher: *Ronald Firbank A Memoir,* p. 20; Nancy Cunard to MJB London, January 3, 1954.
2. Cf. RF to CVV, London, June, 22, 1925.

failed to function. Once a drunken butler attempted to serve dinner when he had "had too much"; so he was dismissed, and Mrs. Firbank declared afterward that, with the "Household & House" restored to their usual quiet, it seemed "like the millennial." Once there was a question of whether to keep a matched pair of chestnuts, but when Mr. Firbank engaged a new coachman and "hired a Break for a week," the chestnuts looked too "splendid" to let go. But on the whole the household ran smoothly enough with "Bessie, Mrs Brown and Harman" or their replacements managing it.[3] It seemed a source of grace and harmony.

Indeed, the surface perfection of their life at The Coopers made the Firbank children appear to be a trio of Little Lord Fauntleroys with a sister (a Firbank daughter, Heather, was born at The Coopers on August 27, 1888). The intimate family names embellished the impression; these were Daddy and Baba, Joey and Artie and Bertie and Baby, or Lassie, as Heather was called. So did the tea parties which each child gave, complete with written invitations, even to his brothers and sister. They wrote replies, too. One which survives is from Joey to Artie; written at Chislehurst on tiny pink notepaper, it reads, "I shall like to come to your tea party if I am not playing cricket."[4] The day and night nurseries, the separate play boxes, the pony carts and bicycles, the elegant lace-trimmed clothes—Bertie's and Heather's were sometimes indistinguishable—belong to a Victorian dream.

3. HJGF to RF, Chislehurst, May 25, 1902 (Berg); RF to HF, n.p., June 5, 1898.
4. (Berg).

Woodhouse, Deputy Sheriff of Hull and returning officer for East Hull, announced that Firbank had been elected Unionist member for East Hull. His responsibilities meant frequent absences from Chislehurst. The same year Joey had been sent away to school, and in 1896 Ronald, age ten, went too.

Ronald went to the Mortimer Vicarage School, an institution organized privately by the Reverend Mr. Cameron, vicar of the parish of St. Mary the Virgin, Stratfield Mortimer, Berkshire. He housed his students and conducted classes in St. John's House, the box-like, red brick vicarage which stands well back from the main road at the end of a quiet lane. The house was surrounded by fields, and these in turn were bordered by a sparse stand of trees. The school acquired a certain prestige from the fact that Eton College is the patron of the living at Stratfield Mortimer, and Mr. Cameron quietly kept that association before the public. In 1896 forty-nine boys, some bearing such distinguished names as Cadogan, Villiers, Beauclerk, Romilly, and Balgonie, attended the Mortimer Vicarage School. Two boys, Leonard Parker and young Firbank, made up the lower half of Class VIII, the bottom form.

Precisely what Firbank's status meant is now impossible to define. The school's records do not belong to the parish archives, and they may not exist at all. Without doubt, however, the stay at the Vicarage School was important to Firbank. It was his first venture into the hungry, untidy, competitive world of boys. He set down a lingering recollection of it a quarter of a century afterward in the equivocal innocence of Tiny and Tibi, Felix and Chicklet, the cathedral boys of *Concerning the Eccentricities of Cardinal Pirelli*.[3] Firbank appears to have made no impression on that world, inasmuch as none of his schoolmates remembered him. Obviously he was compliant in this first encounter with an institution which, like

3. See below, pp. 277–84.

every other institution, fostered impersonality, routine, and a factitious morality. A gentle, agreeable boy, he did what he was expected to do, even to an awkward participation in sports. When he had leisure, he read, preferably stories of youthful peril, and he often wandered alone in the fields near the vicarage.

It was his way of keeping his personality intact. If that makes Firbank sound solemn, it is misleading. At the age of ten he had a strong sense of the ridiculous and a lively fancy. Indeed, there is much evidence in the schoolboy of what the adult Firbank would be. His appearance was already determined. He was tall for his age and slender; his boyish face, not yet sharpened by illness, showed the features of the man: deep-set eyes, arched nose, long upper lip, a wide, full mouth, and heavy, elongated jaws. The more significant individuality was in his inner life. Away from home and from Baba's love, he found a capacity to absorb and elucidate experience. This ability was to be invaluable to him as a writer. Fabrication, of course, had a substantial role in his works, but they issued first from experience. His emphasis in 1896 was on the recording of experience rather than his reaction to it; but for Firbank action, physical fact, social occurrence were even then analogues for his private realism.

"Lila," that first novel, bears witness to the quality of the boy as well as to the reality of Firbank family life. Of "Lila," composed at Mortimer in 1896 and written in an exercise book, only this scrap survives:

d'you do, who would have [fancied] seeing you here, I thought you were still away." She spoke in a drawl, trying to quiet a rigling lap dog which she was holding in her arms. We returned last week, Lila said & have been staying with some friends of Lady Bonchester's in Wales. Wales is charm-

ing said Mrs Keston, squesing her dog who was making
violent overtuers to Lila's retrever who was laying peacea-
biley on the mat. I've just been over to the Swintons with a
message from my husband. May I perswade you to come &
have lunch with me M^iss Rivers, I'me all alone! Lila hesi-
tated I am afraid—she began. You will come? said M^rs
Keston perswasifley I am *so* dreadfully dull, Harry (aluding
to her husband) has gone rabbit shooting & wont be back
until seven. So Lila consented, & sent word by a village
child, to Lady Bonchester saying that she would not be back
till after lunch, the dog she left with the post mistress until
she returned. Mrs Keston swept out of the post office after
sending a telegram & Lila followed not sorry to have at last
something to do. Mrs Keston talked nonsence the whole
time, hardly giving Lila time to answer they passed up the
drive to the house, it was a lovely old place sairounded by a
park filed with beautiful trees, which was in full sight of the
sea. They went into the dining room, Mrs Keston put the dog
in its basket, tited her hair before a mirror, langwidly sat
down & calved a chicken. She asked the butler when the
master would be home, & then began chatering away to Lila.
It was so funney she said, when I was staying with my sister
we drove one morning to see a cousin of ours who is at a
small girls school, we were asked to stay for lunch. Miss
Raymer the head mistress asked Rachel why she did not eat
her beef, & on being told that she did not care for it under-
done, M^iss Raymer grew angry & said, waste not want not, &
eat it up, but Rachel tossed her head. I have quite good
enough blood in my family without going to a bullock for
more, she said leaving the room & slaming the door & what
did Miss Raymer say laughed Lila. She said she was "exces-
sifley vulger" & gave us a lecture on the decay of modern manners.[4]

4. (MJB). Firbank's misspellings are deliberately retained here. That practice is followed throughout wherever quotations are taken from manuscripts
and letters.

When Firbank rediscovered "Lila" among his mother's papers in 1925, he compared it to *The Young Visiters* and congratulated himself that he had had "the tact as a child not to rush headlong into print."[5] Yet in this scrap of his first novel is the nucleus of Firbank's fiction, characters isolated in self-absorption. These are the people of his later novels who never suffered the pain of individuation. Even the details in "Lila" are exact: Rachel's arrogance, the "rigling" lap dog, the hair "tited" before the mirror, and above all the telegram, which preceded the motor car as a mark of status. But to attribute to a child so keen a vision and the skill to impose it on the imagination is going too far. "Lila" is not a technical achievement. From the distance and objectivity of his first school, Firbank was simply recording his impression of the environment he knew best. It was his parents' and especially his mother's. No one has more convictions about a social group than those who, regretfully, do not belong to it.

Firbank's impression is substantiated by a letter from his sister written a year or two later, when the Firbank family was planning a holiday at an unnamed resort, probably Brighton. Heather's letter predicted in advance "a *hot* long journey" and at the end of it, the Firbank children "fighting & noisy!!!" Heather then described how Baba, their mother, would behave:

> . . . she always says when we get to the Hotel, "now Lassie you must have this room." "Yes, (to the woman who shows us to the rooms!) My little girl will have this room !! & my 2 youngest! Boys can have this, & then my *little girl's* 'Maid' can have this room" (which is up in the Attic!) & then "Sir Thomas M.P.!! can have this room when [he] comes, which

5. RF to CVV, London, June 22, 1925.

is so rare, because he's *so* busy!" & then, the old lady referring to Bertie says, "well, my youngest boy is rather nervous so he better sleep with his brother!" etc. etc.! & then we
go to dinner in the Table d'hote room, & Baba criticising
all the poor people! & then call the waiter to tell him to
complain of the ½ *raw* peas & meat!!![6]

The particulars here are different from those of "Lila," but
both start with the same materials. Both motifs are the same:
the imposition of personality.

The real importance of "Lila" is that in it Artie Firbank
looked at his mother so dispassionately. She had already attached him to her unduly. Often such an attachment derives
from a domineering mother. Mrs. Firbank was capable of
tyranny and often practiced it, but she was capable also of
immeasurable femininity and sentimentality. That was the side
she showed to Artie. The unusual affection between mother
and son came through the cultivation of dependency and an
implication of her need. Baba turned with most obvious affection not to her husband or to Joey but to Artie, and in the
next five years she made him increasingly her confidant. She
wrote to him about her worry and annoyance with Joey when
he was especially difficult, running away from Mr. Rawnsley,
who had been instructed to accompany him to a tutor in the
north of England. When she wanted Lassie to ride a particular horse, Tigress, Baba asked Artie whether it would be "quite
safe" and suggested that he tell her what to "guard against"
with Tigress. She valued his opinion and conveyed it to
Daddy when Artie told her she ought to buy a tea set because
it matched "some you've got." When The Coopers was enlarged, it was Artie with whom she anticipated enjoying the
new wing of the house. "It will be such fun," she said to him,

6. HF to RF, Chislehurst, n.d. (Berg).

"when you come home arranging the Billiard Room."[7]

Yet in "Lila," Firbank's reaction to his mother's egoism is as aggressive as Heather's. It is a fact of psychological observation that such aggression in a child is the result of frustration and is directed against the object responsible in the child's mind for the lack of satisfaction. There was, however, considerable ambiguity in Firbank's attitude toward his mother. Oscar Wilde said that "children begin by loving their parents. After a time they judge them. Rarely, if ever, do they forgive them." Ronald never got to that second stage; he could not bring himself then or ever to judge Baba. Although he resented her exercise of authority, he also admired it. That he did is suggested in verses written in the same notebook as "Lila," an incomplete piece called "Lay of the Last Nursery-maid." Its two surviving stanzas run:

> The hand was raised
> The child was there!
> bending over the back of the chair,
> A step on the staircase, a voice there came,
> Calling the nurse a terrible name
>
> She paused . . . !
> There was not time for more
> The stick went crashing thundering to the floor
> Her eyes spoke volumes, doom & woe.[8]

Too much can be made of these verses as evidence of willing dependency, especially in view of Firbank's age; he was less than twelve when he wrote them. There can be no question, however, that his reliance on his mother and the fervor of his

7. HJGF to RF, Chislehurst, September 29, 1901 (Berg). Cf. HJGF to RF, Brighton, November 7, 1901 (Berg); RF to HJGF, [Uppingham], November 22 or 23, 1900.
8. (MJB).

love for her were strong enough to suppress his aggression. Only once or twice in the next five years did he apply his satiric bent to his mother's environment. When he did, he was insecure with his subject matter and gave the piece which contained it secondary importance.

Indeed for some time to come, Artie fulfilled his mother's view of her son. Continuing at the Mortimer Vicarage School until 1900, he showed himself an obedient, gentle, but very unremarkable boy, and a loving son and brother. He was joined at school in 1897 by his younger brother, Bertie, with whom he shared a room. These two, Bertie and Artie, were not only affectionate brothers but also good friends throughout Bertie's brief life. They enjoyed each other's company. Except for Baba, Bertie probably held more of Ronald's devotion than anyone in or outside his family. He took over Bertie's duties in June 1898 when he thanked Heather for Bertie's birthday flowers and told her how lovely they looked in the room. In the same letter he asked her to take "2ᵈ laying on top of some letters" in his play box, buy two packets of a particular "kind of papper," and send them to him. He told Heather how much he was anticipating the "sports on the 9ᵗʰ of July" and that he hoped Baba would come down; if she did, he said, she must bring Heather.[9] By October 30, Artie and Bertie were marking the time, two weeks and six days, until the end of term and a holiday at Brighton.

Just as these were a schoolboy's typical communications, any of Firbank's writing which may belong to this period was also typical, an effusion meant to please his mother. He wrote this letter to her in October 1898:

I hope you will like this piece of poetary I have written for you. It is not much but I should love you to have it only dont

9. RF to HF, [Stratfield Mortimer, Berkshire], June 5, 1898.

show it any boday else I made it up all my self & as Joey
would say "did not look in a fairy book for it" be sure not to
show it any body.[1]

What he sent was "The Fairies Wood," a set of verses about
"little fairies" dancing under "oak and chesnut shade."[2] Baba
was so delighted that she ignored her son's instructions; ap-
pending the initials A.F., she had the poem printed on a
heavy white card with gilt edges and treasured it to the end of
her days. But however agreeable to Baba "The Fairies Wood"
was, it indicated nothing about Firbank's development as a
writer or about his maturing. It was the poem of a boy who
seemed very likely to grow into an ordinary man shaped by
the most conventional and conservative influences in English
life.

Predominantly, that meant the influence of the public
school. Joey, Ronald's older brother, had been at Wellington,
where he was a resident of Purnell's, later called The Wellesley, slightly longer than a year, that is, from May 1898 to July
1899. For Artie—Ronald—the Firbanks chose Uppingham.
Made notable as a breeding ground of "Christian Gentlemen"
by its great headmaster, Edward Thring, Uppingham did all it
could to turn boys, even those with "philistine" backgrounds,
into men with classical educations and conventional habits.
When he left Mortimer in 1900 (Bertie stayed another year),
Artie went to Uppingham. In May 1900 he moved with thirty-
three other boys into Brooklands, one of the thirteen houses
which formed the school. Brooklands stands at the southern
edge of the town of Uppingham on the crest of a wooded hill
which borders London Road. There Firbank settled himself
into his diminutive study with his schoolbooks: *A Latin Gradual,* Bué's *First French Book,* Gardiner's *Authors of English*

1. RF to HJGF, [Stratfield Mortimer, Berkshire], October 30, 1898.
2. Only one copy is known to exist. It is in a private collection.

History. He studied them dutifully but inattentively, and without enthusiasm he did his exercises in Latin and English and Scripture and history. He was taught these subjects by J. G. Thring, son of the former headmaster; H. H. Chapman instructed him in "Maths." To receive instruction, he pedaled his bicycle to the school's buildings dotted along the streets of the town of Uppingham, and then he pedaled back to Brooklands, where he had his meals under the eye of his housemaster, S. Haslam, and slept fitfully in his cubicle in the dormitory. Because "everyone" in Brooklands joined the Rifle Corps, he joined; though, as he told his mother, he did not want to.[3]

It was his one concession to the spirit of the public school, but neither that nor anything else could make Artie's stay at Uppingham a success. He accumulated, during his lifetime, a hoard of facts, so that the allusions in his novels, such as the one to Scantilla in *Vainglory,* are both esoteric and unexpected.[4] But his learning had none of the standardization or balance at which the public school aimed. He developed none of the friendships which often come from public school life. In all fairness, however, it was not Uppingham's failure. Uppingham had little opportunity to affect him. For some reason he was absent a part of his first term, the summer term of 1900. When he returned in the autumn, he was still in the second (and bottom) form of sixteen boys; and for that term his academic record shows him as eighth in classics, fifteenth in "French etc.," and fourteenth in the "bottom Maths Set." More disastrous was Firbank's health. Throughout the autumn term he had an unending head cold and a harsh cough.[5]

3. Cf. RF to HJGF, [Uppingham], November 22, 1900.
4. London, 1915, p. 52. All references to Firbank novels, unless otherwise indicated, are to the first editions.
5. Cf. Brian Belk, Librarian, Uppingham College, to MJB, Uppingham, March 7, 1965; interview with Mrs. Stanley Fuller, 1966.

When Firbank went home for the Christmas recess, his mother kept him there. His name was still on Uppingham's list for 1901 because the statutory term's notice had not been given, but he never saw Uppingham again. Baba was sure rest and care would rid him of his colds; so, until May, Artie stayed at Chislehurst with her, Baby and Fräulein, and the servants. Joey and Bertie were at school. Busy with Commons, Daddy came and went. Now and then Artie was allowed excursions to London, but he had little to do. To while away the time, he started an autograph album, a heavy, green-cloth book with morocco corners.[6] At first, his pocket money went to buy autographs and matching photographs. Then he began to write letters to anyone of prominence who captured his imagination and ask for a signature. Baba and Heather helped by writing a few, but he made most of the requests. "I have hurd you sing four times," he told Madame Albani, "& if you will excuse my saying it—I think you have *the most* lovely voice I have ever heard."[7] He ended with the statement that he was *"hoping"* she would send her autograph. She sent it, adding the date 1901. Similarly Marie Corelli, Anstie Guthrie, E. F. Benson, Mary E. Kennard, and a host of others responded. Since this activity left plenty of time to devote to his health, Artie was well enough by May to go on with his education, to begin seriously a long preparation for the diplomatic service.

A public school background would have been preferable for this career which the Firbanks planned for their second son, but they accepted the fact that Artie, like Joey, was unsuited for a public school. In 1901 the Firbanks still had hopes for Bertie. He had entered Eton that year and lived in

6. (Berg).
7. *A Letter from Arthur Ronald Firbank to Madame Albani* . . . (London, [1924]).

the house of the last of the Eton Dames, Miss Jane Evans, whose boarding house served Eton more than fifty years. From there he wrote to Artie about his activities, how he had purchased General Booth's autograph "from a man at a shop here who has been to the front" as a present for Artie, how he planned to start a library, and about the "d— nuisance" of having to be vaccinated before he could go home for a family gathering. "They bore 4 holes & then put a cow into them," Bertie wrote. He gave an account of "Little sister" having been taken to the dentist while he was at home: "I should think she got out at every station & spent a 1ᵈ Ladies only; not mixed—Caus' you know little sister is coming on." He looked forward to holidays, giving exact times for "longleave" and hoping, somehow, to advance the date. "With any luck," he told Artie, "we shall breed the Pox down here & then I shall go 'ome." As another possibility, he reported, "am going out for a smoke this afternoon; if you are caught you get 'this day month.' In that case I should be home before you."[8] Whether he was caught or not, his stay at Eton was short, only eighteen months, as his brothers' had been at their public schools. Indeed Joey rarely stayed anywhere very long, so that he was constantly being sent to another tutor, another new place, which the Firbanks were always sure "would do" for him, until, having exhausted both English and continental possibilities, he came back to The Coopers. Artie might well have followed the same pattern. His time at Uppingham had been short—less than a year—and fruitless, and now Baba was sending him to a place which seemed as unlikely as she could find.

By May 1901 Firbank was established at Buxton, Derbyshire, with a tutor, Alexander Macbean, M.A., *Oxon.*, de-

8. Hubert Somerset Firbank to RF, Windsor, October 15, 1901, and February 2, 1902 (Berg).

scribed on his death certificate by his brother Archibald as an
"Army Tutor." Macbean was a product of Repton School and
Keble College, Oxford. There he obtained a third class in
Classical Honour Moderations in 1881, took his B.A. degree
in 1886 and his M.A. in 1896. At Buxton he conducted a
crammer's which emphasized preparation for the army. It had
a reputation for high standards of teaching and scholarship,
and Macbean could boast of "successful preparations" for the
universities and all public examinations; but when his students achieved first place, it was in the "Woolwich Entrance,"[9] the examination for admission to the Royal Military
Academy.

Firbank's presence at this kind of institution may be explained by the fact that his mother turned for advice to her
Annesley cousins. Arthur Annesley, for whom Artie was
named, had been a captain in the Grenadier Guards; Hugh,
heir to the title, was a captain in the Scots Fusilier Guards,
and Robert John in the Eleventh Hussars. The only other
possible reason for selecting Macbean's was its location at
Buxton. Situated in the midst of the Derbyshire hills marked
by outcropping of rock and crisscrossed by stone fences, Buxton had long been a health resort. It offered, at St. Ann's
Hotel, thermal and natural mineral baths, and its air was reputed to be beneficial. Macbean and his sister Mary conducted the cramming establishment on Park Ring at the
southeast edge of Buxton in Park Holm, a large rambling
stone house surrounded by towering trees. The house, unfortunately, was bleak and cold, so that in reality few places
seemed to promise less for the improvement of Firbank's
health and education than this army tutor's at Buxton.

Yet that year, that is the period from May 1901 to July

9. Cf. Ivor E. Burton, Borough Librarian, to MJB, Buxton, July 15, 1966;
Basil Drennan to MJB, Oxford, December 7, 1965.

1902, was extremely influential in Firbank's development. In the first place, his health continued to be good. In July 1901, two months after going to Park Holm, he reminded his mother that he was quite immune to colds as he had had none since leaving Uppingham. And none is mentioned until the next spring, when Baba wrote from Chislehurst early in May 1902 to complain of the wintry weather and to hope Artie's cold was better.[1] Furthermore, during that period Firbank began to establish his own identity. The town of Buxton provided no amusement; indeed, there was so little in Buxton except a sense of isolation that Firbank went "always to the [railway] station—just to 'feel in touch with life.' "[2] His lessons were never important to him, though, according to Macbean, Firbank "worked with consistent steadiness and very fair results."[3] If he showed enough enthusiasm for Park Holm in September 1901 to invite his father for a visit,[4] it was because he had no teams to join, no groups to suggest any kind of conformity. Having left Uppingham, he had left those behind as well. Firbank was free to examine his own tastes and, in order to satisfy a gusto for living to a greater degree than the long bicycle ride from Park Holm to the railway station or the station itself could do, he was forced to exploit them.

Foremost was his interest in books. As always he read: H. Rider Haggard, A. E. W. Mason, Lucy Clifford's *A Wild Proxy*, Anthony Hope, H. G. Wells, Percy White's *West End*, Marie Corelli's *Sorrows of Satan* and *Master Christian* (Corelli was a particular favorite), Justin McCarthy, Martha Kennard, E. F. Benson's *Dodo*, Anstey's *The Brass Bottle*,

1. Cf. RF to HJGF, [Buxton], July 4, 1901; HJGF to RF, [Chislehurst], May 5, 1902 (Berg).
2. R. St. Clair Talboys to RF, Teignmouth, May 24, 1903 (MJB).
3. Alexander Macbean, Document, Buxton, January 24, 1906 (Berg).
4. Cf. HJGF to RF, Chislehurst, September 29, 1901 (Berg).

and the whole range of popular fiction. If he could not have romance, he could read about it; and he bought each book he read and carefully kept it. Of course, Firbank's enthusiasm for collecting accounts for some of his book purchases; like so many young people of his time, he was an ardent collector. By 1901 he was very much concerned with his appearance, and he took pride in his "numerous collection" of waistcoats. He liked to "gather together" in quantities all kinds of property, whether coats or books. These last formed what he and Baba complacently called his library.

The library was also a means for adding to the autograph album which Artie had started before coming to Buxton. He still bought signatures—Henry James's, for instance—but more often he wrote a letter expressing his admiration for a certain book, and the author answered with a quotation from it or some reference to it. Maurice Maeterlinck and Henry Arthur Jones sent only signatures; but Percy White quoted from *The West End,* and a "thank you" for liking his play, probably *Mr. and Mrs. Daventry,* came from Frank Harris.

Firbank was energetic in securing a variety of entries for his album. In addition to writers there were soldiers (Baden-Powell and Roberts), statesmen (Gladstone, Salisbury, Joseph Chamberlain, Balfour), and musicians (A. C. Mackenzie, John Philip Sousa, Melba, Calvé, Paderewski). By July 1901 he had forty-one autographs and was assured of another: the actress Muriel Wilson had promised one with a photograph similar to her picture on the cover of a recent issue of *Lady's Realm.*[5] Autographs of theatrical personalities outnumbered even the literary ones. Firbank began a second album devoted largely to ladies of the theater.[6] In the two albums there were Irving and Beerbohm Tree, Sarah Bern-

5. Cf. RF to HJGF, [Buxton], July 4, 1901.
6. (Berg).

hardt and Lilly Langtry, Réjane and radiant Edna May, Jeanne Granier, the Grossmiths, Rosie Boote, Henry Ainley, La Duse, Marie Tempest, Gaby Deslys, Julia Wilson, the Van Brughs, La Belle Otero, Mrs. Campbell, and many more.

Since signed photographs could be bought in shops everywhere in London, their presence in his albums does not imply that Firbank had seen and admired their subjects on the stage. Nevertheless they reflect his enchantment with the opulence and fantasy of the theater. In it he found beauty. "Lovely" was the term which he applied to Mrs. Brown Potter. The theater was also temptation. In 1901, assuring Baba that he was quite old enough to be up until eleven, he pleaded that as soon as his summer holiday commenced he be allowed to see Réjane in *Sapho*.[7] He could, he said, go with Fräulein. If seats were not available for Réjane's performance, then he might see Calvé as Carmen at Covent Garden, though he preferred *Sapho*. He went and afterward gave such an account of it that he and Bertie named a dog Sapho.[8] If *Sapho* was adventure, Pinero's *Iris* was life. As soon as it opened at the Garrick Theatre on September 21, 1901, Firbank determined to see it. Baba refused her permission for that play, in which a woman's whole existence turned on the acceptance of someone else's checkbook; but early in November Ronald went anyway and took Bertie with him. When both boys confessed that they had seen *Iris,* Baba wrote to Ronald:

> I cannot tell you how grieved I am that you could have so deceived me . . . & taken your younger brother to see one of the lowest pieces now on the stage in London. Also that you could have countenanced his sending that lie of a telegram to Miss Evans to screen which he had to verbally tell another

7. The popular play by Alphonse Daudet and Adolphe Belot in which both Jane Hading and Sarah Bernhardt appeared as well as Réjane.
8. Cf. RF to HJGF, [Buxton], July 4, 1901.

on his arrival. *You* had 10 days at home instead of the 3 as asked for—& you had been 3 or 4 times to the Theatre which should have satisfied you. I have not shown either of your letters to Daddy but if either of you ever deceive me again I must tell him. I have always said we could trust you & Bertie & I am sure you will neither of you again act as you did on Saturday. You cannot have enjoyed yourselves or felt happy knowing all the time you were deceiving "Baba"—but I will forgive you both & try and forget how unhappy I have been—[9]

Baba was on an annual visit to Brighton when she sent that letter. She was happy with the "glorious sunshine" and "Parasols up as if it was August!" in spite of fogs elsewhere in England. She liked being in her "old rooms" and knowing that "the Horses (5)" were at "Nyes the Livery Yard just off Preston S^t & so quite near."[1] But her holiday pleasure was tempered by concern for her two younger sons. That she was uneasy, if not seriously worried, is hardly surprising when Joey's example was always before her. Little more than a month earlier, in a letter dated September 29, 1901, she had told Ronald, "Tomorrow will be Joey's 17th Birthday poor boy he has seen as much of life as a man of 40! but I trust & pray he means now to turn over a new leaf."[2] Joey did not reform until he was sick and dying. At fifteen or sixteen he had learned to escape the conflict between himself and his mother's emotional dominance through drink and dissipation. Over and over he proved his manhood only to be tormented by guilt at desecrating his unseasonable love for Baba. The

9. HJGF to RF, Brighton, November 7, 1901; on this letter Firbank later wrote, "Pinero's '*Iris*' at the Garrick ~ AF—1925!" (Berg).
1. HJGF to RF, Brighton, November 7, 1901.
2. (Berg).

two younger boys, however, were able to make adjustments to the problem of their mother's possessiveness. Each solution was different. Ronald's, in the nature of a compromise, began to unfold while he was at Park Holm.

≈ III ≈

It was a painful and slow development, but that Firbank made it at all was owing in part to Rollo St. Clair Talboys, who later became a famous schoolmaster and one of the great figures at Wellington College. The time of Firbank's first meeting with Talboys cannot be fixed more definitely than the early part of 1902. It took place in Buxton at Park Holm, where Talboys was an instructor. Talboys, the son of J. W. Talboys, a clergyman, was educated at Sunnymede and, like Macbean of Park Holm, at Repton and Oxford, though at the university Talboys was a member of St. John's College. He obtained a First Class in the Final Honour School of Modern History in July 1901 and was admitted to the B.A. degree on December 5, 1901. Soon after that he went to Park Holm. A post at a crammer's was hardly commensurate with his ability, but it may have been the best he could get or he may well have been awaiting an appointment at St. John's College, which never came. Throughout his life he maintained an attitude of love-hate toward the college. Years later, when he was a "lecturer not on the foundation" at Christ Church, Oxford, he talked much about the beauties of St. John's, and he clearly thought its occupants unworthy of the place; but he

was extremely reluctant to enter it.[1] Nor was he happy at
Park Holm. After he left, he told Firbank that he liked to
think of his stay there "as a black episode—with just one
bright memory."[2] That bright memory, of course, was Firbank. Yet according to Talboys, in 1903, when Firbank had
been away from Park Holm almost a year, they had met only
two times. "How absurd!" Talboys wrote, "is this correspondence of ours when we've only set eyes on each other's fair
countenance twice—& that chiefly in the land of the Philistines
or else beset by the presence of Philistia."[3] But he also called
himself Firbank's "quondam . . . Pedagogue." Talboy's letters
cannot always be taken at face value; they were often half-
humorous, half-mocking.

Talboy's disdain for "Philistia" as well as his capacity for
mockery delighted Firbank. They answered his sense of fun.
They were so refreshing a change from The Coopers, and
they complemented so well his own instinctive but suppressed
reactions to the pretensions of convention. In a "weak moment" Talboys might inscribe his name in "the fair" Miss
Macbean's "Corelli Birthday book," but then he ridiculed
himself and others as a part of "Philistia," as in this letter sent
from Wellington:

> I've just come in from watching the sports, feeling too tre-
> mendously hale & vigorous & altogether Philistine to the last
> degree—Open air & ploughed fields you know & the breath
> of the heather you know—nothing like them. . . .[4]

1. Cf. R. E. Clifford to MJB, Oxford, February 16, 1966; T. G. D. Galbraith to MJB, London, February 24, 1966, and November 27, 1967; Graham H. Stainforth to MJB, Crowthorne, Berkshire, March 5 and March 20,
1965; interview with Graham H. Stainforth, 1965; John Thorn to MJB,
Repton, Derbyshire, February 17, 1966; J. Stephen Watson to MJB, Oxford,
April 15, 1966.
2. R. St. Clair Talboys to RF, Teignmouth, May 24, 1903 (MJB).
3. Ibid.
4. R. St. Clair Talboys to RF, Wellington College, April 15, 1904 (MJB).

Once, in an ordinary terminal report, he described a boy to his family as "dirty, lazy, ill-tempered and stupid: he should, in due course, make a typical parent." Talboys was whole-hearted in his belief that the "insensitivity of our forbears" had to be "obliterated."[5]

Sensitivity and taste, on the other hand, merited respect; that is, Talboys was a professed aesthete. When Hugh Trevor-Roper asked for advice in decorating his rooms, Talboys found them impossible to arrange, because "fox brushes, hares' heads, the relics of the chase which are Hugh's delight" covered the walls. Talboys himself preferred rooms with late eighteenth-century effects, rooms free of bric-a-brac. He liked mirrors, small or large, which he called the "eye of a room." When he first did his rooms at Wellington in 1904, he gave Firbank an account:

> I . . . have chosen the paper the very palest green of a rough grainy sort, no pattern of course—white paint & dull ivory silk short curtains—to 3 little casement windows. I am going to London to buy a carpet & one or two little frag-ments of oak—For etchings I must wait—ruin stares me in the face.[6]

Such attitudes may seem somewhat unlikely in a man of his personal attributes; Talboys was a big-boned man and in his final years the flesh on his face was loose and pinkish. He grew bald early and thereafter always wore a gray fedora. But his gestures were calculated and his voice carefully controlled and often theatrical.[7] His voice and gestures were the means

5. J. Stephen Watson to MJB, Oxford, February 15, 1966; R. St. Clair Talboys: *A Victorian School Being the Story of Wellington College* (Oxford, 1943), p. 50.
6. R. St. Clair Talboys to RF, Wellington College, April 15, 1904 (MJB).
7. John Masters to MJB, New City, New York, October 5, 1965; interview with Graham H. Stainforth, 1965; J. Stephen Watson to MJB, Oxford, April 15, 1966.

of engaging boys in a cultivation of "taste." It was his faith
that boys who had "standards growing out of a personal sense
of values created within their home environment or from
other contacts" could be involved unconsciously with what is
best and led to discriminate and to choose. He declared that
"it scarcely matters what a boy learns provided he is . . .
induced to discover and learn for himself."[8]

This faith of Talboys's served Firbank especially well. In
1902, when the two met, Talboys was twenty-five, nine years
Firbank's senior; he was a mature man and, what is more, an
Oxford man familiar with Oxonian fashions and fads of
thought. For that reason he may have been responsible either
then or in the next year or so for Firbank's writing the poem
"The Wind & The Roses,"[9] as full of Pierrots and Pierrettes as

---

8. Talboys: *Victorian School,* pp. 51–2.
9. Privately printed for Alan Clodd, London, 1965. Assigning a date to
pieces unpublished during Firbank's lifetime is hazardous. In a few instances he dated them. Otherwise there is almost no documentary evidence
to fix the time of the compositions except the way in which the author
signed them. For his published works Firbank altered the form of his name
repeatedly until he settled on the name Ronald in 1915. His first two
publications (cf. pp. 54–5) are signed with the name Arthur Firbank. They
had been completed by Christmas 1904. He used that name alone only
once more, for an article which appeared in *The Academy* in 1907 (cf. pp.
94–5). When *Odette D'Antrevernes and A Study in Temperament* appeared,
he used both his full name Arthur Annesley Ronald Firbank and the shorter
signature Arthur Firbank; that was in 1905 (cf. p. 58). Thereafter until
1915, he signed himself with his full name or his initials, A.A.R.F.;
and, although books published in 1915 and thereafter carried the name
Ronald Firbank on their title pages, the dust jackets for publications of both
1915 and 1916 (cf. pp. 134, 148) bore the name A. A. R. Firbank. In a letter
to Carl Van Vechten dated June 22, 1925 (Berg), Firbank listed a number
of his early pieces, including his first publication. Most of them are simply
named under the heading "Short Stories Between 1900–1911." The dates
he mentioned for two are patently mistaken, 1896 for "Lady Appledore's
Mésalliance" (cf. pp. 96–7) and 1900 for "The Mauve Tower" (cf. p. 52).
I have assigned probable dates for these two as well as the other pieces.
In such cases I have based my decision on internal evidence—that is, content, language, relationships to published pieces, or specific topical references such as one in "Her Dearest Friend" (cf. p. 71) to Strauss's opera
Salome, which was first presented on December 9, 1905. Firbank's notori-
ously poor spelling is not a consideration. It persisted throughout his life, a

that Oxford publication of the nineties, *The Spirit Lamp*. Although Firbank later ridiculed *"The Wind & the Roses"* by inserting part of it in his novel *Vainglory* as the work of a poetess who attempted to "out-Chatterton Chatterton," when he wrote the poem he regarded it highly enough to sign it Arthur Firbank and send it to his mother for safekeeping. Certainly Talboys would at no time have belittled the poem. Then, as always, he treated boys without condescension and with good manners. He already valued their spontaneity and friendliness, "their quick response to the ridiculous situation, their zest for the thrust and parry of make-believe."[1]

Nothing could have been more congenial to Firbank's temperament, his high spirits, and his rich imagination. Firbank soon explained his family's plans for him, and they discussed his future as a "great ambassador" and Talboys as Firbank's biographer. Firbank teased Talboys about Miss Macbean— "dear Miss MacB"—and devised for himself an imaginary Edna, a "little trollope" about whom one could "believe *anything*" one heard "& more besides." He could be as fanciful as he liked, and Talboys was amused. Later, after Firbank left Buxton and the two had begun to exchange letters, Talboys told him, "Your letters *are* so absurd—a mingling of the green Room and the Moulin Rouge—with just a soupcon of the 'touf touf.' "[2] With Talboys, Firbank was at ease; what is

fact which is apparent in letters, notebooks, and manuscripts. Typescripts of his early works (those of his later ones do not survive) have few or no misspelled words. His typists made corrections, as this holograph note to the typist of *The Artificial Princess* demonstrates: "Keep punc. & cap. letters. Correct spell only." (Berg). Two unpublished pieces named in Firbank's letter to Van Vechten require special mention. "A Disciple from the Country," read in 1961, was not reexamined for this biography; "The Saint with the Folded Hands," as far as I know, does not exist.

1. Talboys: *Victorian School*, p. 83. Cf. John Masters to MJB, New City, New York, October 5, 1965; interviews with T. G. D. Galbraith, 1966, and Graham H. Stainforth, 1965.
2. R. St. Clair Talboys to RF, Teignmouth, May 24, 1903 (MJB).

more, he was encouraged to discover himself, his likes and dislikes. He learned that his own personality was unique. Sometimes Firbank misunderstood or lost his direction; he confused self-expression and excess. He may have gone too far in what he made of himself in the next decade. But in 1902, at Park Holm, what he and Talboys laughed at, the insensitivity and opacity of human kind and especially of middle-class human kind, with its strained concept of high society, was the most natural thing in the world to ridicule. This attitude persisted, encouraged by letters. In one of May 24, 1903, Talboys wrote, "Not even Dante surrounded by acres of Hell at Drury Lane[3] or Lottie Venne[4] clothed in Leagues of Vulgarity & Paquin can compensate for my small shelf of well worn Balzac. You see," he explained, "I . . . read La Comedie Humaine." And Firbank adjusted to the possibility that his mother's environment and ideals were a part of the comedy.

Partly because he had no steadfast intellectual basis for such a position, Firbank was not ready to develop it as subject matter for his writing, and repeatedly he drew back from it. In the next few years he began to formulate relevant convictions. But despite the fact that those years were prolific ones and that during them he learned much about language and what Talboys called "staging," Firbank focused on another kind of material. In the letter to Firbank dated May 24, 1903, Talboys made that clear (as well as his mild disapproval of the fact). He remarked on a new book by Mrs. Humphrey Ward, probably *Lady Rose's Daughter,* and added that in spite of its excellence Firbank would not like it: "something airy & fantastic being more sympathetic to your literary lingerie— something Ambrosineish & frilly."

3. The play in which Henry B. Irving performed.
4. A popular performer.

By then Firbank had left Park Holm and Buxton. He returned to Chislehurst shortly before the date set for the coronation of Edward VII, June 26, 1902. Baba had plans for that occasion well in advance. In May she wrote to her son:

> Daddy & I are going to The Abbey for the Coronation on the 26th of June & I am going to try . . . to secure a window or seats for all of us to see next days Procession from—it will be a much longer one & finer than on the 26th as most of the Great People! will already have assembled at The Abbey before the King & Queen leave Buckingham Palace.[5]

She told him, too, "The dear old Canon has invested £25 worth of Fire Works to let off here near the Cork Pit the Evening of the 26th." It was to be an unusually great day for the Firbanks and Chislehurst: Daddy was on the honours list and thereafter to be called Sir Thomas. Even Joey, who complained that year of having to "rough it" and of other hardships "among Foreigners," was at home for this event.

The Canon's fireworks and Daddy's reward for his faithful political service had to wait. On the morning of June 24 King Edward underwent serious surgery. It was a shocking, anxious time. As *The Pall Mall Magazine* put it, "The Morning which saw us preparing for the greatest pageant of our time found us a little later waiting anxiously hour by hour for the tidings which were to tell us whether the Angel of Death had been stayed."[6] The King recovered, and on August 9, when much of the pageantry had been dissipated, he was crowned Edward VII; and the Firbanks became Sir Thomas and Lady Firbank.

Ronald could then turn to his own plans for a stay in

5. HJGF to RF, Chislehurst, May 25, 1902 (Berg).
6. Lady Jenne: "The King's Illness and the Coronation," *The Pall Mall Magazine*, XXVII (August 1902), 567.

France so that he might learn the language and thus further his preparations for a diplomatic career. He had been concerned with this project before he left Buxton, that is, since mid-May, when he had urged his mother to make arrangements for a Mr. Scone to escort him to France. Scone was one of a series of traveling companions hired by the Firbanks to escort their sons to a series of destinations. In May his mother thought Ronald too impatient about the matter of Mr. Scone, but she promised to attend to it in a few days. Whether she did or not, Firbank went from Chislehurst to Paris in late September and arrived *chez* Madame Bricogne, Le Mortier de St. Symphorien, a suburb of Tours, by October 3, 1902.[7]

He stayed there nearly a year broken by at least one holiday. Shortly after December 17, as arranged by Sir Thomas, a Mr. Malden joined Firbank at Tours with a gift and this letter:

> You will see I am sending this out by M[r] Malden who is to accompany you on your little travel so its to wish you a very happy & bright Xmas & New Year blessing. Now I hope you will like your companion & that we are doing the right thing in your taking this journey; & that it may turn out right in every way. So I shall hope to hear from you soon how you are getting on. I am sure you will do what is right and pick up all you can. So make the best of your opportunity. Now

7. Mme Bricogne stated in a letter to Lady Firbank written from St. Symphorien on February 8, 1906 (Berg), that Firbank arrived on October 3 and remained until August 1904. More than three years after the event she obviously made a mistake in the dates. Letters of Lady Firbank (cf. letter to RF, Chislehurst, December 28, 1902 [Berg]), and R. St. Clair Talboys (cf. letter to RF, Wellington College, May 24, 1903 [MJB]) confirm Firbank's presence at St. Symphorien in December 1902 and May 1903. Lady Firbank referred to a Christmas gift sent in a box from Tours; Talboys spoke of "La Belle Madame on the banks of the Loire." Mme Bricogne's letter (see below, p. 42) indicates that Firbank made his first acquaintance with the French language in her home.

good bye & God bless you hoping you are well and happy.
Much love From your loving Daddy.[8]

The letter's postscript included "a *kiss* X." Firbank and Mr.
Malden set out promptly, going first by train to Biarritz, with
its sunshine and its beautiful Grande Plage so dear to the
Empress Eugénie. They stayed at Biarritz only a short time;
Ronald posted a letter to Baba, and they went on to Madrid.
In Madrid he had letters dated December 28, 1902, from
Daddy and Baba thanking him for a "Fairy God Father Box"
filled with Christmas presents sent before he left Tours. Sir
Thomas's letter once again urged him to make the most of his
journey, but Baba's was filled with news, affection, and
thanksgiving. She wrote of the fact that Joey and Bertie and
even "little Lassie" had no amusements except the golf links,
she gave an account of her Christmas gifts, she marveled at
his gift to her, which she was sure had taken his entire
"Term's pocket money," and declared herself "touched" by
his message on the accompanying card, and she told him how
painful his absence from Chislehurst was. "We so often talk of
you & I so often miss you these Holidays," she wrote. Her
letter ended by saying, "How good God has been to us darling
all through the year now so nearly past, this its last Sunday.
May the New Year be a bright and happy one for you with
health & good luck attending it."[9] From Madrid, Firbank
went with Malden to Seville. This was his first visit to the city
which inspired his final complete novel, *Concerning the Eccentricities of Cardinal Pirelli,* but what Seville meant to Firbank
in 1902 can not be determined. No record exists of his response
to the Giralda Tower, the dancing boys of the Cathedral, the
Andalusian nights rich with the scent of flowers.

8. (Berg).
9. (Berg).

Indeed, the impression Spain made on him at that time can
only be surmised. Firbank's account of his trip in a letter
written after he left Spain caused Talboys to remark on the
"glorious time" Firbank seemed to have had. A piece which
he composed probably in 1903, "True Love,"[1] makes obvious the fact that he had looked closely at the churches and
museums of Spain. From them he furnished the scene which
opens "True Love" with a door "Gothic in shape," armor,
brocades, tables inlaid with ivory, kneeling saints, and Madonnas "with long pale hands out turned in exaltation."

"True Love" has two aspects which are predictably Fir-
bankian. It is the story of a young poet who has just learned
that he has "the beginnings of consumption" and must leave
Paris. His mistress, a married woman with a "Spanish look"
whom he has loved since they were both children, plans to
leave with him. As soon as she has written a note to her
husband they will go together to Seville. But he takes "a
bunch of blue and white violets" she has dropped, kisses it and
whispers, "She and me," and then leaves without her to avoid
ruining her life. "True Love" obviously derives from Firbank's addiction to reading romances. In it his eyes are shut
to human behavior as he was capable of seeing it. Yet "True
Love" is one of the earliest pieces in which Firbank showed
his concern with interiors and the appearance of things. These
served him in subsequent compositions as an anchor of realism for his deliberate exaggeration. In "True Love," perhaps
for the first time also, Firbank tells a story of extramarital
love. Except in one or two pieces, such as "Lady Appledore"
and *Inclinations* and perhaps *Prancing Nigger,* there is no
happy marriage or even the possibility of one in Firbank's fiction. Mother love, extramarital love, homosexual love occupy

1. Typescript signed Arthur Firbank (Rush Rees Library, The University
of Rochester); a second uniform typescript, unsigned (MJB).

his characters. Speculation of a psychological nature must associate such subject matter with his attachment to his mother. The romance of self-sacrifice in love, a major constituent of many of the novels he read, appealed to his imagination; but the love never ended in marriage, in his mind. At sixteen, marriage was already a psychological impossibility for Firbank. The realization came to him later, well before he stated the fact to his sister in 1912.[2] Now for the first time it plainly manifested itself in "True Love." The relationship between the characters in that tale, however, is neither observed nor transformed. Thus the piece is in the category of writing which Talboys called "Ambrosineish & frilly."

If "True Love" was written soon after its author's visit to Spain in 1902, then it was written at St. Symphorien, as he remained there most of the time until August 1903. Once, apparently, he had planned to enter Scoones's, a cramming establishment in London, in the summer or autumn of 1903. In his letter of May 24, Talboys commented: "Now comes Scoones & the midnight oil like retribution—it will be sad and you will grow pale & thin with the scholar's stoop—& all your coats will have to be altered—." There is nothing to indicate that Firbank went to Scoones's in 1903, and it is more likely that, if he left St. Symphorien at all, he made a visit to Chislehurst in June with occasional trips to London for concerts and the theater. Melba sang in *Romeo and Juliet,* and Mme Albani was one of the vocalists of the Handel Festival at the Crystal Palace in late June. Some of Firbank's favorite actors and actresses were visible that summer too, from Irene Vanbrugh and Henry B. Irving in *The Admirable Crichton* and Edna May in *The School Girl* to Bernhardt and Édouard de Max in *Phèdre.*

More than likely Firbank spent the entire summer with

2. Cf. RF to HF, London, n.d.

Mme Bricogne at Le Mortier de St. Symphorien. One product
of his stay there was his memory of the beauty of the Loire
Valley and the city of Tours. After more than ten years he
described it as "all towers & spires & a great round dome for
St Martin's! The Cathedral has twin-towers . . . & the Loire
sails by under 3 stone bridges amid sand-reefs & Poplars—"[3]
Another was his success with his studies, especially French.
Mme Bricogne declared that "Monsieur Artie Firbank," by
his work and lively intelligence, had quickly learned a language which all too often presented serious difficulties to foreigners. Madame stated further that her family could wish for
no changes of any kind in "Monsieur Artie."[4] Apparently Firbank led a quiet, studious existence at Le Mortier, reading
(Maeterlinck's plays, among other things) and writing. Possibly at this time he set down the unnamed French exercise
having to do with a *"Guinevere, mignonne"* who is not so
stupid as to think lovers can live on *"des mots, des regards et
de la sympathie."*[5]

If Firbank did not write the exercise under Mme Bricogne's
roof, then he did so at the farm Howley Grange near the
village of St. Tulle in the Basses Alpes. In September he went
from St. Symphorien to Howley Grange, where he was under
the care and supervision of M. A. Esclangon. When Lady Firbank requested it three or four years later, M. Esclangon
wrote a testimonial in which he declared that he had the most
agreeable memory of Firbank and would be charmed to receive him again, that his work and conduct left nothing to be
desired.[6] More than likely he spent any time not devoted to

3. RF to GR, Torquay, July 28, 1916.
4. Cf. Mme Bricogne to HJGF, St. Symphorien, February 8, 1906 (Berg).
5. Manuscript unsigned (Berg).
6. Cf. A. Esclangon to HJGF, Sainte-Tulle, Basse Alpes, January 28, 1906
(Berg). This letter states that Firbank was at Howley Grange from September to Christmas 1902. That is impossible. His stay there is assigned to

his studies at work on two short "contes." The first was "When Widows Love."[7] It is a slight tale of the pursuit of a second husband by Mrs. Franley, a widow who "loved looking at herself in a crisis." She manages to secure the husband she wants, detaching him from a second widow; but this one is indifferent to her loss, since she has already found a more materially desirable replacement, a prince. The second "conte" was *A Study in Temperament*,[8] probably commenced at St. Tulle. Except for this writing, his stay at Howley Grange was inconsequential. By Christmas, Firbank had moved on.

When he returned to England for the holiday season he showed either "True Love" or, more likely, "When Widows Love" to Talboys. Whichever it was, Talboys used it as a basis for comparison with some version of *A Study in Temperament*. *A Study* had another title then; but in the first two weeks of 1904, from Chislehurst, Firbank sent an early draft to Talboys for his opinion. Talboys replied on January 24 with what he called a "very casual criticism." He thought it "vastly better" than the piece he had seen in London, because it had "more staging in it—& more *movement*," which he declared to be "everything in this kind of temperamental 'conte.'" Talboys suggested an appropriate name, "A Study in Temperament," and then he went on with a "very few suggestions," most of which Firbank incorporated verbatim into his story. For example, the opening sentences are almost word for word the ones Talboys composed; he wrote,

> Lady Agnes Charteris leaned back in her chair & critically glanced at herself reflected in the tall mirror. Certainly the

---

1903, because 1903 is the only year between 1900 and 1907 in which the period involved, September to Christmas, cannot be otherwise accounted for.
7. Typescript signed Arthur Firbank (Fales).
8. See below, p. 58.

delicate brocade of the grande siècle made a foil for the
dusky crown of her hair, which her women friends charitably
attributed to the deft fingers of Mr Isidore.[9]

Firbank changed his heroine's name to Charters, substitued "a
tall mirror" for "the tall mirror," made the brocade green, and
altered the latter part of the sentence to read "made a foil for
her crown of golden hair which her women friends charitably
attributed to Art."[1] This is only one of a number of specific
suggestions in Talboy's letter which Firbank followed. Since
Talboys thought the piece had "promise in it" and was well
"worth furbishing up," Firbank no doubt did his best to follow Talboys's general recommendations too: "The dialogue
wants a little more mistiness—the figures to be more veiled."

The result is that the elements of Firbank's novels are dis-
cernible in *A Study in Temperament*. In it and in "When
Widows Love" as well, Firbank returned for the first time
since 1896 to the motif of "Lila." It is more sophisticated in *A
Study,* a fact attributable in part to Talboys. For instance,
Talboys provided this Rossetti-like description of a picture of
a "mystical Madonna": "A woman, with a long pale face,
leaning out of the clouds, the sins and sorrows of the whole
world gathered in the wearied eyelids and the red-gold of her
hair."[2] But the design of *A Study in Temperament* is unmis-
takably Firbank's. In it he tells of an attempted seduction
which has less importance to the lady involved than the color

9. (MJB).

1. Cf. *Odette D'Antrevernes and A Study in Temperament* (London, 1905),
p. [31].

2. *A Study,* p. 42; Talboys's version in his letter of January 24, 1904, runs:
"One of Bougerau's [sic] mystical Madonnas—the sins & sorrow of the whole
world gathered in her wearied eyelids—& the red gold of her hair." Talboys
liked the phrase "wearied eyelids"; he used a version of it much later when
he described Edward White Benson, Archbishop of Canterbury, as having "a
serene and beautiful face, with tired eyelids . . ." Cf. Talboys: *Victorian
School,* p. 16.

of her hair. She lives, as do all the characters sketched in this story, within her own consciousness. As the speakers in "Lila" are contained and isolated in some private identity, so are they in *A Study*. They speak wittily and absurdly, but they disregard communication. The touchstone for reality is their home decoration, a carefully smart one and one appropriate to their substitution of a spontaneous irony for their capacity to feel. Although Firbank did not sustain it in his next compositions, he has here, tentatively, the characteristic perspective of his novels.

❧ IV ☙

This vision was compatible with the personality which Firbank was busily "tinting." He had been at it for some time, at least since the visit to Spain and probably since his acquaintance with Talboys. Talboys had made him understand the urgency of being everything he was capable of. Firbank's love for the richness of color and texture was genuine, as it would always be; to open his novels at random demonstrates that. He never lost his sense of the delicacy of "the flushed camellias and the sweet night-jasmines," of wonder at "the top of an apple tree" glimpsed "above a wall." In fact, Firbank was intellectually and emotionally dependent on the radiance of beauty. Its implications were essential to nurture his imagination, and imagination was more and more at the core of his existence. As he told his sister a few years later, "There is bound to be ennui, when things become REAL."[1] Perhaps

1. RF to HF, Cambridge, n.d.

the ennui was a pose; certainly he cultivated others, attitudes belonging to his concept of the exquisite and the man of the world.

There was no better place for such self-development than Paris of the "naughty noughts," of *la belle époque,* where the whole of human pleasure seemed to pass on the great boulevards. Firbank was installed in Paris by April 1904 at 17 rue Tronchet. That is the address of a narrow, featureless gray stone building halfway between the boulevard Haussmann and the Madeleine, whose copper-green roof, dominating Mme Hédiard's spice shop and the gastronomy of Fauchon's, ornaments the entire district. There, at 17 rue Tronchet, Firbank lived "in the studious intimacy" of the family Henry Biais. This family consisted of M. Biais, a small man with a large mustache, his wife, Mme Biais-Cazalis, and their young son. As usual, Firbank was abroad to perfect his French, and according to M. Biais he worked regularly to that end, studying the editions of M. Tollemer, professor at the Lycée Lamartine, 6 rue Crétet, trying voluntarily to write in the French language and interesting himself in French literature.[2] But he also worked at developing an "artificial temperament." He gave unusual care to his appearance, dressing often in black relieved only by a single pearl in his cravat, a gold watch chain with one or two seals, and the whiteness of his linen. He wore a little-finger ring. He dined at Armenonville, and he was *au courant* with the very latest thing— *L'Esbroufe, "le grand succès du moment"* at the Vaudeville, the cakewalk danced with high-flung knees and tossing heads by Mr. and Mrs. Elks at the New Circus, the last ingenuity in the convolutions of Lalique jewelry, the gradations of color in Parma violets already featured that year in a number at the Folies Bergère, or Georges Méliès's film *An Impossible Voyage,*

2. Cf. Henry Biais, Document, Paris, January 26, 1906 (Berg).

exhibited at Théâtre Robert-Houdin. Theater and theatrical personalities, of course, delighted Firbank. He watched eagerly for the bills, green for the Opéra-Comique and wine-red for the Comédie-Française, posted to announce new productions. It was the green which he read more eagerly: the Opéra-Comique never failed to please, and operettas—*La Chauve Souris,* for example—were most amusing. His admiration for La Belle Otéro was devout; he went again and again to the Mathurins to see her in the pantomime *Rêve d'Opium* or in M. Gailhard's *L'Aragonaise,* and he filled pages of his photographic album with her pictures. He sat entranced before Polaire as Fiquet in Willy's *Claudine à Paris* as well as before his old favorites. Réjane was at the Théâtre de Variété; and the Divine Sarah created the part of Marie Antoinette in *Varenne,* which opened on April 23, and recreated Aiglon for twenty performances commencing on October 1. He went through the stage door to visit Mlle Jeanne Granier and Édouard de Max, who was at the Théâtre Sarah Bernhardt or the Théâtre Porte-Saint-Martin. This Romanian actor spoke French with a reverberating "r" and a warm voice to such effect that Bernhardt called him the one perfect Aiglon and André Gide thought him the only actor capable at that time of playing great lyric parts, the roles of Orestes, Nero, and Polyeucte, which de Max so longed to play.[3]

Whether or not Firbank first knew de Max in London in the summer of 1903, when he played Hippolyte in *Phèdre,* he made much of his friendship with de Max now. Firbank looked approvingly on de Max's gold bracelet and jacket of otter fur. He admired the actor's grand style on the stage and the grander disorder of his flat in the rue Caumartin. Firbank

3. Cf. Jean Schlumberger to MJB, Paris, May 2, 1965; André Gide: *Journals of,* ed. Justin O'Brien (2 vols.; New York, 1947), I, 104 *et passim;* Louis Verneuil: *La Vie Merveilleuse de Sarah Bernhardt* (New York, 1942), pp. 245, 208, *et passim.*

visited him there and came away with envy of the bindings de
Max had had made for the books piled everywhere and with
de Max's photograph, inscribed to his "young friend" and
signed *"un vieux Roi de Rome."*

The fact that de Max was reputed to have a bad influence
on young men in no way deterred Firbank from associating
with the actor; to the contrary. Firbank's insouciance in the
matter helped establish his dandyism. This meant something
more than the vast numbers of boots and waistcoats he pos-
sessed and the waves his hairdresser created for him. It also
meant something besides a "perfection of culture's etiquette,"
although he had that too; the distinction of his manners and
the nobility of his tastes aroused M. Biais's commendation. It
even went beyond his addiction to the arts. For Firbank
dandyism involved decadence, if not downright wickedness.
He gave such a picture of his life in Paris in letters to Talboys that Talboys replied by saying Firbank would soon be "a
Parisien mondain of the de Goncourt school—without ever a
trace of the Roast Beef that bred" him. Talboys added his fear
that Firbank was "becoming a slave of the senses—an emotional bon vivant to the last tremolo," and he warned Firbank
"to draw back ere it is too late," since he was threatened, as
Talboys said, with "the cult of the purple orchid insidious &
exotic poison all of it like the rank odour of dead men's
sins."[4] Talboys had encouraged Firbank to explore the uses
of the imagination and the intellect and probably of the
senses, but Firbank had strayed in a direction Talboys had
not intended, one summarized by Pater when he said that
"not the fruit of experience, but experience itself is the end."
An uneasy awareness of responsibility may account for Talboys's concern. Whatever its cause, it pleased Firbank. It implied liking and friendship, but it also meant he had success-

4. R. St. Clair Talboys to RF, Crowthorne, April 15, 1904 (MJB).

fully projected his dandyism, his artfully made personality.

Bravado is only one cause, however, for Firbank's recital of his experiences to Talboys. There was also a compulsion in his boasts, an urgent need to provoke censure. Firbank never lost these mingled attitudes. Almost twenty years later he told Carl Van Vechten about an article which Van Vechten had written: "I hope you said I was wicked & interesting."[5] Certainly Firbank wanted disapproval because he disapproved of his own exotic adventures. They were at once his compromise with his passion for his mother and a violation of it. If he had been able at that time, emotionally and intellectually, to re-create Lady Firbank's world in his fiction, he might have solved his problems, as D. H. Lawrence tried to do in his writing. Instead, Firbank formed an artificial personality almost as fictitious as his novels and surely as extravagant.

Firbank's life in Paris also amplified another side of his imagination and intellect. That it did came out in two ways: what he wrote and what he read. In his reading he began to organize the convictions which underlie the amused exaggerations of his fiction. He was acquiring intellectually a key to the human scene already discovered at home. From his reading, too, he learned something—more than he could apply then—about the uses of technique.

Yet to at least one friend, Jean Pozzi, Firbank's taste in literature seemed as much mere fashion as his awareness of the Paris boulevards. Jean Pozzi is the son of Professor Samuel Pozzi, a surgeon who at one time or another was president of the Academy of Medicine, senator from the Dordogne, book collector, and (along with Henri Bergson, Forain, Proust, Réjane, and others of the "soul and salt" of Paris) a regular attendant at Mme Émile Straus's salon, held each Sat-

5. RF to CVV, Bordighera, February 13, 1923.

urday afternoon at her home on the boulevard Haussman.[6] Jean Pozzi later distinguished himself as writer, diplomat, and soldier, a fact attested by his honors: Croix de Guerre, Military Cross Anglaise, Chevalier de la Légion d'Honneur. In 1904, however, Pozzi, who was two years older than Firbank, was a student. His recollection of his friendship with Firbank, written more than sixty years afterward, runs:

> My parents were closely connected with the family Biais, and I believe even distantly related by our kinship with the poet Jean Lahore. We lived then in the sixteenth arrondissement; communications were not as easy as today. I was preparing a *"licencié ès lettres"* at [the lycée] Condorcet and I took some courses at the Sorbonne: I spent my days, then, in the home of our friends the Biais, who had kindly offered me a corner where I could work. I thus avoided loss of time caused by the distance as well as the confusion of 47 avenue d'Iéna, where my father received his patients.
>
> Arthur Firbank, at that time, was himself *pensionnaire* with the Biais. Like all young men of that period, we walked together often, and we exchanged ideas on art and literature. We were not always in agreement, for I was still an admirer of a school of the *époque* already out of fashion, that of the *grands classiques,* the Augustans, Racine, the Romantics and the *Parnassiens,* while Firbank was a great admirer of the Symbolists, the Pre-Raphaelites, Maurice Maeterlinck, the first works of Claudel, Ruskin, Burne Jones etc.[7]

Firbank left no comment on his reading. To know exactly what he derived from it is impossible. It is certain, however, that in Claudel, for instance, and Ruskin, too, there is an

6. Cf. Barbara W. Tuchman: *The Proud Tower* (New York, 1966), p. 205.
7. Jean Pozzi to MJB, Paris, August 30, 1966 (translated from French by MJB).

implicit statement about the bad faith in which the late Victorians and the Edwardians lived. Firbank recognized its truth. Claudel even specified the conflict which recurs in Firbank's novels, the opposition between ancient values and self-interest. Claudel lamented (as in *L'Otage,* not published until 1911), while Firbank laughed; but the emphasis on the conflict between order and disorder is the same. It was a question of the rational or sensory. Furthermore, those writers whom Firbank admired—Claudel, again, and Maeterlinck, the Pre-Raphaelites, the Symbolists—leaned heavily on technique. For Firbank, expertness in merging comment and scene through form had to wait several years, but in 1904 his awareness of techniques began to show in what he wrote.

His experiments with life, if not with letters, were checked temporarily when he went about July 26 for a holiday in the French Alps. The Biais family took a villa at Meuthen-St. Bernard on Lac d'Annecy for the month of August and part of September, and Firbank accompanied them so as not to interrupt his studies completely. In addition to his preparations for his "Diplomatic Exam," still going forward, he was as active and busy as ever. He wrote and he read. He made several excursions, including a visit to Chamonix, where he had a picture taken, postcard size, showing him surrounded by snow and ice, and sent it off to Bertie at Chislehurst. That was on September 12, and when he returned from Meuthen-St. Bernard to Paris at the end of the month, he had completed *Odette D'Antrevernes. Odette* is a pastiche from Firbank's reading of Francis Jammes,[8] a tale of the power of an innocent, believing child who, in her search for the "Holy Mary," saves a harlot from suicide. Its setting is a saccharine version of St. Symphorien, all flowers and birdsong, a ro-

---

8. Cf. Ernest Jones: "Introduction," in Ronald Firbank: *Three Novels* (London, 1951), p. xiii.

mantic château, and the distant towers of the cathedral . . .
purple in the setting sun." According to a letter dated September 25, 1904, Firbank's mother hoped to receive the manuscript of *Odette* in the next day's post. She promised that she would then have "typewritten" both *Odette* and another piece already in her possession, "The Mauve Tower."[9] She also promised to prefix a dedication to "The Mauve Tower" as Ronald asked: *"A Monsieur Jean Pozzi tres cordialement je dédie ma 'Tour Mauve' en souvenir de l'été mil neuf cent quatre."*

Although *Odette* was to constitute a part of Firbank's first book publication, it had no more importance in his progress as a writer than "The Mauve Tower" and the numerous other pieces of that year. The crucial thing was that he was writing. At the beginning of 1904 he had revised *A Study in Temperament* according to Talboys's suggestions. Then he returned to the contrivances on which he relied, because he had nothing to write about. In the weeks following his arrival at 17 rue Tronchet he wrote "La Princesse aux Soleils (Romance Parlée)" in English and then translated it into French.[1] He copied both texts, decorated them with his own water-color designs, and inscribed the booklet to his mother for her birthday, "Written and painted by Artie to Darling Baba with much love for her birthday 1904." The project was so successful that while he was at Meuthen-St. Bernard he prepared another copy of "La Princesse," though in this one he confined the water-color decorations to the wrappers; he gave it to his sister for her birthday, calling it a "second edition" and dating it September 5, 1904. In mid-summer Firbank had composed "The Mauve Tower" and a piece similar to "La

---

9. Typescript signed Arthur Firbank (Rush Rees Library, The University of Rochester).
1. Cf. *"Les Essais," Revue Mensuelle*, II (November 1904), 78–80.

Princesse," *Far Away,* and subscribed to it "Paris, 24th July 1904."[2] All are mannered and altogether appropriate to Firbank's "artificial temperament." Yet these pieces mark an advance in his literary growth. His content was meager and he had no notion of form, but he was working out a kind of craftsmanship.

His princesses and mysteriously unhappy ladies are excuses for manipulation of language. Its possibilities of tone and color delighted him, and he cultivated perhaps all he understood of Symbolism, what Poe called "a suggestive indefiniteness," through evocative words and phrases. Firbank's concept of the role of language is especially apparent in "The Mauve Tower," subtitled "A Dream Play." Possibly his first attempt at play writing, it fails as literature and drama. A synopsis can give no idea of "The Mauve Tower" because it is all manner and no matter. The characters are a shadowy princess, her slave, and a prince. Without relevance to their development, the action is contrived and the dialogue is deliberately repetitious in the same way as Oscar Wilde's dialogue in *Salomé.* An example from Firbank's play is this speech of the princess:

> Oh! Oh! the flowers! do you smell the flowers? All the forest is perfumed with the flowers. They look like dragons' eyes peering at us through the dark. The scarlet lillies look like bleeding wounds. The great white orchids look like hands. The yellow grasses look like golden swords.

These lines are descriptive, but many are a statement of a vague fear. They all avoid being definite and explicit. To be explicit, as Paul Valéry said of Mallarmé, was "strangely re-

2. Iowa City, 1966 (eighty copies were printed, of which none was for sale).

pugnant" to Firbank. That this attitude and his experiments
with language were influenced by the writers whom he supported in his promenades with Pozzi is confirmed by his dedi-
cating "The Mauve Tower" to Pozzi.

These compositions, with the exception of *Odette,* are set
pieces. Later Firbank constructed his novels in a series of
such scenes so juxtaposed as to measure or emphasize each
other.[3] Yet the method of his novels is barely suggested in
these pieces of 1904. None of the movement, the hustle and
bustle of the scenes of the novels, and none of the "cinematic
cross-cutting" occur in "La Princesse," *Far Away,* or even
"The Mauve Tower." They are only a start. In them Firbank
was beginning to understand the meaning and function of
what Talboys called "staging."

Baba and Ronald were pleased with these works. He liked
them well enough to write the same kind of thing again, a
piece called "Harmonie." It was one of two—the other being
" 'The Lieutenant & the Irise's Wife' a Parable"—included in
"Ideas and Fancies," a pamphlet which Firbank prepared
with nine water colors and eight gold gauze interleaves as a
gift for Baba at Christmas.[4] He had already concluded that
his work was ready for publication; encouraged by de Max
and Pozzi, he submitted the French version of "La Princesse
aux Soleils" to the review *"Les Essais."* This was a new Pari-
sian monthly edited by J.-L. Vaudoyer, who wrote a regular
feature, "Notes d'Art," and any other article needed to fill its
pages. *"Les Essais"* lasted only a short time; but as long as it
was issued, it printed the work of promising writers. In October 1904 *"Les Essais"* published Jean Schlumberger's short
novel "L'Homme Heureux," and in November 1904 Ronald

3. Cf. James Hafley: "Ronald Firbank," *Arizona Quarterly,* XII (Summer
1956), 161–71.
4. Manuscript signed Arthur Firbank (Lord Horder). For "Harmonie" cf.
"Les Essais," Revue Mensuelle, III (February 1905), 305–6.

Firbank's "La Princesse aux Soleils." It was his first publication.

In that month his elder brother Joey, not yet twenty-one, died at The Coopers, Chislehurst. By September, Joey had stopped running from himself and his mother and had come home. Lady Firbank told Ronald in a letter written at Chislehurst and dated September 25, "I found Joey today very depressed & ill. I feel so sad when I see him & to be unable to do anything for him."[5] Indeed she could do nothing but watch him die. According to his death certificate, Joseph Sydney Firbank died of "enteric syncope" on November 22, 1904, in the presence of his mother.

Ronald's reaction to his brother's death was hardly predictable. He went to Chislehurst for the funeral, but he returned to Paris at once. Except insofar as convention demanded it, he in no way altered his habits and routine in Paris, and he remained *en famille Biais* until the time already scheduled for his departure, the end of December. He continued to work on the gift booklet "Ideas and Fancies," and he submitted "Harmonie" to *"Les Essuis"* for publication in February 1905. There is no evidence of grief for Joey. In the following years he sent his mother a formal printed card on the anniversary of Joey's birthday, but there is no indication that he felt a sense of loss. Such lack of feeling is unexpected in a young man whom his tutors and associates described repeatedly as having a gentle disposition and manners. Yet this callousness was an aspect of character which Firbank could display from time to time, as his sister Heather was to learn in the 1920's. Now, the emotion he felt on the occasion of Joey's death was concentrated in a passionate pity for his mother. Because Baba had told him repeatedly, he knew how troublesome Joey had been. Ronald may even have understood her part in Joey's

5. (Berg).

self-destruction, but he loved her too compulsively to acknowledge her responsibility.

By implication he denied it in his next composition, "The
Legend of Saint Gabrielle."[6] It is a short piece, which commences with an account of the young Sister Gabrielle as she
lies dying in a convent. Suddenly at the window of her cell she
sees a woman's face, "bright and wonderful," and "as with
lightning rapidity, sweet childhood's memories of Home and
she who had made it home, seem to fill the soul of the dying
girl." The woman enters, lifts Gabrielle, and disappears "with
her amidst the trees of the garden." There she dies. In the
convent the other nuns are convinced that a miracle has taken
place, that "the Holy Virgin had come down and carried the
Sister Gabrielle away with her to Heaven to be the bride of
her Son The Lord Christ." Firbank concluded his story:
"Through the great forest a mother wandered, and on her
breast as though asleep, lay her daughter who was dead. . . .
Amidst the tall trees, solitary in her grief, she walked alone
weeping and uncomforted." The suggestion that the love of
the Virgin and a mother's love are indistinguishable was one
of Ronald's "soulful ideas" which "thrilled" Baba. The lack of
literary merit was no hindrance; Lady Firbank had "The
Legend" typed and preserved it. It was so conclusive a statement of her son's devotion.

The piece confirms Firbank's evolving homosexuality.[7] He
had not yet made his own assertion of it, but it was surely
implied in the hints of vice against which Talboys had warned
during the preceding year when he urged Firbank to draw
back from the "cult of the purple orchid." It is present as well
in Firbank's need to have his erotic adventures known and con-

6. Typescript signed Arthur Firbank (MJB).
7. No documentary evidence of Firbank's early homosexuality exists. That
his inversion was both real and active in later years is more than rumor. See
below, pp. 241–4.

demned as transgressions against purity, especially his mother's. "The Legend of St. Gabrielle" confirms the basis of Firbank's homosexuality, a prolonged dependence on his mother and a rapturous, idealistic love for her.[8] Both are elemental in many instances of homosexuality, especially when the father's influence is as slight as that of Sir Thomas, whether because of ineffectuality in his household or because of his continual separation from his son. The intensity of Firbank's love permeates the entire "Legend"; and readily apparent in the closing sensence, that is, in St. Gabrielle's head at rest on her mother's breast, is his dependency.

This dependency endured and had a lasting effect on his other relationships. He liked to be protected and looked after. The truth of that statement is obvious in an incident of the early twenties. As Osbert Sitwell told it, one day at "luncheon time in the Café Royal," Firbank asked a friend, Gabriel Atkin, a young painter, to give him lunch. Atkin replied that he could not, because he had no money. According to Sitwell, Firbank promptly "took a pound note out of his pocket, pressed it into the hand of his friend and, sinking at the same time into the seat opposite, exclaimed, 'How wonderful to be a guest!' "[9]

8. See above, pp. 19–20.
9. Sitwell: "Ronald Firbank," *Noble Essences,* p. 85.

❧ V ☙

Whether "The Legend of St. Gabrielle" was written before Firbank left the Biais family in Paris or after is uncertain. He returned to Chislehurst at the end of December 1904 and remained there for the first five or six weeks of 1905. With the preciseness of a dilettante, he devoted much of this time to arranging for the firm of Elkin Mathews, Vigo Street, London, to publish his first book.[1] For it he had chosen *Odette D'Antrevernes* and *A Study in Temperament*. *Odette* was a favorite of Baba's, while *A Study in Temperament* satisfied one side of Ronald's literary inclinations. But he was disposed to suppress his satiric bent; so he gave more importance to *Odette*. In addition to arranging for two wrappers, one sea-green, lettered in gilt, and the other rose, lettered in blue, he had ten copies of *Odette* printed separately and bound in white vellum boards. On all three bindings, only the title *Odette D'Antrevernes* appeared with his name; *A Study* is not mentioned on the covers. He had signed his two periodical publications Arthur Firbank; but for his book he used his full name, Arthur Annesley Ronald Firbank, on the cover and the shorter Arthur Firbank on the title page. The financial agreement which he made with the publishers can not be established because wartime bombing destroyed their records. Certainly he paid Elkin Mathews to bring out the book, and in return he received a percentage of the receipts from sales.[2]

Publication did not take place until June, but in February

---

1. Cf. p. 39, *n.* 9.
2. Cf. MJB: *Bibliography of Ronald Firbank* (London, 1963), A1.

Firbank considered himself well on the way to being a man of letters. The agreement with Elkin Mathews was hardly signed when he wrote a letter to Alfred Douglas as from one author to another. In a way this letter was an extension of those he had once written asking for autographs to embellish his albums, but in this instance Firbank ostensibly wanted information bearing on his library. The library of a few years earlier had become a special book collection with bindings as elegant as de Max's. Firbank asked Douglas how to secure a copy of his *City of the Soul* and the name of the artist who had made the drawing of Douglas which appeared in the French edition of the poems; but he was careful to tell Douglas about the forthcoming publication of *Odette*. The older man replied in kind. In a letter dated February 13, 1905, and addressed to "Mr Fairbank," Douglas wrote that his friend Walter Spindler had done the drawing, but that no copies of *The City of the Soul* were available, though he hoped to have some of the second edition soon. He added, "As you are a 'confrère' & are going to publish a volume yourself, I will have pleasure in sending you a copy as soon as I can get hold of any." Then he declared in a postscript that he would like to see Firbank's book when it appeared.[3]

In writing to Douglas, Firbank acted not only as a budding author but also in accordance with his artfully composed idea of himself as a man of the world. Although Oscar Wilde's trials had occurred ten years before, in 1895, they were not forgotten. Douglas, of whom Wilde had written in 1900 "Boys, brandy, and betting monopolise his soul,"[4] had married Olive Custance in March 1902; but that failed to do much for his reputation. If this was Firbank's way of ac-

---

3. Alfred Douglas to RF, [London], February 13, 1905 (MJB).
4. Oscar Wilde: *The Letters of*, ed. Rupert Hart-Davis (London, 1962), p. 831. The letter was written from Paris about June 29, 1900, to Robert Ross.

knowledging his pederasty, he could hardly have chosen a more appropriate correspondent in all England.

At this time, however, any relationship between Douglas and Firbank was by letter. In his first one, Firbank announced his imminent departure for Spain. It was a country just then of unusual interest to the British, politically because of the Moroccan question and romantically because of Alfonso XIII's interest in Victoria Eugenia of Battenberg, who became his queen in 1906. Douglas's reply suggested that if Firbank planned to be in London *en route* to Madrid, he might call at 31 Walpole Street, Chelsea. "Perhaps you will come & look me up," Douglas wrote.[5]

Without taking advantage of Douglas's invitation, Firbank reached Madrid about February 22, 1905,[6] and went at once to Miss Eliza Briggs's "First Class English Pension." It was at Calle Mayor 92, a location at the western end of the Calle Mayor in a building now attached to the Catedral de Nuestra Señora de la Almudena, rebuilt since the Spanish Civil War. In 1905 the original cathedral was still under construction, and number 92 stood apart on the wide street not far from the birthplaces of Calderón and Lope de Vega, the Italian Embassy, and the Palacio de los Consejos, from which, the next year, Matteo Morales threw a bomb at King Alfonso and his bride as they rode in procession after their marriage ceremony. Miss Briggs afterward moved her pension to Calle Luzon 11; but in Firbank's day it was still at Calle Mayor 92. It advertised itself as providing "Air, Electric light, Lift etc," and with these advantages as well as Miss Briggs's helpfulness it housed innumerable Englishmen in Spain. Wyndham Lewis, for one, had been there in 1902.

On his arrival, Firbank found awaiting him an invitation to

5. Alfred Douglas to RF, London, February 13, 1905 (MJB).
6. Cf. Eliza Briggs, Document, Madrid, January 26, 1906 (Berg).

lunch dated February 13 and a proffer of friendship from his "nearest English neighbours" Mr. and Mrs. George Young.[7] Jessie Young, who had written to Ronald, was one of Sir Ilbert Courtenay's five daughters. Less than a year before, she had married George Young, appointed in 1904 attaché at the British Embassy in Madrid after service in Washington, Athens, and Constantinople. When the Youngs had first come to Madrid, they too had stopped at Miss Briggs's pension, but they had soon moved into a flat at Calle Mayor 95. Mrs. Young had learned—mistakenly as to date—from the English chaplain of Firbank's impending arrival and had hastened to send him a note of welcome. She was to play a considerable part in helping Firbank live up to his idea of himself.

Unfortunately he arrived too late to accept Jessie Young's invitation, and he did not meet the Youngs for some time because he was ill when he reached Madrid. He was only beginning to recover on February 25. Mrs. Young wrote to commiserate with him on that date and to hope he was able to get out into the sun a little. She sent him some "light literature," novels which were "old friends," to help him while away the hours and urged him to come in for tea or lunch when he was "all right again."

Firbank's first concern when he recovered was arranging his rooms in a way he believed suited to his personality. Harold Nicolson has described them as having walls "distempered with a light buff wash" and arranged "with red silk, and walnut furniture, and two large gilt candelabra from a church."[8] Candles burned in them often, and the smell of incense hung over the rooms and permeated the numerous cushions and books.

7. Cf. Jessie H. Young to RF, Madrid, February 13, 1905. (All Mrs. Young's letters cited here are in the Fales Library.)
8. Harold Nicolson: "Lambert Orme," *Some People* (London, 1927), p. 60.

Early in March Firbank began his studies. Still in pursuit of a diplomatic career, he had come to Madrid and to Miss Briggs's pension to learn Spanish, and in his usual, dutiful way he worked at it. He was, as Miss Briggs said, "a very steady hardworking youth."[9] For the four months, March through June, during which he studied Spanish, he "attended his lectures with great regularity." His teacher, Sra. Rafaela Llorens de Herraiz, testified to that and to the fact that he "made a very good progress during his stay."[1] Still, Firbank's Spanish, though fluent, was never as idiomatic or as correct as his French.

At first his deficiency in the language barred Firbank from one of his chief pastimes, the theater. He attended performances of opera (usually Italian) at the Teatro Real, but the subtleties of the performances at the Teatro Español or the Teatro de la Comedia were beyond his immediate comprehension. Eventually he overcame this handicap enough to enjoy the theater from time to time and at least once with a friend, Manuel (Manolo) de Hernandez y Sevilla.[2] But not one Spanish actor or actress appears in his photograph album.

According to Nicolson, Firbank was too "shy and coy" to talk with ease in any language.[3] Just the same, his Spanish teacher gave him for his collection of keepsakes an inscribed *carte de visite* of her cousin Victoria, the Marquesa de Peñafiel, and wrote notes to him ending, "with kindest regards from your affectionate friend who kisses your hands."[4] And when his friend Wyniewski took him to tea with a Sra.

9. Eliza Briggs, Document, Madrid, January 26, 1906 (Berg).
1. Rafaela Llorens de Herraiz, Document, Madrid, January 31, 1906 (Berg).
2. Cf. Manuel de Hernandez y Sevilla to RF, [Madrid], n.d. (Fales).
3. Harold Nicolson to Jocelyn Brooke, Sissinghurst, Cranbrooke, Kent, November 30, 1948 (Berg).
4. Rafaela Llorens de Herraiz to RF, [Madrid], n.d. (Fales; translated from Spanish by Sonja P. Karsen).

Ivaurez, he fully expected Firbank to "be eloquent with charming phrases."[5]

Shy and silent or charming and eloquent, Firbank was very much the man of fashion in Madrid. He entertained at tea in his rooms with great attention to the tea cloth and graceful movements with the tea-things. One guest, Antonio de Hoyos y Vincent, recalled such an afternoon at Calle Mayor 92 and described Firbanks as *"alto, rubio, delgado y un poco presuntuoso, aunque con chic, un tanto afectadillo."*[6] He received all kinds of invitations: to go to public services at the chapel of the Royal Palace with "Manolo" de Hernandes, to have tea with José Gomez Acebo, to visit El Escorial with Guillermo Rolland.[7] He was asked frequently for lunch or tea with the Youngs.

Firbank attended at least one memorable dinner at the Youngs' flat. On May 4, Mrs. Young sent a note across to Firbank, "Will you be neighbourly & come in to dine with us at 8.30 *tonight* to fill the Belgian Ambassador's place who has been detained by a railway accident?" Firbank forgave "the informality" because Jessie Young asked it and went to the dinner party. The lady he took in that May evening was Sra. Ojeda. Their hostess identified her the next day in answer to Firbank's questions as an Australian whose husband had formerly been Spanish Ambassador to the United States and was presently Undersecretary for Foreign Affairs. It was to Sra. Ojeda, at the Youngs' dinner party, that Firbank confided his resolution that "should he ever be obliged to earn his living he would become a gardener," a circumstance later

5. J. Wyniewski to RF, [Madrid], n.d. (Fales; translated from French by MJB).
6. Quoted from Fletcher: *Ronald Firbank A Memoir*, p. 25.
7. Cf. Manuel de Hernandez y Sevilla to RF, [Madrid], n.d.; José Gomez Acebo to RF, Madrid, [March 1905]; Guillermo Rolland to RF, [Madrid], n.d. (Fales).

chronicled in "Lady Appledore's Mésalliance."[8] Firbank and
his confidence must have been a surprise to a lady expecting
to meet the Belgian Ambassador. But with Spanish punctili-
ousness, her husband Sr. Emilio Ojeda afterward left his card
for Firbank at Calle Mayor 92.

Spanish formality fascinated Firbank, and he did his best to
participate in it. He observed the conventions of the bullfights
carefully, and with Guillermo Rolland went to a *"course de
toro."* Dressed in white-duck trousers, a blazer, and a boater,
Firbank even tried some cape-play with a mild bull before the
eyes of mantilla-draped ladies.[9] When he saw fashionable
Madrid on parade late in the afternoon along the Paseo de
Recoletas—ladies in their carriages and gentlemen on horse-
back—Firbank determined to join them. Jessie Young advised him, helped him acquire a horse, and discussed his riding with him over tea. More than once she invited him to
come in at teatime if he had "nothing better to do" and tell
her and her husband how his riding was "getting on."

Firbank rode often with the Youngs and with Harold
Nicolson. Nicolson told how, at the Casa de Campos, Firbank
"mounted his horse and remained there with surprising firmness, and, moreover, with an elegance . . . His languid manner
dropped from him; if his back curved slightly it was but with a
hellenic curve, the forward-seat of some Panathenaic rider."[1]
Firbank had ridden a long time; he had learned at Chislehurst
on the horses (Tigress, for instance) about which Baba had
asked his advice. That he sat so well is hardly remarkable.

In Madrid he saw a great deal of Nicolson, who was there
that winter and spring with his father Sir Arthur Nicolson,
Ambassador from Great Britain to the court of Spain. Since

8. Cf. "Lady Appledore's Mésalliance," in *The New Rythum and Other
Pieces* (London, 1962), p. 37.
9. Cf. Guillermo Rolland to RF, [Madrid], n.d., and photo (Fales).
1. Nicolson: "Lambert Orme," *Some People*, p. 58; cf. letter to RF, Madrid,
n.d. (Fales).

Firbank had come to Madrid with a letter of introduction to the elder Nicolsons—both mothers were Irish and both fathers had been distinguished at King Edward's coronation—and they were kindly people, Firbank had frequent invitations to lunch or dinner.[2] He grew quite familiar with the tinkling chandeliers and the red damask hung in the reception rooms of the old Palace of Cardinal Ximénez, which then housed the Embassy. His association with their son, who was not entirely enthusiastic about Firbank, was adequate to provide young Nicolson with material for his character Lambert Orme in *Some People*. Nicolson said that his account in *Some People* of his meeting with Lambert Orme was "more or less accurate" with respect to Firbank and definitely conveyed the impression Firbank made at the time, definitely gave some "idea of what Firbank seemed at that age to a rather conventional person. . . ."[3] Nicolson described Ronald Firbank—or Lambert Orme—as having "a curved face, a boneless face, a rather pink face, fleshy above the chin." About his walk, Nicolson wrote:

> It was more than sinuous, it did more than undulate: it rippled. At each step a wave was started which passed upwards through his body, convexing his buttocks, concaving the small of his back, convexing again his slightly rounded shoulders, and working itself out in a backward swaying of the neck and head.[4]

He stated that Orme dressed simply, wearing a pin in his cravat and a "velours hat tilted angularly." Photographs taken in Madrid show Nicolson's description to be accurate.

2. Cf. M. C. Nicolson to RF, Madrid, [March 4, March 21, and April 28, 1905], and n.d.; Harold Nicolson to RF, Madrid, March 25, 1905, and n.d. (Fales).
3. Harold Nicolson to Jocelyn Brooke, Sissinghurst, Cranbrook, Kent, November 30, 1948 (Berg).
4. Nicolson: "Lambert Orme," *Some People*, pp. 56, 55.

Firbank is pictured, *sans* hat, holding so as to exhibit his long slender fingers a copy of the special large-paper impression of *Odette*. His hair is gently waved, and his clothes are conspicuous only in their elegance.

Once, at least, Firbank went with Nicolson to "do the pictures" at the Museo del Prado.[5] Thereafter he went alone. He examined with meticulous care the colors and grouping of Velázquez's portraits and the brutal honesty of Goya's. Goya's figures and scenes, whether improvised with the typical or the momentary, taught Firbank something about the exposition of human values and the place of hypocrisy among them.

It hardly matters that Firbank made no immediate use of what he learned. The important thing is that he stored up his learning for literary use; he never lost sight of himself as a coming man of letters. Satisfying that view of himself as well as his worldly-wise role may account for his continued correspondence with Alfred Douglas. Firbank wrote early in March, reminding Douglas of his promise to send a copy of *The City of the Soul*. Douglas's reply, dated March 31, 1905, explained that "owing to that beast Grant Richards having gone bankrupt" all the copies of his book were "in the hands of the official receiver."[6] Firbank's next communication included two photographs of himself made by the fashionable Kaulak of Madrid. Meanwhile, when *Odette D'Antrevernes* came out in June, Firbank had his publisher Elkin Mathews send a copy to Douglas, who duly acknowledged both, remarking that he preferred the full-face photograph to a side view and commenting on the new book, "Though slight it is both attractive and well-written."[7]

5. Harold Nicolson to RF, Madrid, n.d. (on *carte de visite*, Fales).
6. Alfred Douglas to RF, [London], March 31, 1905 (MJB).
7. Alfred Douglas to RF, London, June 16, 1905 (MJB).

How much writing Firbank did in Madrid is uncertain. He showed one essay in French, either "Reverie" or "Flavia," to Jessie Young. "Flavia" is merely a description of an interior. "Reverie" is in the style of the prose poems he had written during his stay in Paris the year before, "La Princesse aux Soleils" and *Far Away*. Mrs. Young thanked him for the "loan" of his "article" and said that it read "very pleasantly & easily." She asked him, "Have you attempted a Spanish essay yet?"[8] That he wrote nothing else during his stay in Madrid seems unlikely; he was rarely without some composition in hand. Yet his next piece, "Mr. White-Morgan the Diamond King," is so specific in its topical references (the imminent general election and unemployment) and its locale (London's Old Compton Street) that it is hard to believe it was composed before his departure from Spain. The following one, "Impression d'Automne," is dated October 7, 1905, well after his return to England.

Although he left Miss Briggs's on July 6, 1905,[9] Firbank did not go to England at once. The Biais family had hoped he would join them once more in their Châlet du Lac at Meuthen-St. Bernard. M. Biais, on April 28, had sent brief greetings on a postcard ornamented with his photograph made in his study. In May, Mme Biais-Cazalis had written a long letter to tell Firbank about La Duse and the *"pièces nouvelles fort inté-ressantes et amusantes"* at the Vaudeville and the Opéra-Comique. She asked whether he meant to join her family at Meuthen in the summer and assured him not only that it would give the Biais family joy to relive the happy days of the past year with him but also that Meuthen was unthinkable

8. Jessie H. Young to RF, Madrid, n.d. (Fales). Both essays are in manuscript, a part of the Fales Library.
9. Miss Briggs stated in a document dated January 26, 1906 (cf. p. 60, n.6), that Firbank left her pension July 6, 1906. Since Miss Briggs was writing almost six months before July 6, 1906, her statement is obviously mistaken.

without him.[1] Instead of joining the Biais family, Firbank
went first to the mountains north of Madrid to Segovia and on
to San Ildefonso and La Granja. Soon after his arrival at La
Granja, he conducted a new acquaintance, Standish Vereker,
to a bullfight, first making plans over dinner to avoid the
"disagreeable details" of the ring for Vereker's sake.[2] From
the Hotel Europeo, La Granja, he wrote to the English booksellers Robson & Co. asking whether they could obtain "the
copy of Wilde's 'Happy Prince' sold at Mrs Brown Potter's
Sale last week, & in which there is a dedication written by the
author." His letter to Robson & Co. ended, "Hoping you have
sold all the copies of my book that you have!"[3] While at the
Hotel Europeo, he acquired a prize for his album, a photograph
of the Infanta Isabel inscribed "To Mr A. A. R. Firbank Isabel
de Bourbon" and dated July 31, 1905, at San Ildefonso. In exchange Firbank graciously presented to her one of the ten
copies of the large-paper impressions of *Odette* bound in
white vellum.[4] Then he moved on to San Sebastian, the summer residence of the royal family and the most fashionable
seaside resort in Spain. It was also the place where most
would-be British diplomats went to perfect their Spanish ac-
cent. At San Sebastian, Firbank spent July and most of the
month of August in lazy enjoyment of the Casino, the promenades skirting the Concha, and the sea bathing (Firbank
swam well) from the beach, where the bathing-machines were
drawn by oxen. Only toward the end of August did he return
to England.

1. Cf. Henry Biais to RF, Paris, April 28, 1905; L. Biais-Cazalis to RF,
Paris, May 7, 1905 (Fales).
2. Cf. Standish Vereker to RF, San Jeronimo, June 19, 1905 (Fales).
3. RF to [Robson & Co.], La Granja, [June 22, 1905] (MJB).
4. Cf. RF to CVV, London, June 29, 1922.

⚛ VI ⚛

The next year was a varied one, with frequent moves and much activity of both a social and literary kind. Promptly on reaching Chislehurst, Firbank took up his literary life. He began at The Coopers by sending the copies of *"Les Essais"* containing his "La Princesse aux Soleils" and "Harmonie" to Alfred Douglas. If Firbank had any purpose except to reaffirm his stature as an author, it came to nothing. Douglas wrote a letter of thanks for the "two French Reviews," declared he thought the "poems in prose charming" and said he was leaving for Scotland but would have Firbank in for lunch in October.[1] Firbank was also busy with new compositions. "Mr. White-Morgan the Diamond King" occupied him first.[2] What survives of this piece, a rough draft, demonstrates that once more Firbank was giving free rein to his satirical bent, once more was writing a piece directly out of his own and Baba's environment. The hero, Mr. White-Morgan, is a "typical type of a self made nouveau riche" who is happiest when he sees his picture in the newspapers. His first success "in notarity" had been with a balloon. He and his wife made a practice of lunching in their balloon above Piccadilly until the police stopped them because Mrs. White-Morgan let fell a salad plate, which "severely cut an omnibus horse." London forgot the general election[3] and the "Unemployed Question"

---

1. Alfred Douglas to RF, [London], September 3, 1905 (MJB).
2. Manuscript unsigned and incomplete (private collection).
3. Prepared for and talked about in 1905 but actually held in January 1906.

when the White-Morgans bought a whole street of houses near Piccadilly Circus to make a garden. In June, at the height of the London season, they gave a "Hay party" to exhibit the garden on "Old Cumpton Street" and to celebrate their daughter's birthday. The remainder of the manuscript tells about the party and the guests. It breaks off after the guest of honor, Miss Cicely White-Morgan, "dressed as a Bergere with Crook & bearing a little white lamb in her arms," has danced a "gavotte with the Premier danseur" from the Paris Opera. This tale is inconsequential, but in it Firbank is less the reporter than he had been in "Lila" and even *A Study in Temperament.* He has transformed his material imaginatively, and his dialogue for the first time depends on association.

"Impression d'Automne," Firbank's next piece, was completed by October 7. It tells of the meditations of the autumn leaves as they lie on the ground; at last they understand the summer music of the nightingale who "sang of the coming of Death." After it was typed, Firbank changed the name to "Souvenir d'Automne," but he kept the subtitle, "A Poem in Prose." In the spirit of Pierre Louÿs, Firbank had already experimented with prose poems during his stay in Paris. Both Pozzi and Douglas referred to Firbank's compositions of that time as "poems in prose." Besides, Firbank's subtitle had an exotic quality, inasmuch as Oscar Wilde's prose poems had been privately printed in Paris that year and were for sale in England at a shilling a copy. Firbank submitted "Souvenir d'Automne" to *The King and His Navy and Army,* where it was published with artistic illustrations in December.[4] This was the first piece to which he put his full name only, Arthur Annesley Ronald Firbank; after December 1905 he signed the name Arthur Firbank exactly two more times, once for

4. P. 11.

published material and once for an unpublished piece.

The latter was "Her Dearest Friend," composed either in December 1905 or January 1906.[5] This is a set of three pictures: the arrival of Lady Clio Say for an "at home," the "at home" with the hostess and guests, and Lady Clio's departure. As she leaves, she learns that her lover and her hostess are planning to be married, and she silently considers her next maneuver. Although the characters are too lightly sketched and the comment too specific, "Her Dearest Friend" is an advance from the single set piece such as *Far Away* to a series in counterpoint.

Two other pieces belong to this twelve-month period. One, in an untitled rough draft, begins (after two paragraphs marked for deletion), "The Roses were never called before seven." It is a description of the roses' grief at the death of the gardener's small daughter, Winnie.[6] The second is "The Singing Bird & The Moon."[7] It tells of an ardent love between a bird and the moon. Because the bird loves passionately, her song is sweet enough to lull Queen Caridad to sleep. When the song fails, the queen's people ceremonially kill the bird, and the moon's tears of grief water the crops. This elaborate contrivance, similar to "The Mauve Tower" and "Souvenir d'Automne," is without literary value.

"The Singing Bird & The Moon" was the last such effusion Firbank wrote. With its abundance of epithets and images and its want of substance, it provided no basis for growth. Its reliance on stylization, never adequate as a sole vehicle of representation, was confining. Firbank's two excursions at this time into his own projection of reality—one, "Mr. White-Morgan the Diamond King," probably left unfinished, and the

5. Typescript signed Arthur Firbank (MJB).
6. Manuscript unsigned (Academic Center Library, University of Texas).
7. Typescript signed Arthur Annesley Ronald Firbank (Rush Rees Library, University of Rochester).

other, "Her Dearest Friend," inadequately developed—exhibit his creative sense breaking out of self-imposed limitations. Works such as "The Roses were never called" and "The Singing Bird" unquestionably began in his relationship with his mother, but they also exemplified his artistic convictions. He was, however, groping toward another kind of expression, or, to put it more precisely, away from the blind alley of "The Singing Bird," "Souvenir d'Automne," and even *Odette*. His effort is demonstrated by his showing the typescript of an article to Alfred Douglas, probably in November 1905, and asking his advice about submitting it to *The English Review,* a periodical in which Douglas published.[8] The article does not survive. The only source of information about it is an undated letter which Douglas began by telling Firbank that the article was "no good for the English Review." Douglas went on:

> It is not long enough, it is not worked out, & it has nothing particularly new in it. In fact from the point of view of journalism it is absolutely worthless. If you want to go in for journalism you must write on actual topics or learn not to waste space by such phrases as "in the short space at our disposal" et cet: which are cliches of the worst type.

He explained that he spoke so plainly because he believed Firbank "had something" in him. Douglas reaffirmed that opinion in another letter after Firbank had sent him a copy of "Souvenir d'Automne." Douglas said that he thought the "Poem in Prose" quite charming. "You are much better," he wrote, "when you stick to your own line of imaginative & descriptive suggestion than when you are trying to be practical."[9] His praise of "Souvenir d'Automne" was mistaken, but

8. *The English Review* appeared from October 21, 1905, to February 17, 1906.
9. Alfred Douglas to RF, [London], December 23, 1905 (MJB).

he was right in principle. Firbank's difficulty was in acknowledging his "own line," perhaps in even knowing what it was. To continue his writing, however, he had to move outside the limitations inherent in "Souvenir d'Automne" and "The Singing Bird."

While Firbank was undergoing this adjustment in his literary perspective, his mode of life was changing too. The past four years had been spent abroad. Beginning with his return from Spain, he would spend the next twelve years in England with frequent excursions elsewhere. He had returned to England to prepare for admission to Trinity Hall, Cambridge, in connection with his and Baba's ambition that he enter the diplomatic service. It was an aim which persisted for a few years and then gave way to an intention to try for a clerkship in the House of Lords. For either career a university education seemed necessary; and Baba had chosen Trinity Hall at Cambridge because her grandfather had matriculated there.

In September or early October, after his arrival from San Sebastian, Firbank entered Scoones's, a crammer mainly for Civil Service candidates, in Garrick Chambers at 19 Garrick Street, London. Mr. Scoones in his time coached men who made a name for themselves, such as Edward Marsh, Maurice Baring, Harold Nicolson, John Mitford, and Edward Lascelles. These last two were fellow students with Firbank. He performed in his usual dutiful way for Scoones, continuing his French with M. Turquet, studying what he was required to, behaving agreeably, and distinguishing himself in no way as a student.

During the one term he was at Scoones's, Firbank lived at 49 Nevern Square in the home of one of the tutors who was also a scholar and a bibliophile, Mr. de Vincheles Payen-Payne, who wrote of Firbank's stay with him:

Mr. Scoones suggested to Firbank that he should live in my house. He was entirely spoiled by his mother, who was the cause of the weakness of his character. When he came to live with us she sent a footman and a housemaid to prepare his room with a new bed, complete with eiderdown, and a special armchair. Mitford and Lascelles dominated this weakling, and used to borrow his eiderdown and anything else they desired. Firbank, although weak, had a sweet nature and perfect manners.[1]

Firbank remembered his time in the tall, red brick house at 49 Nevern Square for another reason. Long afterward he told Payen-Payne, "It was at your house that I first heard of Dowson and read first Verlaine."[2]

Firbank might very well have heard of them from Alfred Douglas. True to his promise made in September, Douglas invited Firbank for lunch in October. Firbank readily accepted and the next day sent such flowers to Lady Douglas that she declared, "When I first saw your beautiful flowers I thought that Autumn herself had passed down the street and left them for me."[3] This was Firbank's initial meeting with the Douglases, and he got on well with them. Lady Douglas wrote that she was delighted to find that they liked the same things, and five days later Douglas wrote to "Dear Arthur" to accept an invitation to *Madame Butterfly*.[4] The performance they attended, on October 24, 1925, was one at which the composer, Puccini, was present; with the conductor and the principal singers, he was called before the curtain for enthusiastic applause.[5]

1. Quoted in Fletcher: *Ronald Firbank A Memoir,* p. 25.
2. Ibid.
3. Olive Douglas to RF, London, October 18, 1905 (MJB).
4. Cf. Alfred Douglas to RF, [London], October 23, 1905 (MJB).
5. Cf. London *Times,* October 25, 1905, p. 5.

This acquaintance with Douglas progressed far enough for him to address Firbank as "My dear Boy" in letters.[6] No doubt Firbank saw Douglas more than once after leaving Scoones's, but only one such meeting, which took place at Cambridge, is certain. He kept alive his correspondence with Douglas throughout the years at the university and paraded his friendship with Douglas at that time. In 1913, Firbank snubbed Oscar Wilde's son Vyvyan Holland for his pleasure at a series of lawsuits which Douglas lost. But Firbank's enthusiasm for what Douglas represented in literature had already begun to fade as his own literary individuality changed and grew; and by 1916 Douglas was no longer among the friends designated to receive copies of Firbank's novels as they appeared. In 1921 Firbank called Douglas an "impossible creature" and declared that if the whole of *De Profundis* were to be published, Douglas would "go down the ages as a type of false & treacherous friend."[7]

During these months in London, Firbank was occupied in many ways which involved neither Douglas nor his studies at Scoones. He may have had lessons in elocution. Before September 15 he sent the actor Henry Ainley a copy of *Odette* and proposed that Ainley assist him in elocution. Ainley refused on the grounds that all his time was fully taken up with the theater. Possibly Firbank found someone less busy than Henry Ainley. Firbank went repeatedly to the theater and opera. He dined at the Savoy or ventured into the Café Royal. He visited his tailor (he had taken up the new dinner jacket and the Norfolk coat), and he spent more than enough time

6. Cf. Alfred Douglas to RF [London, 1906], and February 4, 1906.
7. RF to HJGF, Montreux, November 4, 1921. Cf. holograph list of proposed recipients of *Inclinations* (MJB); Vyvyan Holland to RF, London, April 25, 1913 (Fales); Rupert Croft-Cooke: *Bosie* (Indianapolis, 1963), pp. 232–5, 238, 241–4 *et passim;* see below, pp. 94–5, 98–101.

ordering his shirts, now with heavy stripes instead of the severely plain ones of Paris and Madrid, from Hopkinson and
his ties from Harboroughs.

All this activity left him little time for his studies; so Baba
ended his stay in London. She sent a servant to pack his
belongings and a moving van from Maples to fetch the new
bed, his sheets and pillowcases, as well as the much-borrowed
eiderdown.[8] "We were very sorry to lose your son yesterday,"
Payen-Payne wrote to Lady Firbank in a letter dated December 9, 1905; "he proved quite an ideal member of our small
household."[9]

In the following nine months, Firbank concentrated on
preparing for the "Little Go" at Cambridge. As an entering
student who had not been excused from it, he had to pass this
preliminary examination, the "Little Go," which included
Greek as a compulsory subject. By the second week in December, Firbank was a "resident pupil" at The Parsonage,
Bieldside, Aberdeenshire, under the instruction of the Reverend F. W. S. Sievre. In addition to being the rector of St.
Domenick's Church, Sievre was examiner in French for the
Oxford Delegacy for Local Examinations. He took seriously
his obligation to prepare Firbank for Cambridge, as Baba was
aware. Bertie had spent some time with Sievre in 1902 or
1903, and she knew she could count on his diligence with
Artie. Besides, there were few distractions at Bieldside, and the
winter months were bitterly cold. Firbank had nothing to do
except study, so Sievre could testify that he had "no fault to
find" with Firbank in "either his conduct or industry."[1]

How long Firbank stayed with Sievre is unknown. In April,
he invited Douglas to lunch in London; but Douglas, because

8. Cf. HJGF to Mrs. Payen-Payne, n.p., n.d. (Sewell Stokes).
9. (Berg).
1. F. W. S. Sievre, Document, Bieldside, Aberdeenshire, June 20, 1906
(Berg).

he was at Lake Farm near Salisbury and, he said, "delighted to escape from London," was forced to refuse.[2] Perhaps Firbank was on holiday in April and away from Bieldside only temporarily. By late June or early July he was under the tutelage of R. E. Johnston at The Vicarage, St. Peter's-in-Thanet, Kent, and he remained there until shortly after August 10. Baba concluded that her son was not getting on fast enough with Mr. Johnston and, after making other arrangements, informed him to that effect. Mr. Johnston was sorry to learn her decision, but there was nothing he could do about it, as he said; so he sent good wishes for "Arthur's success in October" and added, "He has been a most pleasant addition to our circle whilst he has been with us & I shall always feel interest in him."[3] Back Ronald went to Bieldside.

In spite of his frequent moves and his real concentration on preparing for Cambridge, Firbank was at work on the short novel later called *The Artificial Princess*. Its name then was "Salomé Or 'Tis A Pity That She Would." The first title reflects his study of Jacobean drama, probable conversations with Alfred Douglas, and his usual attention to current theater and music. Firbank had already demonstrated an interest in the Salomé story by his reference to it in "Her Dearest Friend." In the new piece, he used the story as an underlying theme with almost no hint of what Baudelaire called "the phosphorescence of putrescence." Indeed, eroticism is frustrated in *The Artificial Princess*. Even so, Firbank could not then make the heavy sensuality inherent in the legend of Salomé coincide with the delicate suggestivity of his characterization. "Salomé Or 'Tis A Pity That She Would" was unfinished when Firbank went to Cambridge in October.

For a time in September, his admission to Cambridge was

2. Alfred Douglas to RF, Lake Farm, Salisbury, April 28, 1906 (MJB).
3. R. E. Johnston to HJGF, St. Peter's-in-Thanet, August 10, 1906 (Berg).

in jeopardy. Mr. Sievre discovered that Firbank was preparing in the wrong gospel, in St. Mark instead of the one set
for the "Little Go," St. Luke. Sievre was quick to explain to G.
B. Shirres, Firbank's prospective tutor at Trinity Hall. Sievre
declared that "Mr A Firbank" had been the "victim of a serious
mistake." Sievre went on to say that because of an oversight on
the part of Johnston Firbank had given his attention to St.
Mark, and there was "no possibility of preparing St Luke so
late in the day. Consequently his chances of passing the Little
Go in Oct seem to be destroyed." Sievre's letter to Shirres continued:

> He is getting on well & steadily with his other subjects, &
> would no doubt with sufficient tuition during the October
> term pass in December. So I hope you will not consider this
> untoward circumstance a bar to his entering the college,
> which he is very anxious to do.[4]

Plans for Firbank's going to Cambridge had progressed to the
point where he had already been assigned rooms, Baba had
inquired about furniture for them, and she was gathering together all sorts of small useful objects for him to take with
him.[5] Fortunately Sievre was able to compensate for the mistake about the gospel with a personal recommendation of Firbank. In the same letter to Shirres, Sievre wrote about his
student, "I need not perhaps say that he is a thorough gentleman, & though not perhaps well grounded in the ordinary
Public School subjects has other, useful attainments, & is not
likely to be anything but a credit to his college." Shirres,
acting for Trinity Hall, settled the whole matter in a letter to
Sievre dated September 14, 1906. He stated that under the

---

4. F. W. S. Sievre to G. B. Shirres, n.p., n.d. (Berg).
5. Cf. G. B. Shirres to HJGF, Cambridge, August 6, 1906 (Berg).

circumstances "young Firbank" could defer taking the examination until December, but he would come into residence on October 12.[6]

♋ VII ♋

For many men their university experience is a memorable one. Writers as unlike each other as Abraham Cowley and Matthew Arnold, John Henry Newman and Max Beerbohm have celebrated it. Leonard Woolf described his years at Cambridge as the happiest and the most miserable of his entire life. "One lived," he said, "in a state of continual excitement and strong and deep feeling."[1] Oxford, John Rothenstein wrote, gave him much of what he needed when his "need was greatest" and taught him "what it was like to be constantly happy."[2] Rupert Brooke and Geoffrey Keynes, contemporaries of Firbank, satisfied their passion for friendship and intellectual adventure at Cambridge.

To Ronald Firbank, Cambridge meant almost nothing. Only one important thing happened to him during his time there: his conversion in 1907 to the Roman Catholic faith. Otherwise he might as well have been in Madrid, Berlin, Venice, anywhere. He was half-hearted about his lectures and the languages he read. One of them, German, he never mastered.[3]

6. (Berg).
1. Leonard Woolf: *Sowing* (New York, 1960), p. 173.
2. John Rothenstein: *Summer's Lease* (London, 1966), p. 95.
3. Cf. RF to HF, Tunis, November 12, 1920, where he wrote, "I only wish I could read German, but unfortunately that is a language I have never learnt—."

He participated in several undergraduate activities and, as one of his college mates said, "did his best"; but his heart was not in those either. Firbank had been too successful in the artful composition of his personality for Cambridge to make much impact on him. His existence, self-contained and very private, went on in Cambridge exactly as it would have had he been elsewhere.

As Mr. Shirres, his tutor, had promised, Firbank came into residence at Trinity Hall, Cambridge, on October 12, 1906. He arrived there by hansom cab, driving from the railway station through Cambridge's quiet, country streets, enlivened that day by the sound of horses' hooves and the metal-rimmed wheels of hansoms or growlers. The city of Cambridge maintained two horse-drawn trams and an omnibus which ran from the station to Market Place; but most of the new men, baggage and all, arrived at their colleges in hansoms. That Friday, October 12, more than fifty hansoms plied between the station and the colleges. When Firbank, carefully dressed in a dark suit and his customary velours hat, reached Trinity Hall entrance on Trinity Lane, he was shown halfway down the Front Court and into South Court, popularly called the Small Court, where on the ground floor of F staircase was the set of rooms, F2, he was to occupy for most of the next three years. As instructed by the Head Porter, Firbank then proceeded to a required interview with Shirres. George Buchan Shirres, Head Tutor at Trinity Hall, was a "rather dour Scot from Aberdeen"; most students "were shy of him and never got below the surface." According to Bishop G. A. Chase, who knew him well, Shirres was in fact a kindly man who could be "pretty severe when necessary; but he would do all he could to help anyone who needed help."[4] Only his kindness appeared now as he discussed a private tutor for the study

4. Bishop G. A. Chase to MJB, Cambridge, April 17, 1965.

of German. But the interview was brief and Firbank went on, properly clad in academic gown, to pay his other required calls.

This done, he turned his attention to getting settled, so that by the end of his first week in Cambridge, that is on October 19, he heard Fritz Kreisler in concert and, on November 1, saw *The School for Scandal* enacted at the New Theatre. He gave his real attention, however, to his rooms. He made of them the most elegant Trinity Hall had had and certainly one of the few notable things about his stay there. Forty years afterward a fellow member of Trinity Hall recalled the wonder which the beautiful furnishings of Firbank's rooms aroused.[5] They were not the rooms Harold Nicolson attributed to Lambert Orme: shiny black walls, gray sofas with petunia cushions, a Coromandel cabinet with blue china on the top and hardstone stuff inside.[6] Photographs of his living room attest to light-colored walls and other differences.[7] These photographs suggest, though, that in respect to what the living room was, Nicolson's adjective for Lambert Orme, *"cabotin,"* might well apply to Firbank. A large Oriental rug with smaller ones placed over it lay on the floor along with sizable fat cushions. Four more cushions were placed on a low sofa upholstered in velvet. Numerous small tables dotted the room, and on these sat books piled in groups of four or five, porcelain boxes, statuettes, miniatures on porcelain or ivory, vases filled with flowers, and photographs. There was one of Daddy, one of Baba in court dress, another of Heather appearing demure, and, looming large, a picture taken from his album and framed, the one signed "Isabel de Bourbon." More pictures were on the walls, etchings by Helleu[8] and at least

5. W. H. Adgey-Edgar to MJB, Guildford, December 9, 1965.
6. Cf. Nicolson: "Lambert Orme," *Some People,* p. 61.
7. See Plate V.
8. Cf. Vyvyan Holland: "Ronald Firbank," in Ifan Kyrle Fletcher: *Ronald Firbank A Memoir* (London, 1930), p. 103.

one by Whistler. Over the sofa were two reproductions, a Leonardo Christ and a Madonna possibly by Raphael or Perugino, and over the mantel, a gilt-framed mirror. Deep red silk hung at the windows.[9] But the place of honor went to a grand piano. Firbank was the only undergraduate at the Hall who had a grand piano, and it and the flowers which filled his rooms attracted notice. Shane Leslie "found too much scent and flowers" in the rooms; but G. H. Woodhouse, who "kept" in the neighboring staircase in the same court, remembered that Firbank was "certainly an aesthete and used to have lovely flowers on his Grand Piano."[1]

That he was not "ragged," that the "men of his time" did not "sack his rooms as occurred to other aesthetes" is remarkable.[2] Perhaps, as Shane Leslie speculated, Firbank's contemporaries felt "laughter or pity" for him.[3] A. C. Landsberg, who went up to Cambridge in 1907, did. "I . . . found him a little ridiculous," he wrote, "—and even sometimes pathetic!"[4] On the other hand, Landsberg admitted that he admired Firbank, and he may have inspired enough respect to avoid "ragging." Not all recollections of him emphasize either his pitiable or laughable aspects. Forrest Reid, a member of King's College, characterized him as "extraordinarily feline and sophisticated," with a "polished surface" that was not "merely protective but extremely baffling."[5] A colleague at Trinity Hall, the Reverend L. Whitcombe, said, "The picture I have of him in my mind is that of an ascetic figure of contemplative demeanor, with a gentle smile, hair slightly long, &

9. Cf. Jocelyn Brooke: *Ronald Firbank* (London, 1951), p. 31.
1. Shane Leslie to MJB, London, October 12, 1963; G. H. Woodhouse to MJB, London, June 16, 1965.
2. Forrest Reid states that Firbank's rooms were "ragged" at least once. Cf. *Private Road* (London, 1940), p. 57.
3. Shane Leslie to MJB, London, October 12, 1963.
4. Quoted in Fletcher: *Ronald Firbank A Memoir*, p. 29.
5. Reid: *Private Road*, pp. 55–6.

wearing a grey Norfolk coat and grey flannel trousers."[6] Another Trinity Hall man, David Hughes, who described Firbank's walk as "a wobble—like a duck!" and Firbank as "slightly effeminate," also said he was "not a bad chap—quite decent."[7]

In any event there was little place for an aesthete in the life of Trinity Hall. In 1906 it was a "rough Rowing College," a "very sporting college" with "some of the finest rowing men Cambridge has seen."[8] Trinity Hall went "Head of the River" in those years; and both the stroke of the Cambridge University crew, D. C. R. Stuart, and the cox, B. G. A. Scott, were Trinity Hall members. Several of Firbank's contemporaries remember him only vaguely because he was not an athlete. "I do not think our paths crossed significantly," Sidney H. Haughton said, because Firbank had no interest in sports but was "of a different mind, literary and artistic" or, as another Hall man E. S. Hornidge suggested, "perhaps one of the studious class."[9] Hornidge was mistaken, but the fact is that Firbank was hardly suited to Trinity Hall.

Nevertheless, he adapted to it. He managed to survive wherever he might be. Indeed, he managed so well that even though at the end of the Michaelmas term he made no attempt to take his examination, the "Little Go," Shirres could give a favorable report of him to Baba. Shirres's letter, dated December 14, 1906, ran:

> I write you just a line to say that your son has got on very well in this his first term. He has made quite satisfactory

6. Reverend L. Whitcombe to MJB, London, June 16, 1965.
7. Dr. W. Hywel Jones to MJB, Cynfor, Cemaes Bay, Anglesey, June 15, 1965 (written for David Jones).
8. Shane Leslie to MJB, London, October 12, 1963; W. H. Adgey-Edgar to MJB, Guildford, December 9, 1965.
9. Sidney H. Haughton to MJB, Pretoria, South Africa, June 24, 1965; E. S. Hornidge to MJB, Dunlaoghaire, County Dublin, June 19, 1965.

progress in German with his tutor and has kept up his
French.

Next term he will probably attend some lectures in Literature—the Clark lectures in March and perhaps Mr Macaulay
on the period 1650–1700 or Mr Wyatt (General Course of
English Literature).[1]

This is one of the few mentions of Firbank's academic life.
The records show that almost the only lectures he heard with
any regularity were Morier Hinde's, given at 8 King's Parade,
in French and English. He had some instruction in Italian,
also from Hinde, and he attended a course in Euclid for one
term. In the Lent term there was a suggestion that he take up
shorthand. This was in preparation for a new career. His plan
for a diplomatic one had been replaced by an intention to try
for a parliamentary clerkship, and shorthand might be valuable in such a post. But nothing came of it and he did not
learn shorthand.[2] That was all. Firbank adjusted to the Hall
and the University in his own way. He created his own environment and lived within it. On the surface it was the elegance of his rooms, where he spent much of his time. Several
of his college mates reported him as very quiet, as keeping to
himself a good deal. One said Firbank was not a man "to
stand off through conceit. He gave . . . the impression of being
rather a humble type who spent most of his time in his own
rooms."[3] Obviously his adaptability lay in the fact that he
lived in a "state of preoccupation," that his life consisted
mainly—to paraphrase Mark Twain—not of happenings but
of the "storm of thoughts" forever in his head. He told
Heather in an undated letter from Cambridge, "Life itself is
usually more dull than otherwise. Mentally of course it can be

1. (Berg).
2. Cf. Graham Storey to MJB, Cambridge, January 10, 1967.
3. W. H. Adgey-Edgar to MJB, Guildford, December 9, 1965.

thoroughly exciting." Far from resenting his separation from his fellows, he was indifferent to it. He had learned at his first school, the Mortimer Vicarage School, the reality of private experience and its value.

But he also warned Heather to beware of reading seriously lest she become "too dissatisfied." In other words, that he was separated does not mean that he was isolated. He took part in the life of the college. Of course he avoided the more rowdy occasions. Adgey-Edgar, a contemporary of Firbank, gave a report of one such event. It runs:

> The branch [of the Fabian Society] at the Hall was naturally not very popular as they were a bit scruffy and socially not quite true blue. I happened to go up to London one afternoon and got back about 8 p.m. There was quite a commotion when I arrived as apparently the Rowing Club members had seized the Fabian members and given them a public bath in the main court. I forget what the result was but I know Firbank kept to his room and was not involved.[4]

This sort of thing was worlds away from the walks with Pozzi on the boulevards of Paris. Not so remote, at least in spirit, were the times when he joined other undergraduates in the rooms of one of them who ran a roulette wheel, and on these occasions he was "quite matey."[5] Firbank had already made his first gesture toward conformity at Trinity Hall, the same one he had made at Uppingham and with about the same enthusiasm. Soon after his arrival he became a member of the Rifle Corps.

Firbank naturally showed far more interest in the literary possibilities at the university. Vyvyan Holland described Firbank's arrival at the Hall as sensational, because it was "ru-

4. Ibid. The Fabian Society of Cambridge was organized in 1906.
5. Ibid.

moured that he had actually had a book published."[6] Men at
the college with literary ambitions called on him at a very
early date, and Holland was among the first. Firbank gave
him an inscribed copy of *Odette D'Antrevernes and A Study
in Temperament* and, in turn, Holland asked Firbank to contribute something to *The Crescent*, an undergraduate magazine which he edited. Whatever Firbank submitted—"a fantasy
in true Firbank vein"—was promptly rejected as unsuited
to *The Crescent*. As Holland said, Firbank was more "indignant than hurt, though he pretended to be neither."[7] He
promptly took the same piece or another one to *The
Granta*, a second undergraduate publication. In November
The Granta published Parts I and II of " 'The Wavering Disciple.' A Fantasia." The third part appeared the following
month.[8] " 'The Wavering Disciple' " is the story of Lady East-
lake, who, weary of her fashionable life and influenced by *The
Imitation of Christ*, decides it would be "sweet to live in a cell
. . . to have lovely visions and perhaps see all the beautiful
jewellery there must be in heaven!" After careful preparation
she spends a few moments eating a tinned *pâté* in her version of
a cell under the shadows of Canterbury Cathedral. Then she
goes to join her husband at Aix, where at the Villa des Fleurs
"one gambled side by side with the demi-monde of Paris."

This is the first piece of fiction in which Firbank concerned
himself with the uses and misuses of religion. He dealt with
the same subject in his next publication, which came out in
the November 2, 1907, issue of *The Granta*, "A Study in
Opal."[9] It tells of Lady Henrietta Worthing who has recently

6. Vyvyan Holland: *Son of Oscar Wilde* (London, 1954), p. 181.
7. Holland: "Ronald Firbank," in Fletcher: *Ronald Firbank A Memoir*, p.
106.
8. *The Granta*, XX (November 24, 1906), 110–11 and (December 5,
1906), 130–2.
9. Pp. 54–60.

married a bishop because she thinks it an "immense attraction" to have a "Cathedral growing at the foot of one's garden." In her infatuation with the cathedral she determines to erect in it a stained glass window in her own honor. The Bishop dies almost immediately after the marriage, possibly reclaimed by his first wife's jealous spirit. Lady Henrietta decides then to make the cathedral window a double one, a "Jacob's Ladder panel for the Bishop and a panel decorated with a St. Francis" for herself. She thinks St. Francis is appropriate for hers because he was "devoted to gardens and birds and the Simple Life," which has always attracted her. The story concludes with Lady Henrietta looking for an artist to create the window.

Both pieces are decidedly in Firbank's vein. His studied allusions (Hobbema, Grieg, Thomas à Kempis) and his sense of the eternal loveliness of the natural world are there. More important is the contrast between the values of his characters and those implicit in the religion to which they pretend, a subject which Firbank would treat repeatedly with varying degrees of intensity. He was developing a mode of fiction which embodied the ridiculous and the satiric. The ridiculous is in the disparity between reality and expectation, and the satiric in the ironic contradictions between the characters' confidence in themselves and what the reader knows about them. It was a kind of fiction at which he was to become extremely adept.

Meanwhile, still in 1907, Firbank tried his hand at drama once more. That year he joined the two undergraduate societies devoted to the theater, the Amateur Dramatic Club and the Footlights. Holland reports that Firbank attended rehearsals and gave his considered opinion on theatrical matters, but that he never participated in a performance. He was offered parts and acted them privately before his mirror; but

he could not bring himself to a public performance. He could,
however, write a play, "A Disciple from the Country."[1] It is a
one-act play with at least one character whose name, Blueharnis, occurs again in the later works "A Tragedy in Green"
and *Vainglory*. If he hoped for the production of "A Disciple," he was disappointed. Apparently no one but the editor
of *The Granta* saw anything in Firbank's literary efforts.

Even though Vyvyan Holland did not, he and Firbank
maintained a friendship, which accounts for more than one
memorable party at Cambridge. Firbank enjoyed entertain-
ing; and he took great pains with the guests, with what was
offered to eat and drink, and above all with the *décor*. He
gave much time and thought to how to "do" his dinner table.
A favorite ornament was a quantity of autumn leaves. Forrest
Reid dined once with Firbank in his college rooms at a table
"strewn with orchids."[2] E. J. Dent remembered a dinner
party when white flowers were massed throughout Firbank's
rooms.[3] On this occasion Rupert Brooke was the only other
guest; and the talk ranged from music, Dent's particular interest, to the latest fiction. Firbank read continuously in both
French and English, usually formulating sound literary judg-
ments. Although he still admired Mrs. Ward's books because
they were "very quietly written, & refined," he considered *The
Man of Property* a "great book in its way" and the Comtesse
de Noailles's *Le Visage Emerveillé* "delightful in another
way."[4]

The talk at Firbank's dinner parties was always wide-
ranging. Coleridge Kennard described a gathering when he

1. Typescript unsigned (private collection; see p. 34, *n.* 9). Cf. Holland:
"Ronald Firbank," in Fletcher: *Ronald Firbank A Memoir,* p. 106.
2. Reid: *Private Road,* p. 56.
3. Cf. RF to HF, Cambridge, n.d.; Fletcher: *Ronald Firbank A Memoir,* p.
30.
4. RF to HF, Cambridge, n.d.

motored to Cambridge with Vyvyan Holland, and Firbank entertained them in his Trinity Hall rooms. The flowers, Kennard said, reminded him "of the wreaths stacked in the Windsor Castle courtyards after the death of Queen Victoria." As the evening progressed, "Wine flowed; conversation became wild."[5] That was at some time between the end of Summer term 1907 and Michaelmas term 1908, because Holland was away from Cambridge during that period. In 1909, after he returned, he and Firbank gave a party to honor Robert Ross. Among the guests were Rupert Brooke, Mario Colonna, Ernst Goldschmidt, A. C. Landsberg, and F. G. W. Parish. Firbank supplied the wine, and Ross, in an argument with Colonna over his father's success as syndic of Rome, supplied the conversation.[6]

These men, E. J. Dent and one or two others such as Shane Leslie, Charles Sayle of the University Library, and Coleridge Kennard, who was not at Cambridge at all, were Firbank's friends during his university days. Most of them continued to be his friends long after those days were over. His relationship with Rupert Brooke was brief and casual. Dent had brought them together, and they found common ground in their interest in the literature of the nineties, especially its decadence. Brooke, like Firbank, was fascinated by the Salomé story. Firbank's taste for *fin de siècle* literature and its themes had begun to alter before he came to Cambridge, and Brooke's did not last. Geoffrey Keynes, Brooke's close friend, says that he never heard Brooke mention Firbank's name. Yet the two had more in common than at first appears, the most obvious being tough minds—Firbank's was the tougher although his education was inferior—strong preferences, a love of solitude

5. Sir Coleridge Kennard: "Introduction" in Ronald Firbank: *The Artificial Princess* (London, 1934), p. x.
6. Cf. Holland: "Ronald Firbank," in Fletcher: *Ronald Firbank A Memoir*, pp. 108–9; *Son of Oscar Wilde*, p. 196.

broken by talk and laughter, and a delight in the earth's beauty. Although Firbank eventually thought Brooke's romanticism unreliable, he still maintained enough admiration for Brooke and his poetry to speak warmly of both to Talboys in 1915.[7] The friendship with Vyvyan Holland survived even Holland's attempt to borrow money in 1913, a request which invariably terrified Firbank, but the two men saw less and less of each other as the years went by.[8] Landsberg he continued to see in spite of a misunderstanding in 1913. Fifteen years afterward, Landsberg remembered Firbank well enough to say that he called to mind "portraits of society women by Boldini, . . . always writhing about and admiring his hands."[9] Dent's name was on the list of recipients of *Inclinations* in 1916.

Coleridge Kennard was another matter. Because he was not at Cambridge, he and Firbank seldom met. When Firbank first knew him, Kennard was either at Scoones's in final preparation for taking his diplomatic examination or recently assigned to the Foreign Office. In 1909 he was posted to Rome. His mother, Mrs. Helen Carew, who commissioned Epstein to make the memorial figure for Oscar Wilde's grave in the cemetery of Père Lachaise, in time became one of Firbank's staunchest friends. The kind of "wild" conversation Kennard described as having occurred in Firbank's rooms at Trinity Hall was directly responsible for Firbank's "A Tragedy in Green,"[1] composed in 1907 or 1908. The dedication, "To

7. Cf. A. C. Benson: *Memories and Friends* (New York, 1924), pp. 366–72; Fletcher: *Ronald Firbank A Memoir*, pp. 33–5; Christopher Hassall: *Rupert Brooke* (London, 1964), pp. 97, 130–2 *et passim*; Geoffrey Keynes to MJB, Newmarket, May 15, 1960; R. St. Clair Talboys to RF, Wellington College, May 3, 1915; see below, p. 142.
8. Cf. Vyvyan Holland to RF, London, April 25, 1913 (Fales); Vyvyan Holland to MJB, London, May 21, 1967.
9. Quoted in Fletcher: *Ronald Firbank A Memoir*, p. 30.
1. Typescript unsigned (Fales).

The Inspirer of the Tragedy, Sir Coleridge Kennard," acknowledges the author's indebtedness. "A Tragedy in Green" is a short story telling of Lady Georgia Blueharnis's unexpected acquisition of magical powers and her first use of them to destroy the Foreign Office and in it her husband. It is a bit of charming nonsense which does nothing more than reaffirm Firbank's developing satiric method in the character of Lady Georgia; that is, there is an implicit comparison of Lady Georgia's esteem for her own sins and the normal expectations of social behavior. Lady Georgia was to reappear in Firbank's first full-length novel, *Vainglory*.

A greater and more important influence on Ronald Firbank than Kennard's came from Hugh Benson. Born in 1871, he was the youngest son of Edward White Benson, Archbishop of Canterbury. In 1903, after eight years as a priest of the Church of England, Hugh Benson was received into Roman Communion. Late in that year he was at San Silvestro in Capite, Rome, to prepare for ordination, which came in June 1904. Returning then to England, he went to Llandaff House, Cambridge, to read theology; and in 1905 he moved to the Rectory, Cambridge. There Vyvyan Holland enjoyed a "close acquaintanceship" with Benson in 1906 and 1907, when Benson was working with Frederick Rolfe (who called himself Baron Corvo) on a romantic biography of St. Thomas of Canterbury. There at the Rectory Firbank sought out Benson. They carried on a running dialogue which first led Firbank to join Trinity Hall's most prestigious group, the Rowing Club, and to row in his college's second boat, somewhere, as David Hughes recalled, "about the middle of the boat."[2] Gossip says that Firbank rowed as a penance imposed by Benson; but apparently he worked at it, because a friend of

2. Dr. W. Hywel Jones to MJB, Cynfor, Cemaes Bay, Anglesey, June 15, 1965 (written for David Jones).

Heather's reported that he had seen "Artie" on the river and
that he "shaped" very well.[3] Unfortunately, the exercise was
too strenuous for Firbank: he collapsed in the shell and, in
the eyes of his robust peers, "cut a ludicrous figure."[4] Benson's fervor in friendship outweighed his poor advice, and in
December 1907 Firbank recognized the fact by giving him *Of
The Imitation of Christ* in the Essex House Press's limited
edition, leather-bound with silk ties. He inscribed it "For Father Benson in gratitude & affection from Arthur Firbank."[5]

He gave Benson the book in gratitude for more than
friendship. Before December 1907, under Benson's guidance,
Firbank became convinced of his need for the Catholic
Church. Shane Leslie in *The End of a Chapter* referred to
Benson's "nervous fingers twitching to baptise the next undergraduate he could thrill or mystify into the fold of Rome."[6]
Firbank explained that he attended the services of Cambridge's enormous parish church, The Catholic Church of
Our Lady and the English Martyrs, instead of the undergraduates' mass at Llandaff House because he required vast spaces
for his "uprisings of mysticism."[7] Maybe Benson's charm
drew Firbank to the parish church instead of Llandaff House
and maybe Benson's preaching, powerful and moving despite
a stammer, brought Firbank back again and again. Firbank has
been accused anyway of mere submission to the aesthetic aspects of the mass, the music and color and incense. Such an
accusation gains credence in view of the fact that he surrounded himself with a studied elegance unusual for an un-

3. Note to HG, [Cambridge], n.d.; cf. W. H. Adgey-Edgar to MJB, Guildford, December 9, 1965; Graham Storey to MJB, Cambridge, March 23, 1965.
4. Shane Leslie to MJB, London, October 12, 1963; cf. Shane Leslie to Jocelyn Brooke, Cambridge, January 27, 1952 (Berg).
5. (MJB).
6. Shane Leslie: *The End of a Chapter* (London, 1917), p. 88.
7. Shane Leslie to Jocelyn Brooke, Cambridge, January 27, 1952 (Berg).

dergraduate. Certainly his preference was often for the overly refined; Landsberg said he learned "Yellow Book, Savoy and Oscar Wilde tastes" from Firbank. But a religion dependent on the aesthetic was too limited. As his creative sense had broken out of the confines of aestheticism when he finished "The Singing Bird & The Moon," so now did his moral sense. It was Benson's fierce faith and his willing acceptance of the authority of the Church which impressed Firbank. He had argued with Pozzi about Claudel; and Claudel, who was a convert, looked on Catholicism as the "one universal element in a world of unsatisfying particulars." It provided the comfort of established and authoritative value. It meant moral order. That Firbank saw in principles of Christian faith the highest morality by which to gauge human behavior, he suggested in his two publications in *The Granta*, " 'The Wavering Disciple' " and "A Study in Opal." Whether these two derived from his talks with Benson or simpy represent conclusions reached independently hardly matters. He was concerned with problems of good and evil; he surrendered to an authoritarian solution to them. On December 6, 1907, Firbank was received into the Catholic Church by Monsignor Hugh Benson.[8]

Firbank's religious doubts and decisions may have haunted him, but in general the years 1906 to 1909 were happy ones. Baba, descendant of Protestants who had fought with Cromwell and daughter of an Anglican minister, accepted his conversion probably with less respect for his conscience than with unfaltering love for him, whatever he did. He was still her

8. Cf. Reverend Canon F. Diamond to MJB, Cambridge, November 5, 1966; A. C. Benson: *Hugh; Memoirs of a Brother* (New York, 1915), p. 157 *et passim*; Fletcher: *Ronald Firbank A Memoir*, p. 28 *et passim*; Robert Mallett: "Introduction" in *The Correspondence Between Paul Claudel and André Gide* (New York, 1952), p. 30 *et passim*; C. C. Martindale: *The Life of Monsignor Robert Hugh Benson* (2 vols; London, 1916), II, 3–130.

favorite child. Living at Cambridge was pleasant enough. Firbank's academic obligations were no burden. In his entire
time at Trinity Hall he never took the "Little Go" or any
other examination. He was officially in residence from his
matriculation in the Michaelmas term of 1906 to the end of
the Easter term 1909, but he "kept" only five of the nine
terms involved, being away part of the Michaelmas terms of
1907 and 1908 and the Lent terms of 1908 and 1909.[9] Nothing could upset the pattern Firbank had conceived for himself.
He lived up to his own idea of a man of letters, experiencing
and viewing the world for his own purposes. His summer holidays helped. In June 1907, at the end of his first year at
Cambridge, he made a leisurely visit to Bermuda, and from
there he went in July to Kingston, Jamaica, where he awaited
his boat on the verandah of the Constant Spring Hotel and
admired the island's trees. By late August 1907 he was in
Ghent and had visited a castle complete with dungeon,
"sculls," and bones. That month, probably before going to
Ghent, he was also in Bruges, where he spent some time admiring Flemish paintings.

These paintings—or one in particular, a portrait of the
Emperor Charles V attributed to Jan Gossaert—immediately
prompted Firbank to make another attempt at journalism.
Undeterred by his failure some two years earlier, when Alfred
Douglas had urged him not to try "to be practical,"[1] Firbank
wrote a short article in which he speculated on the identity of
Jan Gossaert, also called Jan de Mabuse. Following Douglas's
advice of 1905 to write on "actual topics," Firbank produced
a piece filled with names and dates. To do so may have curbed
his fanciful inclinations, which Douglas had called his "line";

9. Cf. Graham Storey to MJB, Cambridge, January 10, 1967.
1. See above, p. 72.

but the piece is still unequivocally Firbank's. The opening sentences run:

> At the *Exposition de la Toison d'Or,* at Bruges, there is a wonderful portrait of Charles Quint. The face, long and slightly upturned, appears like a wax mask chiselled to rare distinction against its sombre setting. The eyes, full of thought, seem a little weary; the lips, parted, inhale, one would say, some sweet perfume; the hair, descending low upon the neck, falls from beneath the brim of a black velvet hat, aslant, encrusted with pearls, whilst on a round jewel one reads the inscription: *Sancta Maria, ora pro nobis.*

Alfred Douglas had taken over the editorship of the periodical *The Academy* in the summer of 1907, and Firbank sent the article to him. It appeared, entitled "An Early Flemish Painter" and signed "Arthur Firbank," in the issue of *The Academy* dated September 28, 1907.[2]

Here was justification of Firbank's conscientious pursuit of his own vision. In the summer of 1908 he went abroad again. He spent part of July and all of August in France and Italy, going to Paris, Reims, and Florence. In September he moved on to Venice. Returning to England in time for the opening of the Michaelmas term at Cambridge, Firbank fell ill with jaundice; for that reason the term was well advanced before he went back to the university. When he was at the university, he made frequent excursions to London. Once, in November 1907, he went to attend a dinner party which Robert Ross gave at his home in Kensington (15 Vicarage Gardens) to celebrate Vyvyan Holland's twenty-first birthday. The guest list, in addition to Firbank, Ross's housemate More

2. P. 948.

Adey, and Holland's brother Cyril, included the painter William Richmond, that inseparable pair Charles Shannon and Charles Ricketts, Reginald Turner (who developed a strong dislike for Firbank), William Rothenstein, Coleridge Kennard, and Henry James.[3] There are few occasions like this one. Usually on his visits to London Firbank went to an art exhibition at the Grafton Galleries or the Goupil or to the theater, perhaps to see Granville-Barker's latest production at the Royal Court. He certainly saw the Canadian actress Maud Allan perform *The Vision of Salome* in 1908 at the Palace Theatre, where she appeared "all but naked" and kissed the "waxen mouth of a St. John's head resting on a platter."[4]

Except for his illness in 1908, Firbank's life followed its pleasant ways; but that of his parents changed. Daddy, in addition to losing his parliamentary seat in the Liberal landslide of 1906 after more than twenty years' service, also suffered financial reverses in 1907. Sir Thomas concealed the full seriousness of his financial position, but the Firbanks let "dear home" and moved from The Coopers to live at Tunbridge Wells.

Ronald responded to this move and the situation which caused it by writing "Lady Appledore's Mésalliance (An Artificial Pastoral)."[5] It begins by presenting the emotions of Wildred Forrester as he fills a packing case with his music (Debussy) and his books (Maeterlinck's *Ariane et Barbe-Bleu*) and prepares to leave his grand piano, his Persian carpet, his "thick silk draperies" and his "dainty white and gold room." Out of need he has accepted a job as gardener for

3. Cf. Holland: *Son of Oscar Wilde*, pp. 188–9.
4. Diana Cooper: *The Rainbow Comes and Goes* (London, 1958), pp. 87–8; cf. Leslie Baily: *Scrapbook 1900 to 1914* (London, 1957), pp. 232–3.
5. See *The New Rythum*, pp. [31]–67. First published in *Cornhill Magazine*, CLXXII (Summer 1962), [399]–425. The last page of the typescript, signed A. A. R. Firbank, bears the stamp of a Cambridge typing bureau (MJB).

Lady Appledore instead of going "into some sordid city office
. . . and being gradually dropped" by his friends. Wildred
spends happy days in Lady Appledore's garden until his Aunt
Queenie, the Duchess of St. Andrews, exposes him as a gentleman superior to his job. He ends by marrying Lady Apple
dore so that he may live happily ever after. The novelette is as
fresh as a spring morning after rain in its hero's delight with
his own good looks and in the intimacy among arum lilies,
columbine, parlor maids, canaries, duchesses, and even a sick
orchid with which someone had to sit up all night.

Here at last is the lyricism and effervescent fancy which
prompted S. P. B. Mais to name Firbank "the Mercutio of our
time." In this piece, with the subtitle "An Artificial Pastoral,"
Firbank has escaped finally from what Picasso called the
"tyranny of the thing seen." That word "artificial" or an
equivalent occurs often in Firbank's discourse: he made himself an "artificial temperament"; "A Wavering Disciple," published in *The Granta* was "A Fantasy"; in 1919, his "Fantasia
for Orchestra in F Sharp Minor" appeared in *Art and Letters;*[6] there was eventually *The Artificial Princess.* Now, in
"Lady Appledore's Mésalliance (An Artificial Pastoral),"
Firbank affirmed his independence from the social realism of
such writers as Galsworthy, although he had commended *A
Man of Property* to Heather. Despite the fact that the red
brick wall, the clock in the stable tower, the lime trees of
Lady Appledore's estate are taken directly from The Coopers,
Firbank reaffirmed his kinship with those French writers whom
he and Jean Pozzi had examined in 1904. With his repetition
of "artificial," Firbank acknowledged the greater importance,
as compared with realism, of an artist's constructive skills.

His detachment from his own reaction and his ability to
give that detachment and his family's misfortunes literary

6. Vol. II, New Series (Spring 1919), 64–79; see below, p. 172.

form in "Lady Appledore" make it the work of a man with a true literary vocation. It was André Gide who said that the work of art, because it has form, is an "equilibrium," an "artificial health." The truth of Gide's statement goes far to redeem Firbank's writing "Lady Appledore." As a personal response to an unhappy family situation it may seem outrageous, but it is consistent with his personality. He later told his mother that to "give way" to a merciless world is to put one's self at a disadvantage.[7] His self-created legend protected him. Irony and "volleys of . . . laughter" were Firbank's defense against giving way. In "Lady Appledore" the laughter dominated; he treated as ridiculous a serious circumstance.

His serious treatment of a trivial circumstance ended Firbank's stay at Cambridge. In the spring of 1908 Ragland Somerset, a member of Queen's College and editor of *The Granta,* asked Firbank to get something from Alfred Douglas for publication in the May Week issue of that periodical. That Douglas and Firbank were acquainted was common knowledge among Firbank's associates at Cambridge. His contribution to *The Academy* in the past summer was certainly known as well as the fact that, as soon as Douglas learned in the spring of 1907 he was to take over the editorship of *The Academy,* he gave Firbank a book to review. Firbank's "fitful and half-comical struggles" with the book produced no review, but the possibility of one was no secret.[8] Furthermore, Douglas had visited Firbank at Cambridge in November. Early in the month Lady Douglas recorded in her journal the details of a bitter quarrel with her husband; then under the date November 10, 1907, she wrote, "Bosie has gone off to

7. Cf. RF to HJGF, Florence, July 26, 1914.
8. Cf. Reid: *Private Road,* p. 55. No review by Firbank has been located in *The Academy.*

Cambridge and he never said good-bye to me."[9] When Douglas got there, Firbank provided dinner in his rooms. Ragland Somerset's approach to Douglas through Firbank was a logical and obvious one, and Firbank forwarded the request. At first Douglas refused. In his capacity as editor of *The Academy*, he was, he said, "overwhelmed with work." Somerset then wrote directly to Douglas and told him that his article was "counted on as the principal feature" of a special May Week number. Even though he was "over head and ears in work," Douglas contributed "Art and Sport." His only stipulation was that *The Granta* also publish what he called a "Suggested Editorial Note," a statement Douglas had written about his editorship of *The Academy*. One of its more modest passages runs:

> Lord Alfred Douglas took over the editorship of the *Academy* almost twelve months ago. In that short space of time he has turned the paper from one of the dullest and most dismal to perhaps the liveliest and most brilliant of the London literary weeklies.

Somerset published the note exactly as Douglas had written it, though without his name, as part of a regular feature of *The Granta*, the editor's "Motley Notes."

The complacency of the note and the inflated estimate of his stature as a poet which Douglas included in "Art and Sport" were too much for Somerset. *The Granta* had been running a series entitled "Celebrities I Have Never Met" with articles about G. K. Chesterton and George Bernard Shaw among others. Under the pseudonym "Nemo," Somerset published in *The Granta* of December 8, 1908, a piece called "Celebrities I Have Not Met, Yet Still Am Happy. I.—Lord

9. (Berg).

Alfred Bruce Douglas (or the London Curry-Worry)."

Douglas was furious. True to his pride in his "powers as a controversialist," he wrote a report of these events for the February 20, 1909, number of *The Academy*. He pointed out his own generosity in asking no fee from *The Granta* for "Art and Sport," deplored Somerset's ingratitude, and attacked the "views of honour and honesty current in Cambridge." Not content with one quarrel, Douglas started another with *The Cambridge Review*. In its December 3, 1908, issue that periodical, in its "News and Notes," had disagreed with an article in *The Academy* having to do with the Archbishop of Canterbury. Douglas therefore included *The Cambridge Review* in his attack on *The Granta* and his strictures on Cambridge. In its next appearance *The Cambridge Review* protested at being dragged into the *Granta-Academy* dispute. Meanwhile, *The Granta* apologized for "Nemo's" article with an "Open Letter to Lord Alfred Douglas." By this time Somerset had completed his work at Cambridge and gone to Clifford's Inn, London, but he undertook to defend Cambridge in a letter to the editor of *The Cambridge Review*. As a former editor he accepted full responsibility for what had appeared in *The Granta*, although he did not admit that he was the "Nemo" whose article had angered Douglas. Somerset's letter implied, however, that Douglas had presented the situation to his own advantage and had thus lied. Moreover, the letter exposed Douglas as the author of the "Suggested Editorial Note" and ended with this statement: "I regard Lord Alfred as a weekly and quite unconscious contributor to our national gaiety, who should be preserved at any cost. Far be it from me, Sir, if I may use a trite metaphor, to try to pluck a single feather from the goose which lays such golden eggs."[1] Douglas sued for

1. Raglan H. E. H. Somerset: "The 'Granta' and the 'Academy'," *Cambridge Review*, XXX (March 4, 1909), 306. Cf. Alfred Douglas: "Art and

libel; in *The Academy* for March 6, 1909, he announced that writs were being issued on Somerset and the printers of *The Cambridge Review*.

The next day, March 7, 1909, Firbank wrote this letter from Trinity Hall to Somerset:

> I had always suspected you of exquisite manners, but I had no idea, when last summer you begged me to ask Lᵈ Alfred Douglas to write an article for the "Granta," it was for the purpose of making a personal attack.
>
> I never read the "Granta", & saw nothing of the Article. But I should like to tell you I consider your conduct quite odious, both to me, but (happily!) a thousand times more to yourself. Anything more contemptible or third rate, it would be difficult to imagine.
>
> I resent most bitterly the role of Judas you have caused me to play in delivering a friend into such unscrupulous hands.[2]

Except for his invitation to Douglas to contribute to *The Granta*, this letter represents Firbank's only active part in the affair. The rest of it, the dismissal of the undergraduate editors of *The Cambridge Review* from the university and the payment to Douglas of fifty guineas "in consideration of discontinuance of legal proceedings," does not belong to Firbank's history. Firbank was not dismissed. But the contro-

---

Sport," *The Granta*, XXII (June 11, 1908), 19–20; "News and Notes," *Cambridge Review*, XXX (December 3, 1908), 134; "Nemo": "Celebrities I Have Not Met, Yet Still Am Happy. I.–Lord Alfred Bruce Douglas (or the London Curry-Worry)," *The Granta*, XXII (December 8, 1908), 119–20; "Life and Letters," *The Academy*, LXXVI (February 20, 1909), 796; "News and Notes," *Cambridge Review*, XXX (February 25, 1909), 278; The Editors:"Open Letter to Lord Alfred Douglas," *The Granta*, XXII (February 27, 1909), 233–4. Documents in the Hyde Collection confirm the fact that "Nemo" was Somerset.
2. (MJB).

versy, as only an academic one can, had grown out of all
proportion to its importance. Even an Oxford undergraduate
periodical, *The Varsity,* had taken it up. Anyone at Cambridge involved, however slightly, was no longer welcome
there, and Firbank was aware of the fact. When the Easter
term 1909 ended, so did Firbank's stay at Cambridge.

⚜ VIII ⚜

Before he left Cambridge, Firbank declared his intention of
serving the Church. His ambitions for a career in diplomacy
or a post as a parliamentary clerk had evaporated. He had
resolved to try for an appointment as an officer in the "Papal
Guard." That is the term used by Shane Leslie, an ambiguous
one which might apply to several Vatican services.[1] Which
service has proved impossible to determine. The most obvious
is the Swiss Guard, because Firbank had a profound admiration for the uniform (in the 1920's he was still talking about
how much he would like to wear the black, red, and yellow
uniform, the yellow stockings, and buckled shoes),[2] and he
spoke of preparing for the appointment by going into retreat,
as he put it, "as much for my looks as for the welfare of my
soul."[3] Firbank had every qualification for the Swiss Guard
but one; he was not Swiss, and there was no way to get
around this requirement. He could have aimed only at the
Guardia Nobile, the most distinguished and exclusive corps of

1. Cf. Shane Leslie to MJB, Hove, May 27, 1967.
2. Interview with Sewell Stokes, 1967.
3. Fletcher: *Ronald Firbank A Memoir,* p. 35.

the papal military service. That it is a mounted guard made it especially attractive to Firbank. He could use his horsemanship, so assiduously practiced during his stay in Madrid. Again Firbank answered all conditions for reception into this corps except one; he did not come from nobility recognized in the Papal States. According to report, he offered in compensation a letter of recommendation from the Earl Marshall of England, the head of the Herald's College, an office hereditary in the line of the Duke of Norfolk, who is also a leader of English Catholicism.[4]

Details of Firbank's activities in the months before he abandoned his vain and foolhardy attempt to serve with the Guard are scant. The imbroglio at Cambridge with Ragland Somerset and Alfred Douglas left an aura of unpleasantness. Firbank's bold, flamboyant gesture in openly associating himself with Douglas was unwise. Leslie says that "no doubt undeservedly" Firbank suffered from "unkind rumour" and for a while he "lay low." When he went down from Cambridge, he spent the early part of the summer quietly at Tunbridge Wells. Baba and Daddy were living there, probably at Rosemont, a building listed in directories of the time as offering "furnished apartments."[5] Heather was visiting friends, the Brydones, at Newlands in Petworth, Sussex, and Bertie was preparing to go in October to work in the Canadian forests. An outdoor life, it was thought, might benefit him.

4. Cf. Shane Leslie to Jocelyn Brooke, Cambridge, January 27, 1952 (Berg); Shane Leslie to MJB, Hove, May 27, 1967. The Guardia Nobile has neither confirmed nor denied Firbank's application for membership. If the Duke of Norfolk's letter exists, it is in the Guard's archives. It is not in the archives of the Second Section of the Secretariat of State (cf. Msgr. Martino Giusti, Prefect, Archivio Segreto Vaticano, to MJB, Vatican City, May 26, 1967). The fifteenth Duke of Norfolk left copies of few of his letters, and none having to do with Firbank is known to exist (cf. Francis W. Steer, Archivist and Librarian to the Duke of Norfolk, to MJB, Chichester, May 12, 1967).
5. Cf. Shane Leslie to MJB, Hove, May 27, 1967; R. G. Bird, Borough Librarian, to MJB, Tunbridge Wells, October 17, 1966.

Ronald's peaceful family life came to an end in mid-August. He crossed to the continent from Harwich and went directly to Bruges, where he spent at least a week. As he told Heather in a card dated August 18, 1909, he lived in view of Les Quais du Miroir et Spinola. By October 26, and possibly earlier, he was in Rome. There he lived in the home of elderly people named Bedini, probably a pension.

The only other definite fact about what Shane Leslie called a "rather disastrous period" for Firbank[6] is that his hopes for papal preferment were disappointed. He received no audience with the pope. Whether the Noble Guard failed to make an exception for him and thus he never received his appointment or whether he received it and, as Leslie thinks, then failed because he was "unfitted for military discipline"[7] cannot be established. Another unanswerable question is when Firbank acknowledged his failure. He remained in Rome until late spring 1910, but that may have been owing to pleasant pastimes. Sir Coleridge Kennard was at the British embassy; Mario Colonna, an acquaintance made at Cambridge, was at home near Rome; and as always the British came and went. Possibly, in the aftermath of his failure Firbank stayed on in Rome simply because he was reluctant to return to England.

How seriously he was disappointed will very likely never be known. Unwilling or unable to display his emotional reactions, Firbank was silent about many things which were important to him. To link Firbank's reticence in intimate matters with his inversion is hardly avoidable. A tragedy of the homosexual is that he keeps a large part of his emotional life concealed, and in order to fulfill it is forced into subterfuge and secrecy. Secrecy is his protection against hostile convention. Proust, who knew what he was talking about, testified

6. Shane Leslie to MJB, London, October 12, 1963.
7. Shane Leslie to MJB, Hove, May 27, 1967.

that the homosexual is compelled to travesty his own feelings, to "live in falsehood and perjury." Those were apt observations in the first decade of the twentieth century, particularly in prewar England, which had scarcely emerged from behind the façade of what is loosely called Victorianism. Firbank did not put into letters his moments of greatest emotion. He left no record of his attitude toward Bertie's marriage or the numerous deaths in the family. When his mother died, he shut himself away from help. Even in his greatest agony, when he learned that his own death was imminent, he uttered one anguished cry and then went on steadfastly with his days.[8] He never spoke of his failure at the Vatican except for the one comment which Lord Berners repeated: "The Church of Rome wouldn't have me and so I mock at her."[9] His mockery, however, was not aimed at the Church until some ten years after this Roman episode, that is, when he published *Valmouth*. Before that, indeed before he was received into the Church, Firbank derided those who abuse and misuse her in hypocrisy and self-absorption. His evaluation of human kind, apparent in the pieces already published by 1909, was not altered by his failure; it was merely intensified. The inclusion of the Church in his derision is one more aspect of his gradual alienation from the conventions of society and religion.

At times his religion seems, after all, hardly more than a delusion inspired partly by his instinct for the beautiful and partly by an urgency for order. He was capable of discipline, as he was to prove in a few years, but he had not cultivated it yet. He was careful about ritual and the forms of his religion, faithful in observance of days of obligation, in attendance at mass. At Cambridge he had been one of the many who flocked to hear Hugh Benson preach. Later, heightening the

8. See below, p. 274.
9. Quoted in Fletcher: *Ronald Firbank A Memoir*, p. 33.

significance of the mass for himself by his sense of place, Firbank went often to Notre Dame in Paris or to St. Peter's in Rome. But his introversion, his detachment, and his sense of irony made the overt religiosity of a practicing Catholic distasteful to him. His religion, like much of his life, was private. Vyvyan Holland, his contemporary at Trinity Hall, did not know that Firbank had been received into the Church. Lord Berners, after eight years of friendship, had "never for a moment imagined that Firbank was a Roman Catholic."[1] Some time in the twenties he and Victor Cunard were driving back to Rome from the Ristorante dei Castelli dei Cesare. As they passed a certain point in the road, according to Cunard, Ronald said:

> The last time I dined at the Castelli dei Cesare, two priests asked if I would care to share the transport back to Rome. And when we reached this place they said, "We're so sorry. We thought you were one of us." And then, with his hands fluttering madly at his throat, Firbank asked, "What did they mean, what did they *mean?*"[2]

Now and then he feared a lessening or even a loss of faith. Once, in 1921, he told his mother regretfully that for the time being he had no religion, and occasionally he spent long hours on his knees in prayer trying to recover it.[3] Firbank was sincere in his Catholicism, but he found no ease in it. It gave him no relief from the "nightmare of ugliness" in life, the "ordeal" he found life to be. It did not bolster him against his weaknesses or resolve his conflicts. As his friend Evan Morgan said, it "puzzled more than helped him."

1. Lord Berners: "Ronald Firbank," in Fletcher: *Ronald Firbank A Memoir,* p. 149; cf. Vyvyan Holland to MJB, London, May 12, 1967.
2. Nancy Cunard to MJB, London, January 3, 1954.
3. Cf. RF to HJGF, Montreux, November 17, 1921; Evan Morgan to Richard Buckle, Newport, Monmouthshire, July 25, 1940.

❧ IX ❧

In early May 1910, Firbank moved on from Rome, going first to Girgenti for a few days and then to Taormina and Palermo. From there he returned to Naples for a stay of two weeks. By June 9 he was at Siena and by June 29 at San Gimignano. July and August he spent at Florence in lodgings facing the Pitti Palace. He visited churches and admired statuary—Juno especially pleased him—and enjoyed the "noise & confusion" of the streets of Naples or Siena or wherever he might be.

In the autumn Firbank went back to England, and he was with Baba and Daddy at Rosemont, Tunbridge Wells, when Daddy died suddenly of heart failure on Friday, October 7, 1910. Both the local press and the London *Times* carried notices of the death of Sir Thomas Firbank, T.D., D.L., J.P., a major in the Engineer and Railway Staff Corps, and former Unionist member of Parliament.[1] The *Kent & Sussex Courier* gave an account of his funeral at Chislehurst Churchyard on October 11, listed the mourners, and noted that "Lady Firbank was present at the Church but did not go to the graveside." Her older son was her chief comfort, and once more, as at the death of Joey, she aroused Ronald's compassion. Ronald had maintained a dutiful courtesy and probably a dutiful love toward his father, but he entrusted none of his preoccupations to Sir Thomas. They were too distant from Sir Thom-

1. Cf. *Kent & Sussex Courier,* October 14, 1910, p. 7; London *Times,* October 8, 1910, pp. 1 and 10.

as's respect for games and public service and his calm acceptance of what has been called the "muscular Christianity" of
his time. Ronald's sense of loss was slight in comparison with
his response to his mother's grief, which, as always, evoked an
ardent pity. Even in less important matters he rushed to tell
her how "sorry" he was for her "troubles," how they "sad-
dened" him.[2] He wanted nothing more than to protect and
comfort her.

He was now the male head of the family. Although Lady
Firbank was named executrix of Sir Thomas's will, all practical matters and all financial arrangements devolved on Ronald. Most of Sir Thomas's personal property had passed into
his wife's hands well before his death, so that the value of his
estate bequeathed by will was minimal except for some four
hundred acres in Newport, Monmouthshire, known as St.
Julian's, once the estate of his father. This was entailed on
Ronald as the eldest son, with annuities derived from St. Julian's for Lady Firbank, Bertie, and Heather. There could be
no doubt now as to the amount of the Firbanks' income. It
was less than they had realized. They were not people of large
wealth, but they had the means for very comfortable, upper-
middle-class living.

For the first time Ronald Firbank was acutely aware of
money. What he had taken for granted took on an importance
it never lost. He assumed responsibility for his mother and
began to caution her about expenditures and to urge her to
live within a set amount, in 1914 £100 a month. To
Heather, however, he talked about the "consideration & po-
liteness money brings" and called them a "delight."[3] He put
great emphasis on the appearance of affluence, but he drew
back in horror from anyone's attempt to take advantage of it.

2. RF to HJGF, Florence, n.d.
3. RF to HF, London, [1915].

Soon after Sir Thomas's death, Vyvyan Holland was a visitor in the Firbank home when Ronald produced a crystal cup in the form of a shell and asked Holland to admire it. Holland recounted the incident:

> I did so, and Ronald then said, "That cost me £400." I looked at him severely and said: "That does not impress me any more than if you had said that it cost you fourpence. My dear Ronald, you are beginning to be purse proud." Ronald coloured slightly, took the cup, hesitated and then threw it into the fender, smashing it into many pieces.[4]

Yet when Holland asked for a loan in 1913 to enable him to take advantage of a "present opportunity" that he could not "pass by," Firbank was outraged. He protested his near-poverty so vigorously and so stiffly that Holland felt obliged to apologize and to excuse himself on the ground that he disliked "borrowing from Jews."[5]

In spite of his new apprehension about finances, his new responsibilities, and his generally altered circumstances, Firbank was without prospects or plans. He seemed, indeed, as Harold Nicolson said of Lambert Orme, to have "wandered off" rather uninterestingly. Until late 1912 or early 1913 his life might be described as he described that of a character in *Inclinations,* "one of those shadow-lives," visible only "in flashes." He moved with apparent aimlessness from one country to another, walking the streets of cities and villages "on the balls of his feet and not the reverse way," seeming "to spin jerboa-wise from tuft to tuft." His dress was modish and conspicuous: his suits were somber, but the color of his shirts was "never seen off the stage," and his ties were kindly described as "very bohemian." He had replaced the velours hat with a

4. Vyvyan Holland to MJB, London, October 23, 1963.
5. Vyvyan Holland to RF, [London], April 25, 1913 (Fales).

trilby. Although he suggested in his person not a "Fairbank but a Mountebank," he had the graceful dignity of an English gentleman, especially in foreign places.[6] He sent postcards and letters from every place he visited. In the summer of 1911 they came from France, where he spent two months in the Loire Valley, and from Portugal, with views of Lisbon, Coimbra, Tomar, and Leiria.

That winter the cards were from Egypt and Turkey. Firbank passed Christmas Eve 1911 at El-Wasta, arriving by steamer from Cairo. At some time during his stay in Egypt he bought the scarab which he long treasured to the horror of Coleridge Kennard's mother, Helen Carew, who was convinced that it was "poisonous" and exerted a sinister influence.[7] After an extended stay at Shepheards Hotel in Cairo, Firbank went north by way of Constantinople, where, in the person of Lambert Orme, he provoked Harold Nicolson into calling him a "silly ass" and then evaded Nicolson by sending him an enormous bouquet of lilies.[8]

From Constantinople, Firbank went to Athens. There he absorbed the broken majesty of the Acropolis and the remarkable translucence of the blue-and-white Greek scene. There, too, he watched the English tourists whose involvement in their own affairs was a desecration of Athens's classical perfection. Later he was to employ this circumstance in his novel *Inclinations*.

Firbank was abroad again in 1912. He began by going to Vienna, which, with Berlin, he associated with the "Maud Allen boom & the Straus cult" and long held in his imagination as less a city than the essence of a time and an attitude. He went to Berlin, too, after wandering indolently through

6. Evan Morgan to Richard Buckle, Newport, Monmouthshire, July 25, 1940.
7. Cf. Helen Carew to RF, Hove, September 14, [1918] (Fales).
8. Cf. Nicolson: "Lambert Orme," *Some People*, pp. 67–8.

Salzburg, Munich, and Dresden. As he told Heather, he had "expected to hate" Berlin but instead found it "wonderful."[9] After Berlin he planned a short stop in Paris which would keep him away from England until after the "Whitsuntide horrors." Once in Paris, he had such a pleasant time that he put off leaving day after day. At his hotel, the Crillon, he met his old acquaintance Jack Mitford, a fact which he thought *"tres curieux."* He went, one night, to the Théâtre Porte-Sainte Martin to see Jane Hading in *La Crise* and on another to a "fancy dress ball which was really exquisite." Had it occurred in the twenties it might well have served as a model for a Van Dongen painting. Firbank's account of the ball runs:

> So many interesting people were there, & the Russian dancer Napierkowska did the most extraordinary dance with flowers between everybody on Eastern rugs lying on the floor!
>
> Granier was there in a yellow wig & hareems! De Max also, the Infanta Eulalia & one of the Spanish pretenders— the oddest mixture—[1]

When he reached England, Firbank lived with Baba, briefly at 102 Queen's Gate and then at 33 Curzon Street, London. As in the cities of the continent, he drifted without purpose, a "unique character of cameo fantasy."[2] He sauntered through London's streets, skirting Covent Garden to avoid the "massacre of flowers" and holding a handkerchief before his eyes when he passed a butcher's shop. He avoided ugliness and haste. On Charing Cross Road he strolled "as

9. RF to HF, Berlin, May 14, [1912].
1. RF to HF, Paris, n.d. Jane Hading opened in *La Crise*, May 3, 1912.
2. Evan Morgan to Richard Buckle, Newport, Monmouthshire, July 25, 1940.

though time had no claims on him," pausing to look at some
book in the bins before a shop. His most frequent stop was at
Cyril Beaumont's bookshop, where he often found an addition to his collection of first and rare editions of the nineties
authors. Still following de Max's example, Firbank had these
bound in sky-blue French Morocco.[3] On entering Beaumont's shop, his usual question was, "Have you anything in
my line today; you know, something vague, something
dreamy, something restful?" Beaumont described him in those
years as tall and slender with a physique "almost feminine in its
delicacy." Beaumont's description continued:

> His hair was dark and sleek and brushed flat to the head;
> his eyes were blue or bluish-grey; his features were oval in
> shape, the eyebrows thin and arched, the nose long, the chin
> weak; his complexion was fresh, with a delicate rosy blush
> on the cheekbones. He was clean-shaven.
>
> Firbank was always dressed in a dark, well-fitting lounge
> suit, and he wore a black bowler almost invariably tilted far
> back on his head. He carried gloves and a cane. His hands
> were white and very well kept, the nails long and polished . . .
> and stained a deep carmine.[4]

Several acquaintances denied the bowler, maintaining that his
hat was a trilby. Nancy Cunard denied that Firbank stained
his nails, but his hands were noticeable, being much too long
and nervous. As Evan Morgan said, one never knew where
they might "find themselves."

Firbank was very much concerned with his appearance.
About 1912 he grew so fearful of gaining weight that he reduced his diet and tried all sorts of panaceas to keep himself
slim. His efforts were well enough known for his friend Hol-

3. Cf. F. J. A. Sanders to Richard Buckle, Oxford, August 5, 1940.
4. Quoted in Fletcher: *Ronald Firbank A Memoir*, pp. 48–9.

land to write for help in "preserving the fleeting remnants" of his own figure. Holland complained that even after giving up all his "more simple pleasures" he grew "stouter & stouter."[5] To fix his youth and his youthful looks, Firbank began having his portrait drawn; Charles Shannon, whom he had met in 1907 at Robert Ross's party for Holland, drew the first of many likenesses.

For outright amusement in London, Firbank turned first to the theater. Strauss's *Salome*, moralized and *sans* John the Baptist's head, was at Covent Garden in December 1910, and the other Straus's *Chocolate Soldier* at the Lyric the next year. The American Ragtime Octet was at the Hippodrome in 1912, and the Ballet Russe at Covent Garden. Ballet enthralled Firbank. He was away from London when Diaghilev first brought the Russian company there for the great gala at Covent Garden in Coronation Summer, but he had already seen the Russian dancers in Paris. In London, Firbank went repeatedly during the season which opened in October 1911 and during those which followed in succeeding years until the war interrupted them. Slumped low in his seat with his knees pressed against the seat in front of him and thus level with his head, Firbank observed Leon Bakst's exotic costumes and *décor* with delight and watched with fascination as Nijinsky danced *Le Spectre de la Rose* or *Narcisse*. Firbank was usually alone in order to enjoy the dancers "calmly" and "without platitudes."

He also frequented the Café Royal, invariably occupying the same red plush banquette almost at the center of the room and to the right of the door in that bright blue and gilded room with the marble-topped tables. There he sat, some days from noon to midnight, a slender man in a dark suit and trilby hat, detached from the bookmakers, the journalists, the tarts,

5. Vyvyan Holland to RF, [London], April 25, 1913 (Fales).

the boys down from Oxford or Cambridge to find "life," the artists and their models, the writers, and the mere drinkers who were patrons of the dauntless Café Royal. Characteristically Firbank was at a table alone, sometimes giggling for no apparent reason, observing everything which went on around him, and often reaching with one hand to clasp the opposite shoulder, drawing it inward and sitting "as it were cupped within himself."[6]

X

By the last days of 1912 Firbank reached the point of having contemplated long enough what was "within himself," all he had experienced and stored: nobility and laughter and the beauty of things seen and unseen as well as their opposites, shame and boredom and the irrevocable ugliness of failure. From the garden at Chislehurst and the boys at the Mortimer Vicarage School to the hilarious spectacle of the world going about its business, nothing was lost. He believed he had a novel "radiantly unworded," which he determined to produce and by so doing make a novelist of himself. There was also the question of his capacity for discipline. When he had almost completed the book, *Vainglory,* he wrote to his mother that "nobody could guess of the sacrifice behind" and called that the important thing.[1]

Even in the matter of his writing, Firbank had "wandered

6. Nancy Cunard: "Thoughts About Ronald Firbank" (unpublished typescript signed and dated from Toulouse, November 1954; MJB).
1. Cf. RF to HJGF, Edinburgh, [1914].

off" since leaving Cambridge. In this period of almost three years, that is from 1909 to the end of 1912, he had worked only with the piece he described as a "tender classic," the one later to have the title *The Artificial Princess* but then still called "Salomé Or 'Tis A Pity That She Would." When Firbank rediscovered this short novel among his mother's papers after her death in March 1924, he drafted a preface for it of which two versions exist. One begins, *"The Artificial Princess* was composed while preparing for the Cambridge 'Little go in (A.D.? 1910)." The other version more accurately changes the date to "A.D. 1906"; but it adds, "It was about the time of the Maud Allen boom & the Straus cult (a little previous to the Russian Ballet) & the minds of young boys turned from their Greece towards the Palace Theatre, Vienna & Berlin."[2] In England, as Firbank said, the Strauss cult was just prior to the Ballet Russe. It began in February 1910 when Sir Thomas Beecham presented Strauss's *Elektra* with Strauss himself conducting at Covent Garden, and it reached its height early in December 1910 with the performance of *Salome.* Firbank was in Rome in February 1910, so that he could not have seen *Elektra;* but he could have attended Beecham's mounting of *Salome* exactly two months after his father's death. Whether he did or not, he cannot have been unaware of Strauss, who was by far the most famous composer alive. Saint-Säens and Debussy were in no way as spectacular as Strauss, and by the end of 1910 Stravinsky had had only two commissions from Diaghilev for the ballet, the orchestration of *Les Sylphides* and the music for *L'Oiseau de Feu.* Strauss

2. Quoted from an unpublished holograph foreword written for *The Artificial Princess* (Berg). The Palace Theater herein referred to was the one in which Sarah Bernhardt put Oscar Wilde's *Salomé* into rehearsal in 1892, the year before its publication. The Lord Chamberlain prohibited the play because it treats of a scriptural subject. Maud Allan also danced as Salome at the Palace Theater. (See above, p. 96.)

was internationally famous. Besides, during the late summer
and autumn of 1910 the revision of *Salome* which the Lord
Chamberlain demanded before he would permit its presentation caused innumerable complaints from Beecham and the
cast and as many comments in the press. In 1910, Firbank's
interest in the story of Salomé was reawakened, and he tried
once more to adapt it to his own purposes.

He worked at it seriously, probably using for the first time
the mechanics of composition he thereafter found most productive. Coleridge Kennard recorded the fact that in his Cambridge days, Firbank "had the habit of writing down on long
strips of paper any phrase that particularly struck him and
hoarding these strips in his desk."[3] When he came to actual
composition, he took the "treasured strips of paper" out of the
drawer and placed them "here and there like a piece of velvet
or brocade." By the time he attempted to revive "Salomé Or
'Tis A Pity That She Would," Firbank no longer hoarded his
strips of paper. His constant moves made them too difficult.
Instead he jotted down his phrases in notebooks. One which
contains material for "Salomé," *Vainglory,* and his play of
1920, *The Princess Zoubaroff,* is the earliest of fifty-seven
notebooks. Except for meager suggestions for *The New
Rythum,* the novel he was writing at the time of his death,
Firbank left no work sheets and no plot plans. He apparently
composed directly from his notebooks with their lists of words
and phrases in the graphic combinations which mark his discourse. From these he worked and reworked his materials
with great painstaking. "I think nothing," he later declared,
"of fileing fifty pages down to make a brief, crisp paragraph, or
even a row of dots!"[4]

3. Kennard: "Introduction" in Ronald Firbank: *The Artificial Princess,*
p. viii.
4. RF to Stuart Rose, Rome, May 17, 1924.

Nevertheless, Firbank could make little of "Salomé." He had refined his ability to communicate through form rather than statement. That is, he turned the Biblical account into comedy while allowing its implications to comment on his characters.[5] These are shaped with considerable delicacy and put into appropriate conflict. But obviously he could find no solution to the situation he had created; so once more he put his piece aside, leaving it still unfinished.

That was in May 1911 at the latest. Firbank made no attempt to write anything more until the end of 1912, when he began the novel which he called *Vainglory*. In September 1912 he went again to Italy and on his return extricated himself from London life and his mother's household and settled at Laura Place, Pulteney Street, in Bath. He never produced any work of consequence in immediate proximity to his mother. Even as a boy of ten, when he wrote "Lila," he was away from his mother's enveloping love. It nourished him personally but stifled his artistic capacity. As Gide remarked, the artist works on himself, and for Firbank that meant working on his mother too. In Baba's presence he was incapable of any kind of aggression against her milieu, which he turned into the milieu of his fiction. His recognition of this fact meant that he had at least achieved a compromise with the tensions inherent in his relations with his mother. Firbank knew that in order to detach himself from the matter of his fiction, he must live away from Lady Firbank. This time he chose Bath because he was short of money, a circumstance due to the use of income for improvements on the St. Julian's estate. He saw himself once more in the part of Wildred, "Lady Appledore's" hero. To stay in London he must suffer the indignity of lodgings on Brompton Road or Shaftesbury

5. Cf. James Hafley: "Ronald Firbank," *Arizona Quarterly*, XII (Summer 1956), 166.

Avenue and the impossibility of a life without friends, clothes, or money. Bath, on the other hand, was inexpensive and beautiful. The Georgian houses of Bath were so "soothing" that Firbank talked of settling there one day on Royal Crescent or Lansdown Place with a servant like de Max's elderly, gray-haired Marie. Once in Bath, he resolved to work with courage and constancy to produce a book and thus satisfy his eagerness for fame (which he acknowledged to be as sour as "Gooseberry Fool"). Meanwhile he looked forward to better days, perhaps in the next year.[6] Indeed, a palmist had assured him that, although he had difficulties to encounter, he would fight his way through.

On New Year's Day 1913 Firbank could report progress on his book. It went slowly but well, he told his mother, and he said he might finish it in eighteen months. He planned then to set the book mostly in Venice, to have hardly any cause and effect, but to rely on delicate "intrigue." Because of its delicacy, he had to preserve his "mood."[7]

It was shattered tragically. On February 24, 1913, after a few days' illness, Hubert Somerset Firbank died at Plas Tivion, Glyndyfrdwy, North Wales. Official cause of death was cirrhosis of the liver and cardiac dilatation. He left a widow, Gwendoline Lewis Firbank, and a three-year-old son, Thomas Joseph.[8]

Bertie and Ronald had lost the intimacy of their boyhood. Their schools and their travels had separated them. Since the latter half of 1909, Bertie had spent most of his time in Canada. He had taken his wife there, and their son was born in Canada in 1910. That was the year in which Sir Thomas, only a few months before his death, reduced the amount of the

---

6. Cf. RF to HJGF, January 1, 1913.
7. Ibid.
8. Cf. London *Times,* February 25, 1913, p. 1.

annuity provided in his will for Bertie. Up to 1913 neither
Baba nor Ronald had seen Bertie's son. But Baba soon reme-
died that situation. A month after Bertie's death she wrote to
Ronald:

> Life being so uncertain I am writing this to tell you when I
> am gone how I hope you and darling Heather will be kind &
> good friends to Gwennie & "Boy"—She was a good true wife
> to Bertie & he loved her dearly help her in every way you
> can, either or both, you will only need to see "Boy" & he will
> win his own battle all along the line! he is delightful.[9]

Thereafter the child Tommie was Ronald's concern. As
late as 1924, when the boy was fourteen, Ronald wrote to
Heather, "Do you sometimes hear from Tommy? Let me
know anything I should. Has he proper nourishing food? His
holiday must be difficult & lonely unless there are other children with whom he can play."[1] This solicitude was partly a
response to Baba's plea, but it was also an expression of love
and genuine grief for the gay, wild brother who had been his
schoolfellow.

His brother's death strengthened Firbank in his determination to get on with *Vainglory;* and as soon as he could he
returned to his highly original composition. Disentangling the
influence of established writers on Firbank has fascinated several critics; and they have suggested as direct influences Peacock, Huysmans, Maeterlinck, Beckford, and a number of
French and English writers of the nineties. That Firbank had
read many of these and admired them, Jean Pozzi has testified. That he took what he wanted from them and others is
undeniable. But his taking was eclectic and what he made of

9. HJGF to RF, London, March 25, 1913 (Berg).
1. RF to HF, Rome, August 27, 1924.

it sharply individual. Ronald Firbank was not an imitator.[2]
His mature work can be associated with *fin de siècle* writers,
especially those of France, in his reliance on technique rather
than explicit statement to present his subject, but the technique is his own. His cinematic sequences, so productive of
"multiplied associations," he developed for himself. His materials, which he had recognized with such difficulty in the
environment he knew best, his own and his mother's, are not
unusual. He himself compared "Lila" with *The Young Visiters*. But by the time of *Vainglory* these materials were transformed not only by the application of his technique but also by
his distinctly personal view of them. The flower shop of real-
life Lady Angela Forbes, "My Shop" in George Street, is
hardly recognizable as that of Mrs. Shamefoot in *Vainglory*.
Firbank had patronized Lady Angela's shop, and he thought
Lady Angela "amusing & clever." In 1921 he considered col-
laborating on a book with her.[3] Lady Angela's "My Shop"
was the counterpart of Mrs. Shamefoot's, where it was her
"happiness to slap, delicately, at monotony by selling flowers." Firbank described Mrs. Shamefoot's shop:

> On her walls hung charming flower studies by Fantin-Latour
> and by Nicolson, intermingled with some graceful efforts of
> her own—impressions, mostly, of roses; in which it might be
> observed that she made always a great point of the thorns.[4]

The thorns, of course, are an adaptation of fact to fictional
motifs. That is, Firbank had come to the place where, in the
terms of Jules Renard, he could help himself to his own origi-
nality.

2. Cf. David Duck: "Ronald Firbank," in *Frederick Rolfe and Others*
(Aylesford, 1961), pp. 16–17.
3. Cf. RF to HJGF, Versailles, July 2, 1921.
4. *Vainglory*, p. 50; cf. p. 49.

The contents of *Vainglory* demonstrate that fact. It is a mélange of Firbank's earlier writing. Ladies Appledore and Georgia Blueharnis were named first in "Lady Appledore's Mésalliance" and "Tragedy in Green," although the Blueharnis name had occurred still earlier in "A Disciple from the Country." Titles of works which were imaginary or actually written before 1911 are also present in *Vainglory*. "The Home Life of Lucretia Borgia," reading matter for the heroine of "A Tragedy in Green" and under a slightly different title for that of "The Wavering Disciple," is attributed to Mrs. Asp in *Vainglory;* and a stanza of *"The Wind & The Roses,"* an early poem, is quoted in *Vainglory* as an example of a Miss Hospice's verse.[5] Words and sentences which had pleased him in "Salomé Or 'Tis A Pity That She Would," he used again for *Vainglory.*[6] A favorite, employed in both "Lady Appledore" and "Salomé," occurs in *Vainglory* as "Overhead the sky was so pale that it appeared to have been powdered completely with *poudre-de-riz.*"[7]

A more tenuous exploitation of earlier works is in minor characters. For instance, Miss Dryd of "Her Dearest Friend" and Miss Tail of *A Study in Temperament* become Mrs. Asp in *Vainglory*. The fictitious writers, the Bishop's household, most of the innumerable people who flit in and out of *Vainglory's* pages have all appeared elsewhere previously under other names.

Having collected them and grouped them in a "system of correlated planes,"[8] as he had been learning to do for a long time—certainly since the composition of "Her Dearest Friend"

5. Pp. 32 and 108. Cf. *"The Wind & The Roses,"* [p. 9].
6. Cf. Kennard: "Introduction," in *Ronald Firbank: The Artificial Princess,* p. viii; *The Artificial Princess,* pp. 19, 14, 28, and 29; *Vainglory,* pp. 81, 29, 73.
7. P. 139; cf. "Lady Appledore's Mésalliance," p. 64; *The Artificial Princess,* p. 16.
8. Nicolson: "Lambert Orme," *Some People,* p. 65.

—Firbank then set them into the framework he had invented for "A Study in Opal." The eagerness of the Bishop's widow in that piece to erect a memorial window to herself is reenacted and brought to completion by Mrs. Shamefoot in *Vainglory*. Mrs. Shamefoot is new for Firbank in that she is what Nancy Cunard called a "sweet-sad or yearning" character,[9] perhaps his first, but her story had already been sketched in "A Study in Opal."

Firbank stayed in Bath selecting and adapting and shaping his materials until the end of May. He worked so privately that friends such as Vyvyan Holland did not know what he was doing. Firbank had a letter from Holland dated April 25, 1913, asking whether he was writing anything. "I look in vain for your works in John Lane's summer catalogue," Holland wrote.[1] He tried to induce Firbank to come to London by describing two Japanese vases, recently purchased, and by attempting to seem exciting. "I am wrapping this up in wood coloured paper to make it look mysterious," Holland wrote at the end of one letter. "One usually reserves such things for great moments, such as making assignations with the husbands of beautiful ladies."[2] But Firbank kept steadily at his novel.

He allowed himself a change during the late spring and summer. In January, Firbank had talked of revisiting Vienna.[3] But in May he went first to Salisbury for a brief stay; from there he sent picture postcards to Heather dated May 31. By July 11 Firbank was in Paris, and from Paris he went to the Loire Valley, to Bourges and Orléans, and then north to Amiens.

When he returned to England in the autumn, Firbank vis-

9. Nancy Cunard to MJB, London, October 28, 1958.
1. (Fales).
2. Vyvyan Holland to RF, London, [1913] (Fales).
3. Cf. RF to HJGF, Bath, January 1, [1913].

ited York and then settled in London. Baba had left the house in Curzon Street and taken a flat, first at 45 Parkside, Knightsbridge, and then at 44 Sloane Street. Exactly where Ronald lived is uncertain. He may have moved into his mother's flat or he may have gone to a Jermyn Street location.

Partly because he was in London and partly because he felt more competent to finish his novel than he had a year before, Firbank's life was an active one. When Holland was married in early 1914, with his cousin Father Maturin performing the ceremony and Robert Ross serving as best man, Firbank attended. He had already sent a gift of "charming candlesticks."[4] He was often at the Café Royal, and he took to going to a restaurant on Percy Street, Soho, called the Eiffel Tower (now the White Tower). Its proprietor, Rudolf Stulik, had changed it from a modest eating-house for French families in London to a resort for the artistic and the fashionable. It aroused such feeling in its patrons that Nancy Cunard wrote a poem about it which ends with these lines:

> I think the Tower shall go up to heaven
> One night in a flame of fire, about eleven.
> I always saw our carnal-spiritual home
> Blazing upon the sky symbolically . . .
> If ever we go to heaven in a troop
> The Tower must be our ladder,
> Vertically
> Climbing the ether with its swaying group.
> God will delight to greet this embassy
> Wherein is found no lack
> Of wits and glamour, strong wines, new foods, fine looks,
>   strange sounding languages of diverse men—
> Stulik shall lead the pack

4. Vyvyan Holland to RF, Ramsgate, Kent, December 24, 1913 (Fales).

Until its great disintegration, when
God sets us deftly in a new Zodiac.[5]

The Eiffel Tower Restaurant was haunted by a coterie sometimes called the "Young Souls," because most of them were
descendants of the "Souls," those free and intellectual spirits
of the days of Arthur Balfour, Lady Elcho, and the "Dusty
Duchess," later joined by that "ubiquitous chatterbox" Em-
erald (Maud) Cunard. Many of the coterie called the
"Young Souls" died on the battlefields of France in the First
World War; but many survived: Duff Cooper, Alan Parsons,
and of course the women, among them Diana Manners, Phyl-
lis Boyd, and Nancy Cunard. Other regulars at the Eiffel
Tower were Augustus John, Jacob Epstein, Michael Arlen,
Wyndham Lewis (he and Michael Roberts decorated a room
at the Eiffel Tower), Walter Sickert, Nina Hamnett, Frederick Delius (when well enough), Igor Stravinsky (when in
England), Cecil Gray, his boon companion Peter Warlock,
whose real name was Phillip Hesseltine, and Evan Morgan. It
was at the Eiffel Tower that Firbank first encountered Evan
Morgan. Morgan, seven years Firbank's junior, was the only
son of the third Lord Tredegar of Tredegar, Monmouthshire,
and of Lady Katherine Agnes Blanche, daugher of the ninth
earl of Southesk. Morgan was very attached to his mother, a
lady who rumor says prudently built herself a nest each
spring. Evan had none of his mother's feeling for feathered
creatures, but when in Wales at the family seat he entertained
his guests by going a round or two against his own kangaroo.
In addition to his ability with the gloves, he was a painter, a
poet, a musician. He was also, as Nancy Cunard wrote of

5. Nancy Cunard: "To the Eiffel Tower Restaurant," *Sublunary* (London,
1923), pp. 94–5.

him, "a fantasy who could be most charming and most
bitchy."[6] Morgan described his meeting with Firbank: "A
Sherlock Holmes-like figure, the face characteristically half-
covered with the coat-collar held up with the right hand and
[the other] long hand in an Aubrey Beardsley attitude pointing out towards infinity suddenly whispered . . . 'Your name is
Rameses.' "[7] Precisely when this happened is unknown, but
when it did Firbank insisted on showing Morgan "his original" at the British Museum.[8] Augustus John wrote of seeing
them both at the Eiffel Tower, Firbank "struggling manfully
with his asparagus and a bottle of wine, while following in-
termittently the bird-like flights of the Honble. Evan Morgan."[9] John may have been recounting a postwar scene.
Their intimacy no doubt waited until after 1918; but certainly
before the war Morgan and Firbank were what Morgan
called "fairly close acquaintances," and Morgan took delight
in Firbank's conversation, which, he said, was "of a most
speculative and dubious character."[1] But usually Firbank,
who came irregularly to the Soho restaurant, talked with no
one. He sat apart from the "coterie," the "Young Souls" to
which he did not belong—they were extremely jealous of that
privilege—and most of the other habitués, whom he did not
know.

However Firbank spent his nights and wherever he was, his
progress with *Vainglory* was nonetheless sure and steady.
When he traveled he took his manuscript with him; and he
worked at it on trains and in hotel rooms. When he returned

6. Nancy Cunard to MJB, Lamothe-Fénelon, Lot, July 27, 1963.
7. Evan Morgan to Richard Buckle, Newport, Monmouthshire, July 25,
1940.
8. Cf. Fletcher: *Ronald Firbank A Memoir*, p. 47.
9. Augustus John: *Chiaroscuro* (London, 1952), p. 137.
1. Evan Morgan to Richard Buckle, Newport, Monmouthshire, July 25,
1940.

to England, he resumed his writing almost without interruption. And at last, by mid-June 1914, he was ready to begin final revisions.

Although he planned to complete these in late August at either Salisbury or York, Firbank made many "excellent alterations" that summer on a trip to France and Italy.[2] Before June 20 he had arrived in Paris and taken a room at the Hotel Wagram; on that date he wrote to tell his mother than Madame de Thèbes, the renowned fortuneteller, had predicted long life for Lady Firbank and great success for his book. As always, Firbank had a happy time in Paris. He visited the Biais family and saw both de Max and Jeanne Granier. One sunny day he made an excursion to Versailles. He went for a drive in a new motor car with his friend of Cambridge days, A. C. Landsberg, and together they inspected flats available at about £60 a year. Firbank made no move to hire a flat, but he thought it might be nice to be "settled." He watched the spectacle at La Cigale, and he saw Evelyn Nesbit Thaw and Jack Clifford dance together at the Folies Marigny.[3]

On the afternoon of July 11, Firbank left Paris for Rome. By then Sophie Chotek and her husband, the Archduke Franz Ferdinand of Austria, had been dead for two weeks, killed by an assassin's bullet at Sarajevo. Firbank's concern when he first wrote to his mother from Rome, however, was with the fatigue and discomfort of his journey; he had missed his train connection at Turin and with four hours to get through had walked about the city.[4] His stay in Rome was brief but full of "bustle." It interfered with work on *Vainglory*, although he was slowly erasing the "strained" parts. Eventually he quit all attempts at revision, consoling himself with the benefits he

2. Cf. RF to HJGF, Rome, [July 16, 1914].
3. Cf. RF to HJGF, Paris, [July 9, 1914].
4. Cf. RF to HJGF, Rome, July [14], 1914.

would reap later from this trip to Italy, precisely what he needed for the book. He was sure that when he reached Salisbury or York at the end of the summer he could finally polish the book, which he said was "only thistledown," anyway. Firbank gave himself up to the enjoyment of Rome. His hotel, the Grand Hotel de la Minerva, pleased him for its associations as well as its garden, from which he could see the "venerable" Pantheon. The quantity of paintings and statues at the Vatican left him "dazed." He was gratified to have a flower shop's assistant remember him after three years. He visited the Spada Palace's gardens and the Villa Medici; he went to Orvieto and returned to Rome, all in one day. Evenings he spent in gardens on the Palatine. He observed the light of Italy. In Rome he compared it with fine music and later, in Pisa, with the light on the first day of creation.[5]

On July 20 he started northward in Italy, spending two or three days in Assisi and a day in Perugia, so that, hot and dusty, he reached Florence on the afternoon of July 24, the day after Austria's ultimatum to Serbia. Although he regarded it as a rather sinister city, Firbank was happy to be in Florence again. He went to the same hotel as he had in 1910, one in the Piazza Pitti, where he secured a room for five lire a night. He liked being remembered at the hotel, he liked the cost, and he anticipated having his lunches on the street, concealed only by a tub of flowers.[6]

In Florence, Firbank took time to attend to family affairs. He advised his mother about subletting the flat at 44 Sloane Street, urging her to arrange the rooms herself so that her taste and her "style" would make the place attractive enough to double her income. On June 30 he signed a lease for a flat

5. Cf. to HJGF, Rome, [July 14, 15, 16, 17, and 19, 1914].
6. Cf. RF to HJGF, Assisi, July 21, 1914; Perugia, July 23, [1914]; Florence, [July 24, 1914]; Venice, August 3, 1914.

in Basil Mansions, Basil Street, as she had asked him to do, and posted it back to her. The flat was not for Lady Firbank, who stayed at Sloane Street after all, but for Heather, who took it alone.

That done, Firbank turned his full attention to Heather. He began by sending his sympathy to Baba, realizing, he said, how "weary" she must be with the problems her children had made for her. Then he offered strong recommendations to Heather of which the keynote was "valour." In 1911 or 1912 Heather had fallen in love with someone whose name is still a mystery. He was a man of independent means, a member of Parliament, and enough in love with Heather to want to marry her. Unfortunately, he was already married. Early in this love affair, his divorce seemed possible, and the lovers' dilemma promised to end happily. At that time, probably in the summer of 1912, Firbank wrote to Heather:

> dear you have *all* my sympathy. But if things turn out for you as I hope they will, you should not regret anything you are suffering now; it will make you twice the woman & also you will enjoy life far more than most people, & things that would have escaped you had you always had everything you will *see* now, & they will give you pleasure. . . . I feel sure that one day you will have a good time, the misery is waiting for it to come. You must think of yourself as waiting for a train to pass, the silly people in the signal box all fast asleep! But you must remember no trains worth catching pass by Broadstairs.[7]

Ronald Firbank firmly believed in "grappling with the cruelty of the world,"[8] in facing life and justifying one's existence; but he overestimated Heather. She was unable to seize happiness.

7. RF to HF, London, n.d.; cf. RF to HJGF, Florence, July 24, 26, and 30, 1914.
8. RF to HF, Rome, July 19, 1924.

She had beauty, and she adorned it with exquisite clothes of a heather color to complement her name.[9] These were usually made by the famous dressmaker Lady Duff-Gordon, known as Lucile. But all her life Heather remained at the figurative Broadstairs against which her brother had warned until, after Baba's death, she took as her lover her chauffeur, an Italian whose first name was Giovanni, to relieve her loneliness and frustrations. They began in 1914, when the wife of the man Heather yearned to marry refused to divorce him, and Heather's romance terminated. Her nerves, raw from long uncertainty, gave way. Now, from Florence, her brother implored her to help herself, to forget her health, to travel, above all to face the world with valor, for her own protection.

Firbank's stay in Florence lasted about ten days. Although he knew that *Vainglory* would be "richer" because of his expedition, he was impatient to get through the revisions and find a publisher. Florence was so hot that the afternoons were a problem. Still, he went several times to the gardens at Fiesole. One day, July 31, he spent at Pisa and climbed the tower to view the mountains and the sea. During his last night in Florence he was awakened by a storm, and for an hour, in his nightshirt and barefooted, he watched the lightning play over the tower of the Palazzo Vecchio.[1]

The next afternoon, August 3, the day after Germany's ultimatum to Belgium, Firbank arrived in Venice. He took a "divine" room at the Grand Hotel facing the "Salute Church" and went round at once to the Café Florian, where once more he was pleased to be remembered. The following day he spent the afternoon in the sea, which he found "delicious," and

9. Many are now a part of the collection at the Victoria and Albert Museum, London, as examples of an Edwardian lady's wardrobe. They were shown in the winter of 1960–1 in a handsomely mounted exhibition.
1. Cf. RF to HJGF, Florence, July 25, 1914, July 30 [1914], August 1, 1914; Venice, August 3, 1914.

then, returning from the Lido in a gondola, extended his ride through the canals. That was August 4, 1914. By midnight of August 4, Great Britain was at war with Germany, and the whole intricacy of experience which had shaped Ronald Firbank was at an end.[2]

Firbank was faced with two difficulties, getting north through a Europe mobilizing for war and then, either from France or Holland, crossing the Channel to England. This was a totally unexpected development; according to a letter which he wrote to his mother from Florence on July 28, he had seen no newspapers since leaving home. But he was fearless and resourceful enough to act promptly. He anticipated a long delay in making his way to England, but luckily, since no money could be transferred from England, he had adequate cash for about a month, and he looked ahead to help from Landsberg if he could get to Paris. Because Venice was expensive Firbank moved on to Milan on August 6 with the idea of continuing to Como. He preferred Como to Milan in case he had to wait any time to cross the border. In one morning in Milan he visited two picture galleries and the British consul, who hoped to arrange Firbank's departure from Italy within four or five days. Firbank was far more composed about the whole situation than Baba, who was racked with anxiety about him. She had had no letters written after July 30, though he had posted several. She had sent a telegram to him from Victoria Station, aware that there was little likelihood of its delivery. Then she had called at the Italian embassy to ask if there were any sure way of reaching her son and had come away with the knowledge that until French mobilization was "over" no one could travel and letters or telegrams would take days, even weeks. She worried that his money might be "getting short," but reassured herself that with Italy still neu-

2. Cf. RF to HJGF, Venice, August 3, 1914, and [August 4, 1914].

tral her son was probably safe. On August 7 she wrote from London to tell him all this, and then she said:

> I am sure there are terrible times before us eggs already are 3^d each bacon by taking a whole side is 1/8 a lb. a tiny cauliflower 8^d sugar 6^d a lb & so on and this is only the first week of the war. One would think the German Emperor had gone mad or he would never have run amuck (with all the other Great European Powers against him) as he has done he will repent too late! Germany will never again be a Power to fear![3]

Baba ended by hoping that he was "well & calm," as indeed he was. On August 8 he went on to Como to await word from the British consulate and enjoy the loveliness of the lake.[4]

How long he remained there and how he got to Paris and then to the British Isles are unrecorded. By early September Firbank had arrived in England and fled to the North in search of a place where he could live and work. He went first to York, but in spite of the fact that it had "magnificent moments," he moved on to Harrogate. It was so "disgusting" that after one day he left for Edinburgh. There, from the Princes Street Station Hotel, Firbank arranged for a sitting room, bedroom, and bath on the ground floor of 4 Coates Crescent, an address just off Princes Street, and on September 10 he moved into his new quarters.[5]

Firbank devoted most of his time in Edinburgh to the revision of *Vainglory*. Once at least he visited Father John Gray, the author of *Silverpoints*, who had been the friend of Aubrey Beardsley and reputedly the original of Oscar Wilde's Dorian Gray. Apparently none of this meant a thing to Firbank; he

3. (Berg).
4. Cf. RF to HJGF, Venice, August 6, [1914]; Milan, August 7, [1914].
5. Cf. RF to HJGF, Harrogate, September 8, [1914]; Edinburgh, [September 9, 1914], and September 11, [1914].

commented on Gray only as the "nicest" of priests. He tended
to business matters—road building—having to do with the
Firbank properties in Wales, and sometimes at night he
watched the searchlights play on the sea beyond Edinburgh.
But as a rule Firbank worked steadily at his book. When he
was within a week or so of finishing his revisions, he read the
book through at one sitting and declared it was exactly what
he had thought, "a souflé."[6]

Even so he wanted to publish it. To arrange for publication, Firbank decided to return to London. By the time he
made that decision Edinburgh was very cold, and he complained of having no winter clothes. Nevertheless he went first
to Glasgow and proceeded south by way of Durham and Car-
lisle. Any reaction he may have had to Durham as the site of
the Firbanks' origins is not available. He had considered
going to Hampton Court for a week and then taking rooms in
the neighborhood of the British Museum. In fact he hired a
"tiny flat" at 19 Old Square, Lincoln's Inn.

Firbank commenced residence there well before Christmas
1914. From that address he wrote to Heather, probably at the
Bedford Hotel, Brighton, to thank her for a gift of Alfred
Douglas's collected poems and to say he would be glad, "especially this year in town," when Christmas was past. "At
present," he told her about London, "it is not sympathetic at
all. How I wish it were Spring always with no grey depressing
sky above."[7]

His impatience for Christmas to be over involved more
than London or the weather. Firbank was anxious about the
fate of *Vainglory*. Early in December he had submitted it to
Martin Secker, whom Firbank considered sufficiently ven-

6. RF to HJGF, Edinburgh, [1914]; cf. RF to HJGF, Edinburgh, September
11, [1914].
7. RF to HF, London, [December 1914]; cf. RF to HJGF, Edinburgh,
[1914].

turesome to publish his book. Secker refused it as too great a financial risk, but suggested that Firbank try Grant Richards. Here was a publisher whom Wilde had described as "daring" and Shaw called tragic because he had let himself fall in love with literature. Firbank took *Vainglory* to Richards's office in St. Martin's Street, and Richards read it during the Christmas weekend. Then, by appointment, he and Firbank discussed it the next Monday, December 28. According to Richards, he too refused *Vainglory;* though he thought it curiously fascinating, he also thought it too slight and too unusual to have much of a sale.[8] But Firbank was persuasive, and they talked about the financial arrangements under which Richards might publish, that is, that Firbank pay the costs of publication and thereby assume the risks. They reached no agreement, and when Firbank left St. Martin's Street he took his typescript with him. Later that day he wrote to Richards:

> Thinking over our interview this morning I cannot see my way to pay any more than £80. Half now, and the balance in April. My income is derived solely from a developing Property, and with increased taxation, and the war, everything is at a standstill. Perhaps you could let me know this evening if under these circumstances, I may bring you my manuscript tomorrow.[9]

Firbank returned the manuscript to Richards the next day and at the same time signed an informal contract for production of five hundred copies of *Vainglory* as similar as possible in type, paper, and binding—black, not red—to Arthur Machen's *Hill of Dreams.*[1]

8. Cf. GR: *Author Hunting* (London, 1960), pp. 199–200.
9. (UCL).
1. For a full account of Firbank's financial arrangements with Richards for *Vainglory* and subsequent books see MJB: *Bibliography of Ronald Firbank.*

After seeing a specimen page of the text in Richards's office on January 5 and making a decision about the covers on January 7, Firbank began to take an active part in the book's production. He told Richards, "that expression of not being able to 'put a book down' I'm convinced has nothing to do with the inside"; and he urged Richards, "Do please let the book be delightful to hold."[2] To help make it so, Firbank decided to have a pictorial frontispiece and dust jacket at an additional cost of £12.17s.6d. He suggested the use of one of Felicien Rops's crayon drawings already in his possession, but because he feared it was too delicate to reproduce adequately he changed his mind. He tried to get an illustration from Augustus John, who was away from London. Meanwhile Richards assured Firbank that Rops's drawing could be used; it presented no greater difficulty than pictures by Conder, Richards said. So Firbank took the Rops back to Richards with the suggestion that it might succeed on "rather rough paper." The position of the drawing on the page was a serious matter; "the angle is vital to the effect," he told George Wiggins, Richards's manager.[3] Firbank was anxious lest the Rops drawing be mistaken for a Beardsley. There was, he told Wiggins, an "important nuance" between the two, and confusion might be avoided by naming the artist on the dust jacket. He was thinking, he said, of "hostile critics." He insisted, too, that A. A. R. Firbank instead of his Christian name appear on the jacket, although the title page carried his name as Ronald Firbank. He was sure the book would sell better that way, since "one's acquaintance" would more easily identify the author and purchase the book. He was concerned about the lettering on the jacket and its paper, and he sent samples of the paper he preferred to Wiggins "as a

2. RF to GR, London, January 25, 1915 (Copy, UCL).
3. RF to George Wiggins, London, March 3, 1915 (Copy, UCL).

guide." To Richards, Firbank sent a book with all edges stained green; he said it offered "quite a thrilling contrast" to the black covers. Richards declared the green should be confined to the top, but in almost every other respect he deferred to Firbank's wishes. "Every one of your admonitions," Richards wrote, "shall be carefully considered and if possible carried out."[4]

That promise also referred to the proofs. Firbank returned them on January 25 with a letter expressing his grief at the loss of his "beautiful capital letters," removed in the printing. He insisted on retaining two and then sent word that the printers were to replace none of the capitals. "I dare say," Firbank wrote, "it will be all the chaster without."[5] He demanded revises of the first two signatures and wanted them for the entire book.

At last, on March 31, 1915, two weeks before publication, Firbank received a copy of *Vainglory*. He had told George Wiggins that he wanted his book "to be beautiful & attractive more than anything in the world," and when he saw the book he knew his wish had come true. He wrote to Richards, "A line to tell you how delighted I am with Vainglory. In such charming looks who could have the heart to be horrid?"[6]

Vainglory was published on April 15, 1915.

4. GR to RF, London, January 29, 1915.
5. RF to GR, London, January 25, [1915] (Copy, UCL).
6. RF to George Wiggins, London, February 28, 1915 (MJB); RF to GR, London, March 31, 1915 (Alan Anderson).

Part II

1915–1926

AMONG THE MORE ORTHODOX TYPES
THAT STOCKED THE LAKE, SUCH AS CARP, COD,
TENCH, EELS, SPRATS, SHRIMPS, ETC.,
THIS EXCEPTIONAL FISH [A DISTINGUISHED
MAUVISH FISH WITH VIVID SCARLET SPOTS]
MUST HAVE KNOWN ITS TRIALS AND PERSECUTIONS,
ITS HOURS OF SUPERIOR DIFFICULTY . . .
The Flower Beneath the Foot, p. 162.

❧ I ❧

Although Ronald Firbank maintained that the real importance of *Vainglory* as far as he was concerned was the "sacrifice behind," the self-discipline, he very much wanted his book to sell. Baba, of course, wanted the same thing. Even before it was published she wrote to Grant Richards asking him to do everything possible to get her son's book *"well reviewed"* to ensure his success. She said that a "kind review from Mr. Robert Ross for instance would be such a stimulus."[1] She also solicited W. H. Smith & Son, who thereupon agreed to take copies of *Vainglory* for a number of their bookstalls and shops on terms of "sale or return."[2] Ronald, too, was free with suggestions. His agreement with Richards had provided £20 for advertising, a sum meant particularly for *The Morning Post.* Richards made the arrangements, but choosing the dates involved considerable correspondence. Whether to quote from the two reviews *Vainglory* had had by early July was also a vital question. "I think," Firbank wrote to Richards, "it would be much better not to use the Times. One becomes a mineral-water instantly. Or would you omit the Observer instead? Whichever sounds the least like Gingerale."[3] There was little to choose between. *The Observer* echoed *The Times,* and *The Times* was no more perceptive about *Vainglory* than it had been about *Odette D'Antre-*

---

1. HJGF to GR, London, March 18, 1915 (MJB).
2. Cf. GR to RF, London, May 4, 1915.
3. RF to GR, London, July 11, 1915 (Copy UCL).

vernes and A Study in Temperament in 1905. Then it had described Firbank's first book as consisting of two pieces, "one a pretty old world story, and the other, less successful, of modern society." Now, about *Vainglory* and its author, *The Times* wrote in part:

> If Mr. Firbank would only introduce some slabs of good, honest commonplace dullness he might write a very amusing novel. He can be witty enough and gives a neat turn to his sentences, but his endless flow of scintillating nonsense is most exhausting. Moreover though we give him credit for a perpetual sparkle, we are by no means certain that our poor dazzled eyes have always seen the right point.[4]

The scarcity of notices as well as their lack of approval concerned Firbank greatly, and he asked Richards what could be done for a "really good" review. "It is almost embarrassing," he wrote, "to have 'exhausted' two reviewers. I feel so positive there must be critics who would not feel the 'strain.' "[5] He suggested sending a copy of *Vainglory* to George Calderon, who had written a preface to an edition of Chekhov's plays, and he urged Richards to get a special notice into *The Morning Post,* a feat Richards gently refused to attempt. Firbank was sure the book only needed "placing."[6]

Firbank himself arranged to have his portrait, drawn by Augustus John, published in *The Tatler* with his name, "Mr. A. Ronald Firbank." He had hoped for a review at the same time. The portrait had occupied Firbank in the early days of 1915. The drawing of his hair did not seem right, the back of

4. *The Times Literary Supplement,* June 9, 1905, p. 187; April 22, 1915. Cf. *The Observer,* July 4, 1915.
5. RF to GR, London, April 29, 1915 (Copy UCL).
6. Cf. RF to GR, London, [May 1915] (Copy UCL); GR to RF, London, April 29, 1915, and July 8, 1915; GR to George Calderon, London, April 29, 1915.

his head "got somehow out of focus," his mother had to be
pleased, and John was "so slow." Firbank went repeatedly to
John's Mallord Street studio. At last, on January 27, John
sent the drawing and this letter:

> It is no obvious portrait of course but you will not think it
> devoid of quality on that account. I think there was a slight
> improvement in your posing—Perhaps I may yet do a more
> perfect drawing some day when you are in a more stable
> mood.[7]

Firbank was pleased, although he promised to let John make
another attempt for his own satisfaction; and *The Tatler* readily published John's work in its issue of April 28, 1915. Almost two weeks after the book had come out, *The Tatler*
announced *Vainglory* as "shortly to be published" and gave
Firbank a few remarks beneath the picture: that he had succeeded to St. Julian's estate in Monmouthshire, that he was
"artistic," had traveled, and had joined the "Church of
Rome" under the influence of Monsignor Hugh Benson while
at Cambridge. There was no review.[8]

Indeed, the reviews were scant, and the count of books sold
in 1915 totaled only 179 copies.[9] Nevertheless Firbank had
much pleasure from his book. He enjoyed Robbie Ross's opinion that it was "very clever" and John's that the first half was
"immensely" amusing but in the rest there was "too much
cackle and nobody *did* anything."[1] He had copies sent around
liberally, including among the recipients Lord Alfred Doug-

7. Augustus John to RF, London, [January 27, 1915]; cf. Augustus John
to RF, London, [January 1915] (Fales).
8. Cf. *The Tatler*, p. 108; Augustus John to RF, London, [February 8,
1915] (Fales); GR to RF, London, April 29, 1915; RF to GR, London,
April 29, 1915 (Copy UCL).
9. GR to RF, London, December 6, 1915.
1. Augustus John to RF, London, n.d. (Fales); cf. GR to RF, April 26,
1915.

las, Mrs. Cosmo Bevan (a family friend living in Kent), the
Annesley Garretts (an uncle and aunt), Charles Shannon,
Vyvyan Holland. The copy intended for R. St. Clair Talboys,
Firbank wanted to deliver personally, and he invited Talboys
for a visit as soon as *Vainglory* appeared.

The two spent an afternoon together, which may have been
satisfactory to Firbank but was highly unsatisfactory to Talboys. Without quite knowing why, he admired Firbank's living room at Old Square—a room aglow from the "patina of
old wood" which paneled the walls and decorated only with
one of Gordon Craig's drawings and a recently purchased
carpet covering the floor. They talked of many matters but
chiefly of Rupert Brooke, whose name and poetry were new
to Talboys. And Talboys went back to Wellington College
and wrote to Firbank:

> I still think of your beautiful room—even though I cannot
> understand all that is in it—the period of it & the sense of
> things eliminated leaves in the mind a delightful remem-
> brance of repose—I could live there & write very quiet books
> —the converse of "Vainglory"—but I must not speak of
> that with the humiliating sense of misunderstanding.[2]

This had been Firbank's chance to justify all the pains Talboys had taken with him and to meet Talboys as an intellectual equal. But the visit obviously was not a success. Perhaps
Talboys suffered from the uneasiness of the teacher who suddenly realizes that his student has "sprung ahead," far ahead.
Or it may be that with Talboys Firbank overdid his role as a
man in the vanguard of literature and life.

He was inclined to exaggerate his reactions, even to be
somewhat shrill in his response to comments on his book,

2. R. St. Clair Talboys to RF, Crowthorne, May 3, 1915 (MJB); cf.
Ifan Kyrle Fletcher: *Ronald Firbank A Memoir* (London, 1930), pp. 51–2.

such as those of Mrs. Ernest Leverson, the "Sphinx" who had
been so kind to Oscar Wilde. She told Richards that *Vainglory* had given her much pleasure but that it was "restless and
witty and allusive enough to give anyone who understands it a
nervous breakdown." She thought Firbank should write another "more reposeful" novel in which all the characters did
not talk alike. The book, she said, was "too Meredithian."[3]
Firbank was delighted and derisive. " 'Meredithian' is marvellous, and I am sure must be intended as an epigramme," he
told Richards. Firbank went on, "I would adore to write a
really charming soothing novel. A sort of Moorish massage . . .
Or a play—that would begin before the theatre opened &
evapourate while the 'Star' was still en toilette de ville.
Wouldn't it be wonderful?"[4]

ꙮ II ꙮ

Before Firbank got very far with his next piece of writing, not
a play but the novel *Inclinations,* he had left London. By mid-
July he was at Stratford-on-Avon, and no later than July 27
he went to Pangbourne in Berkshire, where he spent the summer. He went back to London reluctantly, and London in
wartime was no place for him. Kitchener's face with the legend "We want you" stared from every hoarding. His friends
and acquaintances—Evan Morgan, R. St. Clair Talboys, Augustus John, Vyvyan Holland—were in service. The newspapers were filled with battles and long lists of the dead. Lon-

3. GR to RF, London, May 10, 1915.
4. RF to GR, London, May 11, [1915] (Copy UCL).

don had become a hurried, harried city where Firbank felt
alien. He had complained about it to Heather at Christmas
1914; the gloom and the tension increased each month.
Then, on October 13, not long after his return from Pangbourne to 19 Old Square, London, a bomb fell from a German zeppelin on Old Square and exploded, doing considerable damage to the square and the chapel in it. Unafraid for
his physical safety but very agitated by the confusion and
disorder, Firbank determined to leave London.

Partly under the influence of Talboys's grudging love of the
place, Firbank decided to retreat to Oxford. He settled first in
rooms opposite Longwall at 71 High Street; then, before the
end of November, he moved to 66 High. Twenty-five years
later, with a greater reliance on fabrication than memory, the
Oxford bookseller F. J. A. Sanders described these rooms as
having a "scheme of decoration completely in black with exotic designs painted on the walls. One sat on cushions on the
floor." Firbank had with him his collection of books, about a
thousand in all, many of which were "bound in sky-blue
French Morocco." Among the books were a "complete set of
Machen's Casanova, the complete set of the large paper Wilde
in cream vellum and Uzannes Fan, Sunshade, etc."[1] Because
Firbank had no servant, he lived largely on cold chicken.[2]
Except for occasional excursions to London, one to Torquay
in August 1916, and another to Brighton in 1918 or 1919,
Firbank spent almost four years at 66 High Street. There he
completed his next three novels and saw them as well as a
reprint of *Odette* through the press.

He had started *Inclinations* before leaving London. In November, from Oxford, he wrote to say that the new book went
slowly, but that he did not "quite despair about it." He was

1. F. J. A. Sanders to Richard Buckle, Oxford, August 5, 1940.
2. Cf. Siegfried Sassoon: *Siegfried's Journey* (London, 1945), p. 136.

sure it would create "'curiosity'" in *Vainglory,* and he worked steadily. When Firbank went to London for Christmas with Baba, he discussed his progress with Richards, who decided that *Inclinations* ought to be on his spring list. He sent a letter dated January 7, 1916, urging the author "to get typewritten immediately" that part of the novel which was done. The letter ran, "I had better read that part now, decide about it, and get it into my Spring list."³ Firbank was hesitant about complying. He said that he could send all but one chapter by the seventeenth and that chapter by the end of January so that the book could go to press at once; but he told Richards, "I am afraid I have hurried & spoilt my book although I can make it quite complete by compression."⁴ But he rushed along so that the last chapter reached the publisher by January 31. Meanwhile he had gone once more to London to talk over the book with Richards, and on January 20 they completed an agreement for the manufacture of five hundred copies of *Inclinations* at a cost to Firbank of £80.

By February 6 he was frantic for proofs. "Every hour," he told Richards, "is really of consequence! There are so many revisions for me to make—."⁵ As late as May 28, little more than two weeks before *Inclinations* appeared, he was still trying to improve on it. On that date he asked to have "weary fingers" changed to "psychic fingers."⁶ Inability to get proofs because of a printers' strike nagged him throughout the production of the book. When they were delayed in April, he

3. Cf. RF to GR, Oxford, [November 1915] and December 12, 1915 (Copies UCL).
4. RF to GR, January 12, 1916.
5. RF to GR, Oxford, February 6, 1916; cf. Grant Richards Ltd to Riverside Press, Ltd, London, January 31, 1916, and February 2, 1916; GR to RF, London, January 20, 1916.
6. *Inclinations* (London, 1916), p. 22; cf. RF to George Wiggins, Oxford, May 28, 1916 (MJB).

thought of rewriting and extending the second part. "This long delay with the printers & my horrid ending," he said, "go so badly together—Had I forseen a 'strike' I would have been more mature! . . . I feel so ashamed of my flimsy endings & all the heavy Time!"[7] When he got the proofs, he was disappointed. He complained, "I wanted so few 'commas' more capital-letters & dots instead of dashes. . . . By changing the punctuation all 'goes.' Since one never attempted to be classic . . . I feel like 'a waiter' in evening dress!"[8] He worried about the number of pages in the book; 199 were too few. He suggested having at least two hundred and then wondered whether the pages needed numbering at all; he said it was "so much more restful *not* knowing." He also suggested that the edges be tinted the pink of a "malmaison . . . a sort of 'Sumerun'-Bakst."[9]

All this time Firbank was busy getting a drawing for the frontispiece and wrapper. After the successful use of the Rops drawing for *Vainglory,* Richards encouraged Firbank to have something similar in quality for *Inclinations.* He wanted John to design the jacket, but was persuaded by Richards to approach Albert Rothenstein. Although the artist was "laid up" in February, by March 15 he had made two drawings and suggested their exact place in the book and on the dust jacket. The question of color or black and white reproductions and of size of lettering entailed countless communications.[1] Before anything was decided, Rothenstein and Firbank had a serious disagreement. Rothenstein, on April 4, 1916, changed

7. RF to GR, Oxford, April 24 and 16, 1916.
8. RF to GR, Oxford, March 26, 1916.
9. RF to GR, Oxford, March 9, 1916, and April 19, 1916.
1. Cf. RF to GR, Oxford, January 12, 1916, February 13, 1916, April 19, 26, and 30, 1916; GR to RF, London, March 15, 22, and 24, 1916, April 18 and 20, 1916; George Wiggins to Albert Rutherston, London, May 27, 1916; Albert Rutherston to RF, London, n.d. (MJB); Albert Rutherston to GR, London, March 16, 1916 (MJB).

his name to Rutherston. He asked to have his name appear in that form on the title page of *Inclinations,* and he lettered the design for the dust jacket with the name Albert Rutherston. Firbank learned about the change only when he examined a proof of the jacket. He promptly went to London and to Richards's office, where he explained his attitude to Wiggins, who in turn explained to the artist that Firbank "set great store" on having the name appear in the book as Rothenstein on the ground that the name Albert Rutherston would mean nothing to the general public. Two days later, when Firbank was back at Oxford, he confirmed his position in a letter to Richards. Firbank demanded that if Rutherston were unwilling to sign himself Rothenstein his name be omitted entirely from *Inclinations.* If neither alternative were agreeable, Firbank offered to return the drawings for the money he had paid. He told Richards, "I do not wish my book to be 'confusing' or 'mysterious' do you understand—!"[2] Rutherston stood firm. He had had to insist before he got his name in any form on the title page. It had been agreed to only after he told Richards in March that he thought Firbank "scarcely a writer of sufficient weight or name" to warrant having drawings in the book "unannounced." Rutherston protested that it was "quite the usual thing for a designer's name to appear on the Title page" and that he preferred to be "conventional in the matter."[3] Furthermore, his change of name had separated him to some extent from his brother William, who had decided against the same course of action. Albert was nervous about the situation, and he maintained that, since Rutherston was now his name, he must be so designated in print. Richards resolved the dilemma with a compromise; the jacket went

2. RF to GR, Oxford, May 21, 1916; cf. George Wiggins to Albert Rutherston, London, May 19 and 27, 1916; Robert Speaight: *William Rothenstein* (London, 1962), pp. 278–80.
3. Albert Rutherston to GR, London, March 16, 1916 (MJB).

unchanged with Rutherston on it, and both versions of the artist's name appeared on the title page.[4]

This was a sensible solution. Everyone was pleased, including Richards. He could get on with his work. Rutherston and Firbank became fast friends, and *Inclinations,* a book which Firbank said "ought to have followed on the heels of the other —instead of the train,"[5] appeared on June 17, 1916. The day before that, Firbank arranged with Richards for presentation copies to go out to friends and relations: six to Baba, one each to Alfred Douglas, John, Talboys, the Annesley Garretts, Joan Evans, Charles Shannon, Alys Lister of the Shakespeare Head Press, Stella Benson, and others. He was diligent in advertising *Inclinations.* And once again he read the Sphinx's opinion of his work: she considered *Inclinations* "quite amusing and jolly and deliciously quaint and old fashioned."[6]

Firbank was already planning a new publication. He had decided to reprint *Odette D'Antrevernes.* In June or early July he revised the text of *Odette,* working directly on a copy of the 1905 version. One or two changes alter syntax slightly, as "then she would sit silently" became "then silently she would sit." Most, however, are verbal revisions: "crimson roses" became "clustering roses" and "imagine," "picture"; he changed "the little white village church" to "the homely lichened church"; "her heart beating against her nightgown" was shortened to "her heart beating"; a "sad wreck of a human soul" became a "shattered wreck." Another stage of revision occurred, very likely on proofs. The effect of all the changes, as Firbank later told Carl Van Vechten, was to make this

4. Cf. George Wiggins to RF, London, May 30, 1916.
5. RF to GR, Oxford, April 24, 1916.
6. GR to RF, London, June 21, 1916. Cf. RF to GR, [London], June 16, 1916, and July 2, 1916; Torquay, August 25, 1916 (Copy UCL), and September 11, 1916 (UCL); GR to RF, London, June 24, 1916.

Odette "less naïf" than the 1905 version.[7] Still, the piece remains essentially the same in both versions; even poor and atypical work by Firbank is impossible to disguise or alter.

On July 18, 1916, Firbank delivered his revised book to Richards and signed an agreement to pay £65 for two thousand copies of *Odette*. Heretofore he had paid for illustrations separately and in addition to the amount paid Richards. In the case of *Odette*, the £65 included the cost of illustrations, though before they were done the artist asked for another £2. 2s., and Firbank finally paid it.[8] As soon as the agreement was signed, he began as usual to participate in the production of the book. The first problem, of course, was the matter of the illustrations. Firbank thought Hans Henning Voight, who signed himself Alastair, was "sufficiently Catholic" and very likely to give the book a "Gothic air—tres 'St Sulpice.' "[9] But Richards engaged Albert Buhrer, about whom Firbank commented only, "Two Alberts in one year. In Wartime too."[1] He was pleased with Buhrer's drawings, though in the process of getting satisfactory ones he rejected one or two and had second thoughts about style, subject matter, and color. He told Richards, "I long for the book to be really captivating & lovely."[2] The plates had to be named, and that entailed careful selection. Then there was the question of the book's title. The original one was discarded, but Firbank could not choose another at once. Although he was inclined to think it "clumsy," Firbank with Richards decided on "Odette A Fairy

7. RF to CVV, London, June 29, [1922]; cf. the revised copy of *Odette D'Antrevernes*, pp. 9, 14, 8, 17 *et passim* (MJB).
8. Cf. GR to RF, London, July 18, 1916, and December 21, 1916; Albert Buhrer to GR, London, September 1916 and October 17, 1916 (Illinois); RF to GR, n.p., n.d. (The Lilly Library, Indiana University).
9. RF to GR, [London], n.d.
1. RF to GR, Torquay, September 11, 1916 (Copy UCL). Buhrer later changed his name to Adrian Bury.
2. RF to GR, Torquay, July 28, 1916.

Tale for Weary People." He worried about the size of the
book. He objected to the words "one shilling net" on the
cover; "there need be *no* price marked as the book is not net,"
he stated.[3]

Despite this flurry of activity, Firbank's main concern was
getting the book out. Production was slow because printers
and pressmen were being called up for military service. As
early as November 3, a Friday, he asked whether the book
might be ready the following Wednesday, when he wanted it
to "go extensively out for review." He explained that he
would never again "be so respectable."[4] On November 26,
writing from Oxford, Firbank told Wiggins that because the
drawings were dated 1916, he feared the book would "be
dismissed as 'last years goods'" in a week or two. It was "an
agony to think about," he said. He was so importunate that
Wiggins and Richards considered having the book printed on
a hand press;[5] but that idea was abandoned, and the book
was printed by ordinary means. It appeared on December 13,
1916.

Firbank had been at work on another novel since August.
From Torquay on August 25 he wrote to Grant Richards,
saying he had just begun a "new one" which he wanted to
announce in *Odette* as "in Preparation." He added, "Its to be
called Caprice."[6] He referred to it again the next month, saying once more that he wanted to announce *Caprice,* as well as
Vainglory and *Inclinations,* in *Odette.*[7] Richards inquired
about Firbank's progress in December and again late in April,

3. RF to [GR], n.p., n.d. (The Lilly Library, Indiana University); cf. RF to
GR, Torquay, September 11, 1916, and Oxford, November 3, 1916 (Copies
UCL); GR to RF, London, November 13 and 15, 1916.
4. RF to GR, Oxford, November 3, 1916 (Copy UCL).
5. Cf. GR to RF, London, November 27, 1916.
6. (Copy UCL).
7. Cf. RF to GR, Torquay, September 11, 1916 (UCL).

when he asked whether the book was finished.[8] Firbank replied from Oxford on April 29 that he hoped to finish in ten or twelve weeks. He went on, "I expect you will think it scandalously short 3000—5 words about, but I wont bore you with a Queen's Hall resumé of the 'charactcrs and situa tions.' "[9] Richards had urged him to get the novel done in time for publication in autumn; but in the same letter Firbank protested that his book was hardly "solid enough for an Autumn novel," that *Caprice* would make a "ravishing Spring novel" the next year and give him "leisure to pull it about."

Richards wrote twice more to encourage the author to get the novel ready for autumn production.[1] In view of the publisher's persistence, Firbank took the manuscript of *Caprice* to Richards's London office in St. Martin Street on June 19 and immediately afterward wrote this note, "I fear you will find Caprice 'nothing'—there is still a good deal of revision required . . . Perhaps you will let me hear to Oxford what you think & advise about Caprice." Richards advised publication. He sent an informal contract dated June 22, 1917, to Firbank, who replied the next day, "I agree to the agreement . . . entirely."[2] Thus Firbank was to pay £70 for an edition of five hundred copies of *Caprice* and additional charges as they developed for frontispiece and wrapper; the publisher was to forfeit £10 if the book did not appear by the end of October.

The production of *Caprice* was singularly free of difficulties. Again Firbank wanted Augustus John to design the frontispiece and dust jacket. Even before signing Richards's memorandum, he "ran about" looking for John without success. The Chenil Gallery suggested Althea Giles instead, and

8. Cf. GR to RF, London, December 13, 1916, April 27, 1917.
9. (Copy UCL).
1. Cf. GR to RF, May 1, 1917, and June 13, 1917.
2. RF to GR, Oxford, June 23, [1917].

Richards advocated Miss A. H. Fish, and Firbank had in
mind William Strang, who might do "a rather lurid frontispiece & wrapper of figures dancing supremely well."[3] But on
July 1 Firbank could write from Oxford to say to Richards
that John had tentatively agreed to consider the drawing for
Caprice, though Firbank hardly expected him to make it; to
his "horror," Firbank had remembered references in the
manuscript to John as Judy Johncock. "In future," Firbank
told Richards, "I shall only give my characters numbers so as
to be quite safe."[4] Two weeks later, John promised to make a
drawing before the end of July. The one he produced was
unsatisfactory—"A dancing subject—only rather over Oriental to suit Caprice perhaps"—but by August 10, Firbank had
in hand an illustration "Less Nautch" and entirely appropriate.[5] Problems arose over Firbank's spelling of Tybalt and
Tchekhov, but these were easily settled. The printers tam-
pered very little with his capital letters, and proofs, even to
the extent of three revisions, were prompt. Because Firbank
had selected October 17 as a day of good omen for publication, Richards sent prepublication copies "got very specially"
to *The Morning Post,* Baba, and the author. The author responded with a telegram so enthusiastic that it made his publisher "quite cheerful."[6]

 Caprice was not actually published, not available in any
quantity, before November 9. On that day Richards distrib-

3. RF to GR, Oxford, July 9, 1917 (Copy UCL); cf. RF to GR, Oxford,
June 23, [1917]; GR to RF, London, June 25, 1917; GR to A. H. Fish,
London, June 25, 1917.
4. (Copy UCL).
5. RF to GR, Oxford, July 29, 1917 (Copy UCL); cf. RF to GR, Oxford,
July 15, 1917, and August 10, 1917 (Copies UCL).
6. GR to RF, London, October 17, 1917; cf. GR to RF, London, August
17 and 21, 1917, June 25, 1917, September 27, 1917, and two letters dated
October 16, 1917; Grant Richards Ltd to RF, London, July 4, 1917; RF
to GR, Oxford, June 23, [1917], July 9, 1917, and August 18, 1917
(Copies UCL).

uted copies in Firbank's behalf and sent five more to him and Baba. Only after that date did Firbank enjoy the questionable pleasure of hearing from Augustus John that while *Caprice* had its "charming light quality" he preferred *Vainglory* as "perhaps more idyllic—like a Fête galante" and from Richards that he advised an expenditure for advertising of no more than £20.[7]

At first the peripheral activities of authorship seem to have been more important to Firbank than the writing. In fact, he made elaborate preparations for his books and worked on them with great care and patience. That is true of every one of his novels, even *Inclinations,* which he thought so "spoilt" by haste that as late as April 1925 he was concerned enough about it to rewrite the fourth chapter of the second part, the "dinner party chapter."[8] Indeed, his procedure with *Inclinations* is a reasonable example of how he worked. He left no record of the genesis of this or any of the early novels. Obviously "Lady Appledore" began with an amused idealization of himself and his family's circumstances. The piece eventually called *The Artificial Princess* can be associated with a schoolboy's fascination with *fin de siècle* taste for the lush and the overripe and a public revival of interest in Salomé between 1906 and 1910. *Vainglory* rests on Firbank's previous work, especially his publication of Cambridge days, "A Study in Opal." But unless this can be associated with Firbank's reorientation of his religious needs, a process which took place at the same time as his composition of "A Study in Opal," any attempt to find the real origin of *Vainglory* comes to nothing. In the case of *Inclinations,* conjecture can supply nothing more precise than his brief visit to Greece and his encounters there

---

7. Augustus John to RF, Renvyle House, County Galway, n.d. (Fales); cf. GR to RF, London, November 10, 1917.
8. Cf. RF: *The Works of* (2 vols.; London, 1929), II, 133–41.

and elsewhere with the English female abroad. Yet an examination of his procedures with *Inclinations* gives a clear idea of his method.

It begins with his notebooks. Firbank had a series of these in all sizes for every book commencing with *The Artificial Princess* ("Salomé"), and for *Inclinations* he had ten.[9] Almost the whole novel is related by the kind of phrases Firbank customarily recorded in his notebooks. *Inclinations,* as its title announces, is about the propensities, and more specifically about the sexual propensities, of a number of women. The men in this novel are shadowy and undeveloped. They are sketched in the vaguest way as the objects for which some of the women have inclinations. One of these, really a girl, is Mabel Collins, who ends by marrying an Italian count. She is contrasted with another woman, Geraldine O'Brookomore— Gerald to her friends—whose inclinations are toward Mabel. The contrast is implicit, not stated. It is Firbank's characteristic means of making a comment, in this instance on the human female's various propensities. Since he depicts Gerald as a Lesbian and a bluestocking, takes both Gerald and Mabel as tourists to Athens, and surrounds them with more tourists, Firbank comments on a number of things in addition to inclinations. All this he achieved by means of the notebooks, so that in a way his method of composition represents what Coleridge Kennard described as fitting phrases in "mosaic-wise."

The procedure was a painstaking one. First came phrases or sentences jotted down as they occurred to him. Then, working backward and forward in a single notebook with no apparent system, Firbank assembled these into larger units; that is, phrases are put into sentences, and sentences, appearing first separately on various pages, are placed together in

9. (Fales).

groups of two or three. In each case Firbank revised, adding
something, eliminating a word here, changing a word there.
In one notebook Mabel Collins's statement, "I could clap my
feet in the air"[1] occurs three times in slightly different con-
texts, revised each time. The letter in which Miss Collins announced her marriage[2] is derived from two versions, both
much revised, in the notebooks; one of its sentences is tried
out elsewhere twice. The pages of the notebooks, then, constitute Firbank's work sheets. Some form of nearly all the novel
is in the ten notebooks, though not in the same order as in the
text. When the material was transferred to the text of *Inclinations,* the sentences in the notebooks were crossed out in
order to avoid repetition.

Later Firbank told Stuart Rose, the young American associated with Brentano's, "I am all design—once I get going."[3]
What emerges from Firbank's notebooks for *Inclinations* is a
considerable design. That is, the novel moves, if it does move,
only through the phrases and sentences organized as dialogue.
All of *Inclinations*—characterization, such action as there is,
and comment—is exposed (not presented) in dialogue between characters. Narrative tags, such as "she said," and indi-
rect discourse are hardly present, especially after the first
chapters. Individuation of characters, except through what
they say or through what someone says about them, does not
exist. Description of movement or environment is a bare
skeleton which occurs only when it is essential to clarify the
dialogue and sometimes not then.

The success of such construction depends on the nature of
the dialogue, or more precisely the exchange of words, since
there is often no communication. In any case it must function

1. *Inclinations,* p. 18.
2. Cf. p. 146.
3. RF to Stuart Rose, Rome, [July 1924].

in several ways. In *Inclinations* speeches which are complete
with well-made sentences and some internal logic, at least,
belong properly to Mabel. She is the more conventional of the
two main characters and possibly the most conventional in all
Firbank's fiction. Many speeches are fragmentary and stac-
cato in rhythm, a fact which is emphasized by the use of the
exclamation point. The rhythm suggests movement. It implies
the characters' restlessness. It also enforces the incomplete or
very short speeches and thereby something else which Firbank
conveys, his characters's self-absorption. This is again emphasized by the fact that the sequence of dialogue depends on
seemingly illogical associations occurring from speech to
speech, from speaker to speaker. Here is an exchange between
Geraldine and Mabel which Mabel commences:

> "Which would you prefer," she inquired, "a wedding or a
> funeral out at sea?"
> "I'd prefer there was no unpacking."
> "For the one emergency I've enough, of course, of white
> . . . and for the other, I dare say I could lean from the
> ship-side in a silver hat crowned with black Scotch roses."
> "Were it mine, I'd give that hat to Palmer [the maid]."
> "Poor thing, every time the ship rolls she seems to hear
> something say: *The captain*—his telescope."
> "She will see the land very soon now with her naked eye."
> . . .
> "I look forward first to eleven o'clock, . . . when the ship
> boy goes round with bananas."[4]

The dots above are not Firbank's. They indicate omissions
from his printed text. Frequently, however, to convey the self-
interest of his characters and the consequent lack of communication among them, Firbank broke his sentences with dots

4. *Inclinations*, pp. 42–3.

and dashes or terminated them with exclamation points. The dots do not indicate innuendo or represent naughtiness, which is sometimes present too, as much as they do fragmented consciousness, the "consciousness disjunct" of Pound. The exclamatory breaks may also be emotional ones. When Mabel deserts Gerald for marriage, Gerald's reaction occupies one entire chapter consisting of "Mabel!" repeated eight times. Not the speeches but their patterns disclose inclinations and mindless tenacity in fulfilling them. By the time Firbank concluded *The Artificial Princess* in 1925, he had reduced this method to a mere device. In *Inclinations* the dialogue is the novel.

The fact provoked *The Times Literary Supplement* to sharp criticism. Its review in the issue of June 22, 1916, reads:

> There is some humour, if one could get at it, underlying this tale . . . But as it is written almost entirely in snappy dialogue in which it is impossible to make out who is speaking without close and prolonged calculations, and as the characters have an inveterate habit of not finishing their sentences we cannot honestly say that the humour is worth the trouble.[5]

Nevertheless, *Inclinations* was a considerable achievement for Firbank. Its characters and content mark a detachment from his environment and a freedom from the artistically crippling reliance on his mother. The form of the novel is a refinement of what he had learned from the nineteenth-century French writers and adjusted to his personal view of the world. It perpetuates the "conversational-ironic tradition" of the Symbolists, but the book is too original to warrant a label, a niche. It is a wholly original piece of fiction, the first long one Firbank created for its own sake.

5. P. 299.

If Malraux was correct in saying that every artist masters and transforms the meaning of the world by mastering and modifying the forms of a predecessor, then Firbank had advanced far toward literary artistry. *Caprice* took him farther. In it, since he was technically more conventional, he could consolidate his earlier experiments. *Caprice* is about a "flight from the provinces," the hazards of success, the emptiness of fame. All this is contained in the plot. It tells of Sarah Sinquier, who gathers together her heirloom pearls and the family silver and flees from a cathedral town to the London stage. With the hypocritical guidance of Mrs. Sixsmith, Sarah opens triumphantly at her own theater as Juliet, only to die the next dawn. Happy in her "delicious" success, she approaches the empty stage, breaks into a private dance, and falls into a mousetrap, where she dies. Mrs. Sixsmith, unable now to "make out the score," to present her account to Sarah, invades the cathedral town determined to get what she can from Sarah's father. Instead of relying here so heavily on his notebooks—there are only four for *Caprice*[6]—Firbank employs much of the usual machinery of fiction. The dialogue has the same character as that of *Inclinations,* but it is only one element of *Caprice.* His distinctive words and phrases are integrated with ordinary narrative with which he fills many of the "gaps between scenes" and characters. The characters are depicted by the means novelists usually employ: action, descrip tion, and dialogue.

Despite this fictional conventionality, greater than that of the two preceding novels, *Caprice* is peculiarly Firbank's. For example, in *Caprice* the author is specific in his use of names and place-names (Augustus John, Buxton, London). Because these are real and identifiable, they give the extravagances of *Caprice* credibility. On the other hand, Firbank's

6. (Harvard).

description of these real places makes no pretense at representation. When the heroine, Sarah Sinquier, goes in search of "some nice tea-shop, some cool creamery," she finds the Café Royal:

> Such a noise!
>
> Everyone seemed to be chattering, smoking, lunching, casting dice, or playing dominoes.
>
> She advanced slowly through a veil of opal mist, feeling her way from side to side with her parasol.
>
> It was like penetrating deeper and deeper into a bath.[7]

This is not the Café Royal, but the effect it produced. The heroine of *Caprice,* like the heroine of *Vainglory,* is another of Firbank's yearning souls, an example of the "pathetic-ironic" which recurs in his novels.

Caprice allowed Firbank to test and evaluate his own methods because it contained so many techniques already tried and so few untried. It was a sound preparation for his next book *Valmouth,* a novel which began with one detail at least in Firbank's awareness of Rabindranath Tagore, who, after several visits to England commencing in 1912, had received his Knighthood in 1915. The surface of Tagore's mysticism interested Firbank enough to name the heroine of his new book Mrs. Yajñavalkya, after the Hindu goddess of the same name. The novel began also with place-names which had caught his attention. One was the village he saw repeatedly as he traveled between Oxford and London, Hare Hatch, complete with Hare Hatch House. The other was the Welsh town where his brother had died, Glyndyfrdwy, corrupted by Ronald to Glennyfurry and then removed from his book. Firbank was planning *Valmouth* as he completed *Caprice.* Soon

7. *Caprice* (London, 1917), p. 38.

after June 11, 1917, the day on which he was discharged as "permanently and totally disabled for Service under the Military Service (Review of Exceptions) Act,"[8] he wrote to Grant Richards, "I have an idea for another!! I think of going to America to write it—since I am free again."[9] Firbank did not go to America, but on July 1 he reported, also to Richards, that he had started a new book which was to be his last and best.[1] A few days later he asked Richards's advice about announcing it in *Caprice*. He wrote also about the names he was considering for his book, either "The Centenarians of Glenfurry" or, if Richards thought that too "outlandish," "Glennyfurry: a Romance." Richards disliked both, and Firbank changed it first to "Glenmouth: A Romantic Novel," the name under which it was announced in *Caprice,* and then to "Valmouth." He did not alter his faith in the novel. "You will be astonished," he told Richards, "how different it will be to anything yet of mine."[2]

III

The difference and the consequent complexity of *Valmouth,* because they meant long, intense hours of work, were a blessing to Firbank. Similarly, the effort spent on the other two books written in Oxford and his attention to their production and that of *Valmouth* were his salvation. These literary mat-

8. Certificate of discharge (Beinecke Rare Book and Manuscript Library, Yale University).
9. RF to GR, Oxford, n.d.
1. RF to GR, Oxford, July 1, 1917 (Copy UCL).
2. RF to GR, Oxford, July 9, 1917 (Copy UCL).

ters claimed his attention during one of the most difficult pe-
riods of his life. Firbank's stay in Oxford was an unhappy one
with a lasting effect.

He thought very little about the war. By July 17, when he
began to write *Valmouth,* Britain had survived the ghastly
slaughter of the Somme and the Battle of Verdun. That
spring, Russia had been forced out of the cause of the Allies
and the United States forced in. Firbank, however, seemed little
affected by any of it. If he felt throughout those years, as
Lady Ottoline Morrell says she did, "a haunting fear of something dark and terrible,"[1] he never hinted it. Only one of his
extant letters written from Oxford made direct reference to
the war. That one, to Heather, undated but very likely belonging to 1916, said, "It must be a change to have a quiet sky
overhead again." He had heard, Firbank continued, that
"there was an attempted raid on London . . . a few nights ago
but the fog baffled them." No one dear to him was killed in
action. His friends—Talboys, John, Evan Morgan, Kennard,
Holland—survived the war. Firbank saw them seldom, but he
took notice of their comings and goings. When Holland, still
in service after the armistice of 1918, returned to France after
a leave in England, Helen Carew wrote to thank him in Holland's behalf for "divine Malmaison flowers . . . delicate and
fragrant cigarettes," and, above all, "perfectly chosen books."
She assured Firbank that all he had done for Holland was "an
act of Charity" which had given "infinite pleasure to one who
was feeling very desolate and lonely."[2] Those men who had
frequented the Eiffel Tower as Firbank had and who died in
the war to England's immeasurable loss—Patrick Shaw-
Stewart, Raymond Asquith, Edward Horner—were hardly

1. Lady Ottoline Morrell: *The Early Memoirs,* ed. Robert Gathorne-Hardy
(London, 1963), p. 281.
2. Helen Carew to RF, London, November 23, [1918] (Fales).

acquaintances. The loss of Rupert Brooke touched Firbank; but he felt regret, not grief, and he failed to understand the promise for which Geoffrey Keynes and Edward Marsh mourned. After Brooke's death, Firbank asked Marsh in their one meeting, an incident which Marsh said was "beneath the dignity of biography," whether he had admired Rupert Brooke. Marsh answered affirmatively, and Firbank replied, "You're wrong—I'm better than he."[3]

Firbank's capacity for such remarks enlarged during his stay in Oxford, a consequence of his unhappiness there. The weather depressed him; he still remembered in 1921 "the dreary Oxford winters" and "what one suffered from lack of sun."[4] He had to cope with illness. In September 1916 he was threatened with surgery. Richards inquired twice about Firbank's "projected operation," but it eventually proved unnecessary.[5] Baba, however, had cataracts removed. Ronald rejoiced when the "ordeal" was over and offered to give her a week at Brighton so that the sea might "blow away" all remembrance of her discomfort.[6]

The worst part was the loneliness. It took from Firbank his natural exuberance and changed his sweet, genial nature into a suspicious, hypersensitive one. "Solitude I adore," he told Heather in 1923, "but I do not think without a very definite object it is good for one, as all isolation unfits one for 'society' making it very difficult to return."[7] His solitude in Oxford, especially when he first went there, was almost complete. He

3. Edward Marsh to MJB, London, October 14, 1952. The incident as narrated by Fletcher (*Ronald Firbank A Memoir*, p. 35) is placed in 1914. If it happened after Brooke's death, as the account implies, then the date is mistaken. Brooke enlisted in September 1914 and died of septicaemia on April 23, 1915.
4. RF to HF, Tunis, February 18, 1921.
5. Cf. GR to RF, London, September 6 and 27, 1916.
6. Cf. RF to HJGF, Oxford, n.d.
7. RF to HF, Rome, August 11, [1924].

was reduced to lone excursions by bicycle, such as the one he described to Heather, a ride along a road which skirted the River Turl all the way to the site of a Roman camp.[8] He slowly developed a "nervous apprehension about life" so that, as he said himself, "the thought of London or anywhere among people quite paralysed" him.[9] His journeys to London for talks with Richards were real trials, and Firbank began to shy away from companionship. Richards remembered an occasion when he lunched with Firbank at the Café Royal. After they were seated, the artist C. R. W. Nevinson approached their table and insisted on joining them. Richards introduced the two, but Firbank was far from cordial; he whispered that he thought Nevinson "sinister." They eventually became friends because they shared a strong dislike of "the mob," a taste for drink, and a "worship of beauty"; and in the years to come Firbank attended Nevinson's summer parties in Hampstead. On this occasion, though, Firbank so openly considered Nevinson intrusive that Richards felt the need to apologize. He wrote:

> At the moment I must confess to having been annoyed at Nevinson's suggestion that he should come and sit at our table, but putting him off was too difficult a proposition for me to tackle . . . but I enjoyed my lunch all the same; and you must come and sit with me while I lunch again one day.[1]

Firbank's "nervous apprehension" was intensified by his frustration and disappointment at the reception of his novels. He longed for recognition. The Oxford bookseller Sanders re-

8. Cf. RF to HF, Oxford, November 8, 1915.
9. RF to HF, Rome, August 11, [1924].
1. GR to RF, London, January 9, 1918. Cf. GR: *Author Hunting* (London, 1960), p. 202; Fletcher: *Ronald Firbank A Memoir*, p. 78.

called Firbank as having a "very sensitive personality rather exotic and I would say effeminate in the nicer meaning of the word, eager to be understood by those he felt in sympathy. Almost tragic in the appeal to be appreciated."[2] The sales of his books hardly indicated that he was. With ninety-two copies sold in 1916, *Inclinations* went less well than *Vainglory* had in its first year. The reviews, moreover, were scant. *Inclinations* had had only nine notices by August 25, 1916, more than two months after publication. On that day Firbank sent a letter from Torquay suggesting that Richards "insert fearlessly from those nine newspapers & announce the book as a success." He thought it might "help Odette & a new one . . . just begun."[3] The 1916 *Odette*, however, was largely disregarded. Both publisher and author thought it "an attractive book and, what is more, distinguished[4]; but nobody noticed. It was sent out for review, and Firbank spent £10 for five announcements, authorizing them on December 31, 1916, when he wrote, "So far I've seen no reviews. I expect Odette is looked upon as a kind of Christmas-card—or a Peace Pamphlet."[5] At the end of January 1917 he explained his mother's idea to alter the cover of *Odette* so as to produce an "Easter version."[6] When Richards discouraged this as too expensive, and when, by April 1917, there had been no review of *Odette*, Firbank was resigned to its failure. He wrote to Richards, "I am so sorry it didn't take as it looked so nice."[7]

Lady Firbank, disappointed for her son, sent a letter to Richards well in advance of the appearance of *Caprice* asking him to promote that novel vigorously. He promised to do

2. F. J. A. Sanders to Richard Buckle, Oxford, August 5, 1940.
3. (Copy UCL).
4. GR to RF, London, December 13, 1916.
5. (Copy UCL).
6. Cf. RF to GR, Oxford, January 31, 1917 (UCL).
7. RF to GR, Oxford, April 29, 1917 (Copy UCL); cf. GR to RF, London, February 3, 1917.

everything possible. He said he thought its chances better than its predecessor's because it would look attractive and would make a more "popular appeal." He proved himself a sympathetic and understanding publisher in what he replied about Ronald:

> In the two previous books he was very obviously feeling his way towards a method, and as he made no capitulations and conceded nothing to the public they presented all sorts of difficulties. The book should really help him towards a reputation even though the number of people who care for the kind of cleverness and ability he shows is limited.[8]

But Richards's efforts to arouse interest in the novel offended Firbank and led to his first quarrel with the publisher. In an advertisement which appeared in the October 25, 1917, issue of *The Times Literary Supplement,* Richards spoke of *Caprice* as "like nothing else on earth." Firbank was affronted and, because he was, Lady Firbank was also affronted. Richards wrote two letters to defend himself. He said he had shown the advertisement to several people who thought it "excellent" and that he himself thought it "good." He maintained that the offending phrase applied to *Caprice* in the same way as it would to "some of the greatly admired paintings by the very modern men"; he thought no one would have "minded" if he had called the book "unique," which is, he added, the same thing but an "ugly word." His final justification was that G. P. Putnam's Sons, attracted by Richards's reference to *Caprice,* had asked to consider it for America.[9] Whatever Richards did—advertising the book and asking for reviews and getting Firbank's latest photograph, one made by

8. GR to HJGF, London, August 22, 1917.
9. Cf. GR to RF, London, October 27 and 31, 1917.

the fashionable Bertram Park, published in *The Tatler*[1]—the reception of *Caprice* fell short of Firbank's expectations. He called the reviews a "frost," as indeed they were. *The Times Literary Supplement* for November 1, 1917, spoke of his "explosive style, his continuous barrage of crisp paragraphs and chippy talk," which, they said, made it "hard to get any continuity or sense of character and atmosphere, or to feel much interest in the very unlikely experiences" of the book's heroine. The best review, one in *Town Topics* for November 17, 1917, characterized *Caprice* as a "strange novel" which might be "intensely" amusing. Firbank was disappointed with the number of copies sold, and he took no comfort when Richards told him,

> If you want to sell large numbers you must write like Conan Doyle or Miss Dell, or Mrs. Barclay. Personally, if I were in your place I would prefer to write as you do write. But you cannot expect to please the great public at the same time.[2]

When appreciation finally came to Firbank near the end of his stay in Oxford, he was too withdrawn to enjoy it. In either late September or early October 1918, Firbank had a call from Lord Berners. Helen Carew had come once to spend a "peaceful afternoon at no 66," Ronald's rooms on the High. But she was disturbed by his having an "ill-omened relic from Egypt" and she urged him to bury it and so avoid its evil influence.[3] Nevertheless, she sent Berners to visit Firbank there too. Lord Berners was a musician whose motor car then or shortly afterward was outfitted with a small harmonium;

1. January 30, 1918, p. 418. Cf. GR to RF, London, October 24, 1917, January 9 and 31, 1918.
2. GR to RF, London, December 10, 1917; cf. GR to RF, London, November 2, 1917, December 1, 1917.
3. Helen Carew to RF, Hove, September 14, [1918] (Fales).

he composed on it, deriving motifs from the countryside
through which he drove. Mme Jacques Balsan heard him
making music when she passed him once on the roads of
southern France in his "drawn-up car." He was "sitting at his
harmonium with butterflies as a halo round his head, an
ironic smile on his lips and a monocle in his eye."[4] To quote
Osbert Sitwell, Berners had indeed the "particular gift of rec-
onciling the irreconcilable, both in people and circumstances."[5] He did so with enough detachment to keep Firbank
comfortable. Yet he had hard going with Firbank. Helen
Carew had prepared the way by writing that Berners was "a
great musician" who admired Firbank's works and by urging
Firbank to see him because he was sure to be interesting. But
Berners declared that "to know Ronald Firbank doesn't mean
that one got to know anything about himself or his opinions
and any direct question was invariably answered by the words
'I wonder.' "[6]

A second letter from Mrs. Carew, also dated September,
brought other, more intense and more uneasy associations. In
this letter she added to an account of a visit to London the
fact that she had seen "two great friends" of hers, "the Sitwell
brothers (both in the Grenadiers and both Poets)," who
turned out to be "great admirers" of Firbank's work. They
had surprised her, Firbank read, by making "long and accurate quotations from both 'Caprice' and from 'Vainglory.' "
The letter ran:

> They . . . begged to meet you. They are nearly as aloof as
> yourself and live together in a tiny house in Chelsea, when

4. Consuelo Vanderbilt Balsan: *The Glitter and the Gold* (New York, 1952), p. 278.
5. *Laughter in the Next Room* (London, 1949), p. 180.
6. Lord Berners to Jocelyn Brooke, Berkshire, November 19, 1948 (Berg); cf. Helen Carew to RF, n.p., September 25, [1918] (Fales).

not persecuted by Military duties. At the request of the Elder
(Osbert) I am to send you a copy of some poems recently
published by the Younger Brother, "Sachie." Both are extremely talented, and their chief work has been published in
'Wheels'. . . .[7]

Firbank was pleased enough to respond with a "delightful and
a wonderful letter" which Mrs. Carew "shared" with the
"Poet Brothers" and then wrote to assure Firbank that they
had "a cult" for him and all his work.[8] The following January, well after November 11, 1918, had duly passed with
three nights of riotous joy, the older of the "Poet Brothers,"
Osbert, went to Oxford to visit the younger, Sacheverell, by
then in residence at Balliol College. They called on Firbank,
taking Siegfried Sassoon with them. According to Sassoon,
Firbank received them in a "closely-curtained room lighted
by numerous candles and filled with a profusion of exotic
flowers." There was an "enormous fire" and a large table was
"elaborately set out with a banquet of rich confectionery and
hothouse fruits." Firbank's speech was "almost inaudible, and
he was too nervous to sit still for more than half a minute at a
time." Neither Sassoon nor the Sitwells could "elicit anything
except the disconnected utterances which were his method of
evading direct explanations." When Sacheverell expressed
admiration for *Caprice*, Firbank "turned his head away and
remarked in a choking voice, 'I can't bear calceolarias! Can
you?'" He seemed to Sassoon "as unreal and anomalous as
his writings, and the room—with its exquisite refinements and
virtuosities of taste—seemed a pathetically contrived refuge."[9]
Perhaps Firbank was more profound than epigrammatic
(at least about himself) when he told Sassoon later, "I

7. Helen Carew to RF, Hove, September 14, [1918] (Fales).
8. Cf. Helen Carew to RF, London, November 23, [1918] (Fales).
9. Sassoon: *Siegfried's Journey*, pp. 135 ff.

am Pavlova, chasing butterflies . . . You are Tolstoy, digging for worms."[1] Nevertheless, he was interested in Sassoon. In June 1918, months before meeting him, Firbank had ordered Sassoon's book of poems *The Old Huntsman* in a first edition. A few days after the visit, he accepted Sassoon's invitation to tea and appeared "powdered, ninetyish, and insuperably shy" at 14 Merton Street, where Sassoon had rooms. His host reported that Ronald "absorbed a single grape" instead of the chocolate cake and crumpets offered him and when confronted with a discussion of literature and art said only, "I adore italics, don't you?"[2]

Furthermore, he allowed himself to be honored by his new acquaintances with a dinner party; that is, he agreed to arrive with the dessert and read a chapter of the still unfinished *Valmouth*. Nine men gathered in the oak-beamed dining room of the Golden Cross Inn. They were, in addition to the three hosts, Gabriel Atkin, Wilfred Childe, V. de Sola Pinto, Frank Rewitt, Gerald Crowe, and Thomas Earp. Atkin drew the party at table, but unhappily he chose a moment before dessert to fix on paper; so Ronald Firbank is not shown. When he came, he sauntered in with apparent indifference to everyone in the room and then, after some coaxing, sat down at the appointed table but "sideways" to the others, showing only his profile, described by Osbert Sitwell as "waving in and out with something of the line of a seacoast." After a taste of port, as Sitwell has related, Firbank "began to read in a voice which contained in it the strangled notes of a curate's first sermon, but was warmed from time to time—indeed, fairly frequently—by fits of genial, deep chuckling." He managed to get through one version of what amounted to the eighth chap-

1. Ibid., p. 137.
2. Ibid., p. 136; cf. RF to [Cyril Beaumont], Oxford, June 25, 1918 (Iowa).

ter of *Valmouth*, continuing while he read "to pluck wildly at
his tie and feverishly to avoid the gaze of those watching him
and concentrating on his words."[3]

According to Sanders, this "period of post war Oxford"
was a "time of the blatant and the strident." It was, he said,
"entirely foreign to such a sensitive soul" as Firbank and
"would account for his loneliness."[4] Certainly Sassoon, a
poet, a lover of the outdoors, a man of painful conviction, did
not find Oxford distasteful. He makes that clear in *Siegfried's
Journey*. And in a letter written from Oxford on March 4,
1919, to his aunt Mrs. Frederick Beer, he told about seeing "a
lot of interesting people" even though they were "mostly
young & unknown" and about his plans for lunching with
John Masefield that very day.[5] Certainly, the group at the
dinner party was receptive to Firbank, and there were others
in or near Oxford who might have been. Besides Masefield,
living at Boar's Hill, there was Lady Ottoline Morrell, the
friend of D. H. Lawrence and Mark Gertler, with a home at
Garsington.

Somehow Firbank had lost the quality which introduced
him to de Max's flat in the rue Caumartin and charmed Jean
Pozzi. Firbank was no longer (if he had ever been) a suitable
replacement for the Belgian Ambassador at a dinner where he
could confess his love of gardens to the lady on his right.
Perhaps those people, as Cocteau said of de Max, were "igno-
rant of codes and formulas" in life as well as in the theater
and thus capable of more variety in their acquaintances than
the residents of an English university town were. More likely
the difficulty lay with Firbank. The effect of the solitude

3. Sitwell: *Laughter in the Next Room*, p. 182; "Ronald Firbank," *Noble
Essences* (London, 1950), pp. 74–6. The drawing by Gerald Atkin is reproduced opposite p. 69 in Sitwell's *Noble Essences*.
4. F. J. A. Sanders to Richard Buckle, Oxford, August 5, 1940.
5. (MJB).

forced on him when he first went to Oxford was magnified by the demands of his work. When he spoke of the sacrifice and discipline for which he prized *Vainglory,* he referred to more than routine or physical comfort, which he retained, or the loss of society, which he valued. He meant the loss of his adaptability to society; it could not survive his obsession with his work. That was the price he paid for the writing itself, the intense conscious effort which drove him too far into himself, the desperation of the search for how to say what he had to say—what Virginia Woolf called "stumbling after" one's "own voice"—and at last the intoxication of finding it. It was impossible without a conviction that his work was important, and having that, Firbank very likely expected more forbearance and more of the moral support of adulation than he had a right to. Or possibly he had cultivated too artificial a temperament.

In any case, before the end of February 1919, the month in which Sassoon and the Sitwells had entertained him, Firbank acted with unexpected coolness toward Sacheverell Sitwell. A mutual acquaintance, Willie King, who eventually became keeper of ceramics at the British Museum, had reported that Sacheverell was interested in Firbank only as a curiosity, something to be examined minutely as if by microscope and then dropped. When Sitwell came to call at 66 High Street on February 21, Firbank implied that he resented the disturbance and that he believed what Willie King had said. Sitwell, sensitive, gifted, and young (only twenty-two), left Firbank abruptly and that evening wrote to him:

> I am writing to say how much I hope you were not angry with me for disturbing you this afternoon. I have been very upset about it. I am afraid I left you rather curtly but I had been a *little* hurt by what you said about my "microscope." If only you would realize that I don't come to see you & read

your books because they're *"extraordinary,"* but because
you appeal to me & interest me, and because your books
are the best things of their kind.[6]

Despite this letter, Firbank maintained his reserve with Sitwell
until some time in May.

Then he regretted his behavior and the consequent loss of
possible intimacy with the Sitwells. He even made a fruitless
attempt to recapture it. Osbert Sitwell had liked the chapter
from *Valmouth* read aloud at the Golden Cross well enough
to solicit it at once for publication in *Art and Letters*. When
arrangements were complete, Osbert wrote from Monte Carlo
on March 20, 1919, to say how delighted he was to have the
opportunity of publishing Firbank's work. Sitwell's letter said:

> If people are such fools as not to appreciate the wit and
> beauty of "Vain Glory" or "Caprice" they must, somehow
> or other, be made to.
>
> I think myself that, much as I love your other work,
> "Chapter VIII" is almost the best thing I've seen of yours.[7]

When the piece appeared in May with the title "Fantasia for
Orchestra in F Sharp Minor,"[8] Firbank was extremely
pleased. He called it to Richards's attention, wrote happy letters to both Osbert and Sachie, and called on Sachie in
Oxford. Sachie had obviously not told his brother about Firbank's behavior in Oxford, inasmuch as the letter which Osbert sent from Monte Carlo to remark on "Chapter VIII" has
as a postscript, "I have never told you how nice you were to
Sachie and me. I hope that—Bulls of Bashan as we are—we
did not trample too much on your seclusion!" But Sachie was
not easily appeased. He told Firbank that he was "touched" to

6. Sacheverell Sitwell to RF, Oxford, February 21, 1919 (Iowa).
7. (Iowa).
8. *Art and Letters,* II, New Series (Spring 1919), 64–79.

I

Sir Thomas Firbank

Lady Firbank

Ronald Firbank,
London, 1917

Ronald Firbank,
Chamonix, 1904

III

Evan Morgan

R. St. Clair Talboys

Henry Biais

Édouard de Max

V

Ronald Firbank's room at Trinity Hall, Cambridge University, 1907

Ronald Firbank,
drawing by
Wyndham Lewis,
1922

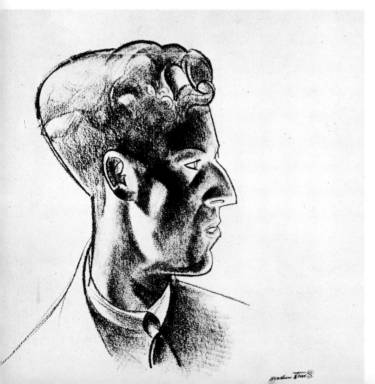

Ronald Firbank,
drawing by
Wyndham Lewis,
1922

VII The Café Royal

From a notebook used for *Valmouth* and *The Princess Zoubaroff*

Ronald Firbank,
drawing by
Augustus John,
about 1915

IX

Ronald Firbank,
drawing by
Augustus John,
about 1922

By Albert Rutherston, 1916

By Augustus John, 1917

X DUST JACKETS FOR FOUR FIRST EDITIONS

By Michel Sevier, 1920

By C. R. W. Nevinson, 1923

XI

Hunter Stagg

Sewell Stokes

Grant Richards

Carl Van Vechten

have his letter and liked seeing him, but he felt that an explanation was needed. Sitwell wrote:

> You may remember that I arrived on the scene rather, perhaps, like one of the three Magi, drawn by your star so to speak, or at any rate by what I admired of your writing. I saw a great deal of you in January and February, and took it, I think for granted, that I had your friendship.
>
> I then went abroad during which time I wrote you two letters, neither of which you answered. On my return here you showed not the faintest pleasure at seeing me, although I came round to your house within ½ hour of my arrival in Oxford . . . My feelings were naturally very much hurt.[9]

He once more denied Willie King's accusation by saying he had seen King neither during the last term at Oxford nor in London before going to Spain. The letter ended, "Apart from the lack of opportunity, I think you ought to have known for certain that I am not in the habit of talking about my friends to somebody who had proved a very mischievous and false friend in the past." Sachie offered to make no further reference to the incident in exchange for a "tiny letter" of understanding from Firbank, but Firbank did not respond. Although he saw the Sitwells afterward in London and Florence and Rome, the relationship with them was never what it had promised to be.[1] Usually Firbank played the role of the injured party in telling his mother about the Sitwells, but his own capabilities for friendship had proved inadequate. He did not admit that. Because he did not, he rationalized his own behavior and blamed Willie King and Sitwell. Certainly this incident was one of the "many stages" by which he came to

9. Sacheverell Sitwell to RF, Oxford, May 23, 1919 (Iowa). Cf. GR to RF, London, May 8, 1919.
1. Osbert Sitwell in *Noble Essences* (p. 78) ascribes minor and brief differences between the Sitwells and Firbank to Firbank's amusing imagination.

the "lonely and isolated" existence which he wrote about to Heather in 1922.[2] It was a wounding incident, which convinced him, as he told Nancy Cunard, that permanent relationships cannot be created, that "one person replaces another."[3] He went even farther when, in 1923, he said to his sister, "All lies in oneself, people wound & contribute too much or too little, & to rely on them is always grief!"[4] Thereafter Oxford was a synonym to Firbank for the "jealous & spiteful."[5]

Still Firbank lingered on in Oxford. His staying there was no longer the result of his "apprehension about life." Either late in 1918 or in the spring of 1919, he had taken to Brighton a "clever sympathetic Swede" who "got him out" of himself and his fears.[6] From time to time, now, he went to London to see the Ballet Russe, which Diaghilev showed at the Alhambra that spring of 1919. Firbank was often visible in the foyer of the Alhambra to at least one other patron of ballet, "walking about in a curious crab-like manner in the intervals."[7] Furthermore, he was able to face without too many qualms the *bon voyage* banquet which Grant Richards gave in May 1919 at the Café Royal to honor C. R. W. Nevinson, soon to depart for America and a one-man show. It was a splendid occasion, with food and drink to please the palate of Richards, a real gourmet. Walter Sickert was in the chair and J. L. Garvin, the well-known and gifted journalist, the principal speaker. Firbank sat among the hundred or more distinguished guests (artists, poets, novelists, journalists, and publishers), since, after the first unhappy meeting with Nevinson the year before,

2. RF to HF, Fiesole, March 13, 1922.
3. Nancy Cunard to RF, Paris, n.d. (MJB).
4. RF to HF, Rome, December 30, 1923.
5. RF to HJGF, Rome, October 1923.
6. RF to HF, Rome, August 11, [1924].
7. Alan Harris to Richard Buckle, London, July 24, 1940.

Firbank had been won over by the artist. Anyway, Richards thought it would be "good" for Firbank to attend. When Garvin rose to speak, his praise of Nevinson was so pompous and high-flown that Firbank found it ridiculous. He began to laugh, and he laughed and laughed until finally Alvaro Guevara, the Chilean painter, had to lead him out. Firbank went straight back to Oxford and a day or two later had a letter from Richards containing only one remark about the banquet: "I believe J. L. Garvin is still looking for you with a knife!"[8]

Firbank remained in Oxford because he preferred not to disturb himself before *Valmouth* was well along toward publication. In May and June he was still at work on it. It was July 5, 1919, before Richards had read the book and was ready to talk about it. Five days later Firbank signed a memorandum for the production of *Valmouth*. For an edition of five hundred copies he paid £116 6s. 2d. plus the cost of revisions and advertisements. He had begun to consider the frontispiece and wrapper before the novel was done. He had wanted to use for them a "Gauguin negress," but he could find nothing from which to make a suitable reproduction. He chose instead a black and white drawing "of a lady in eighteenth century dress" which he had seen on Augustus John's mantelpiece in his Mallord Street studio. Richards arranged for the use of the drawing, but the cost, £25, was settled between John and Firbank.[9] Proofs began to reach him in August. Sanders, who had been called in to purchase Firbank's library, stayed to help with what proofs had come.[1]

8. GR to RF, London, May 1, 1919. Cf. Guy Deghy and Keith Waterhouse: *Café Royal* (London, 1955), pp. 169–71.
9. Cf. GR to RF, London, July 5 and 10, 1919, May 8, 1919, July 12, 1919; GR to Augustus John, London, July 10, 1919; Augustus John to RF, London, July 16, [1919] (Fales).
1. Cf. F. J. A. Sanders to Richard Buckle, Oxford, August 5, 1940.

❦ IV ❦

Before he had all the proofs, Firbank had sold his library of about a thousand books and a number of autographs of people of the nineties, packed up his personal belongings, and moved permanently from Oxford. In July he had considered returning to London "for 'good.'" In early September he went from Oxford to Bath, a city which he declared had always impressed him as picturesque. Besides, it was the place to which he had retreated in 1913 with *Vainglory*. There he had once exercised discipline and balance. Whether he hoped to regain them in Bath, whether he still yearned for a house on the Royal Crescent with a servant like de Max's cannot be known. In any case, he gave up the thought of going on to Gloucester and stayed in Bath, enjoying the pleasures available to him, such as Mrs. Annie Besant's talk on India in the Assembly Rooms. But he was fretful over additional proofs for *Valmouth*. On September 21 they had not yet arrived; his room at the Pultney Hotel was let for the first week in October; and he could only conclude that, with all the problems he had had, it was "wonderful" to have survived his five books "written on other peoples tables and other peoples chairs."[1]

The proofs came on September 26, and the following week he returned to London, taking a flat at 48 Jermyn Street.

1. RF to HJGF, Bath, September 21, 1919; cf. RF to GR, [London, July 10, 1919]; RF to HJGF, Bath, September 12, 1919, n.d., September 21 and 25, 1919.

Duncan Grant remembered meeting Firbank at about that time on Jermyn Street behind St. James's Church. Alvaro Guevara introduced them, and according to Grant it was "rather like being introduced to an elegant grasshopper in white kid gloves and boots."[2]

Once more Firbank was ready to take up his life in London, where he remained until the next summer. Even while awaiting publication of *Valmouth,* he had started what was to be his next work, a play, *The Princess Zoubaroff;* and that determined the pattern of his days. He wrote usually well past noon and often until tea time. Then he emerged from his flat to return to his old habits and haunts. Perhaps Bath had given him back some of his earlier self. He was certainly not averse to companionship and social life. That winter he had his portrait done by "Chile" Guevara, a view of an acutely uncomfortable Firbank seated on a straight chair like another piece of bric-a-brac in the *décor* of his flat, where the picture was painted. Firbank described the portrait as "a perfectly brutal little study" of himself "huddled up in a black suit by a jar of Orchids, in a decor suggestive of Opium—or (even) worse!"[3] When the picture was done, it was entitled "Ronald Firbank Esq." and shown early the next year in an exhibition of the New English Art Club at the Gallery of the Old Water-Colour Society. Firbank went repeatedly to the theater. He heard over and over again the Southern Syncopated Orchestra and their Negro spirituals. And he attended the ballet, which danced at the Empire that winter and at Covent Garden in the spring of 1920. One observer says that Firbank invariably retired to the bar as soon as the ballet began.[4] That

2. Duncan Grant to Richard Buckle, [London], December 21, 1941.
3. RF to CVV, Paris, June 10, 1922.
4. Cf. Alan Harris to Richard Buckle, London, July 24, 1940.

statement is an exaggeration, but Firbank spent considerable
time now if not at bars then with a drink in his hand. He went
occasionally to the Café Monaco on Regent Street and often
to the Café Royal, taking up his accustomed place at the
right, halfway down the room. There he sat, "writhing like a
basket of serpents"[5] and paying for endless drinks. The very
fat, round-faced waiter George kept a full glass of brandy
before Firbank (*fine champagne,* he called it) without a word
exchanged between them. This might go on all day and into
the night; Firbank never moved over to the back part of the
room reserved for those who wanted food. When he was
ready to leave his place under the angels which graced the
ceiling, he left the Café. But before going he turned his head
apologetically as though to make himself invisible and applied
a *papier-poudre,* one of those pink, rice powder-coated
papers, to his face.[6] His favorite haunt, however, was the
Eiffel Tower, sometimes alone, sometimes with Augustus
John, but more often with Evan Morgan.

On November 17, 1919, *Valmouth* appeared, a novel in
every way superior to his earlier work. In this book Firbank
defined sharply the subject with which he was preoccupied,
the "complex interplay of value and disorder."[7] He expresses
it in *Valmouth* by balancing a natural and primitive love of
beauty against the love of Catholic discipline and form without Christianity. For the first time in Firbank's fiction the
Church itself (in the person of the priest Father Mahoney) is
an out and out part of the disorder. Heretofore in his novels,
the lay practice of religion had been measured by the ideals
inherent in Catholicism. Here the Church is measured by

5. Fletcher: *Ronald Firbank A Memoir,* p. 68.
6. Interview with Sewell Stokes, 1967.
7. James Hafley: "Ronald Firbank," *Arizona Quarterly,* XII (Summer
1956), 167.

Christianity and found wanting. That motif is not the focus of *Valmouth*, but Firbank's admitted mockery of the Church reported by Berners[8] is well under way in *Valmouth*. His moral evaluation, of course, is not stated. In a watering place called Valmouth, so healthful that most of its inhabitants and habitués have had a hundred years to develop their vices, Firbank puts the Negro woman Mrs. "Yaj," a masseuse, and her niece Niri-Esther. Neither the inhabitants nor these two exotic newcomers have anything to do with actuality. Nor does their environment. Yet they evolved from Firbank's perception of the disparity between the expectations of Christianity and the reality of its practice. His principle of organization is implicit contrast in a "self-contained structure." Kaleidoscopic scenes studded with dialogue expose what his characters are and what, self-absorbed and obstinate as always, they think they are. Even as the entire *dramatis personae* of *Valmouth* awaits the formal marriage ceremony of Niri-Esther, already pregnant with her second child, she has "run out of the house (old, grey, grim, satanic Hare) into the garden, where with her bride's bouquet of malmaisons and vanessa violets, she was waywardly in pursuit of—a butterfly."[9] The function of the parts of Firbank's novel is a matter of poetry and proportion. That is, by proportion he presented a moral judgment; by poetry, a virtual experience. Indeed, like Harold Nicolson's Lambert Orme, Firbank succeeded in this and later work because of reference to "unapparent reality." That statement fails to convey the comic absurdity of Firbank's situations and characters in *Valmouth*—what Mrs. Leverson, the "Sphinx," described as amusing but "wilful"—or the recurrent melancholy, as delicate as a pastel sketch. Augustus

8. See above, p. 105.
9. *Valmouth* (London, 1919), p. 209.

John said it was "perfectly wonderful. Better than all the others." He wrote to Firbank, "I wouldn't alter a word—and you know how captious I can be—"[1]

What with *Valmouth,* his portrait on show with the New English Art Club exhibition, and the Sitwells having publicized him as "fabulous," Firbank's acquaintance enlarged. At the Eiffel Tower Restaurant, its patron Stulik, who made "masses of money but . . . lost yet more through being kind, and through being drunk and through family upsets,"[2] welcomed Firbank almost nightly. Stulik had a "flair for genius," a delight in personalities, and he made sure Firbank got his chicken livers, strawberries, and champagne. Stulik encouraged this diet, although it "seemed already an understood thing" that Firbank was ill, "consumptive." Nancy Cunard recalled his face at about the time of *Valmouth*'s publication as flushed with illness. He was, she said, "tall, thin, narrow, erect, with a most sensitive, intelligent, aquiline face and cheeks rather high in colour."[3] Nancy was one of Firbank's new acquaintances. Another was Iris Tree, who, with Nancy Cunard and Diana Manners, was one of the great beauties of her time and place. Still another new friend was Jacob Epstein, whom Firbank wanted to sculpt his portrait; but that idea came to nothing. He also met Nina Hamnett at about this time. In view of her elongated drawings of the elongated Alan Odle and Lytton Strachey, it is surprising that there is none of Firbank. At times, still, Firbank sheltered behind the huge brass pots and palms in the restaurant, or "had the illusion of so doing," but more often he sat in conversation with his new friends. At no time did he allow any illness to intrude. Nancy

1. Augustus John to RF, London, December 1, 1919 (Fales).
2. Nancy Cunard to MJB, Lamothe-Fénelon, Lot, August 12, 1957.
3. Nancy Cunard: "Thoughts About Ronald Firbank" (unpublished typescript signed and dated from Toulouse, November 1954), p. 2 (MJB).

Cunard reported that "if he was really ill, then he was brave and adroit indeed, for one noticed nothing of the kind, save, at moments, a sort of asthmatic conflict between words, breathing and laughter, as his quips popped into the conversation." A few times, she said, she had seen him "really paroxysmal, as if savouring some private joke." Then would come that "ecstatic, special gesture of his," one hand grasping the other shoulder and, when he was "all cupped within himself," then "some astonishing point would be made which had everyone immediately rocking." And then he disappeared. In such exits and similarly sudden entrances, Firbank could, Miss Cunard said, appear "enchantingly caricatural," as if everything about him were heightened in tone, "so light was the touch, so deft the *glissando.*"[4]

That was his amusement, but his emotions were centered on the Honorable Evan Morgan, who, according to Nancy, could lay as much claim as Firbank to the word "fabulous" in view of Morgan's "generous brand of 'milordism.' "[5] His attachment to Morgan lifted Firbank for a while out of himself. He displayed a gaiety and joyousness missing from his personality since his Cambridge days. With these, he charmed Morgan. "More often than not," Morgan said, Firbank "appeared to be under the influence of Bacchus . . . at least you could never tell, because his conversation was equally wild either way."[6] But Morgan turned his own affections toward the musician Philip Heseltine, who called himself Peter Warlock and who was the model for Halliday in Lawrence's *Women in Love.* Jack Lindsay wrote about him with a mixture of detachment and compassion, but Jacob Epstein de-

4. Ibid.
5. Ibid.
6. Evan Morgan to Richard Buckle, Newport, Monmouthshire, July 25, 1940.

scribed Warlock—or Heseltine—as childish and cruel.[7] As
for Firbank, Morgan declared that he looked upon him "as
one might some rare bird to be cherished for its exquisite
exotic qualities rather than as a human being." Yet their relationship was unmistakable, a matter of "deep concern," said
Morgan, to his "distinguished father and in fact to other older
members" of his family. Firbank's practice, said Morgan, "of
running his fingers through his hair 'just like a woman my
dear' all pointed to the same sinister suspicions concerning
him."[8] To demonstrate his regard, Firbank wanted to dedicate his next piece of fiction, *The Princess Zoubaroff*, to
Morgan. Long before the book went to the printer's with a
printing order issued on July 24, 1920, Fairbank showed the
proposed dedication to Evan Morgan. He was not familiar with
the contents or tone of the book, but he agreed to accept the
dedication. It read, "To the Hon. Evan Morgan in Souvenir
Amicale of a 'Previous Incarnation.' "

During this period Firbank was as faithful as ever in his
attention to literary and financial affairs. Baba had been eager
to move from 44 Sloane Street in 1914, but she had stayed
on there throughout the war. As soon as the war ended, she
began once more to consider a change of residence. Firbank
advised her in 1918 not to let but to sell her lease, and in
December of that year he offered to meet a reasonable rent if
she would find a pleasing cottage suitable for herself and
Heather near London. Meanwhile the matter of a mortgage
on the St. Julian's property in Wales had to be faced, because
interest rates were rising. Firbank preferred to pay off the
mortgage by the sale of dwellings instead of land; their up-
keep was expensive, and he regarded land as a more desirable

7. Cf. Jack Lindsay: *Fanfrolico and After* (London, 1962), pp. 82–93;
Jacob Epstein: *Autobiography* (London, 1955), p. 116.
8. Evan Morgan to Richard Buckle, Newport, Monmouthshire, July 25,
1940; cf. Nancy Cunard to MJB, Lamothe-Fénelon, Lot, July 27, 1963.

investment than shares. But he was determined to clear the mortgage, and the only way to do it immediately was to sell several acres at one end of the estate needed to enlarge a nearby cemetery. By this means he hoped to raise a considerable sum before the end of 1919. While these negotiations went on, Baba found a place at Richmond in Surrey, Denbigh Cottage, a part of Spring Grove estate, and early in 1920 Ronald agreed to purchase a ninety-nine-year lease on Denbigh Cottage for £1,450 payable only after he had received payment for the Christchurch fields in Wales. The cottage, he assured his mother, was being bought not for speculation but for her use.[9]

Firbank's literary affairs were varied. He kept at Grant Richards in the matter of getting out review copies of *Valmouth* and advertising it.[1] In the summer of 1920 Baba asked to have twelve copies of the 1916 version of *Odette,* without illustrations, bound especially for her. Although most of the arrangements for this binding were made by Richards and Lady Firbank, Ronald oversaw their start.[2] All the while, that is, throughout the latter part of 1919 and almost the first half of 1920, he was composing *The Princess Zoubaroff.* He worked hard at it, hoping, as he told his sister, that it would be amusing.[3] Not until June 7, 1920, did he reach an agreement with Richards for an edition of five hundred copies; more than a month later, Firbank signed a memorandum providing for frontispiece and wrapper, at a total expenditure of £207 9s. 6d. (advertising included). Firbank chose Michel Sevier to make two drawings for the new book, one for the

9. Cf. RF to HJGF, London, [1918]; n.p., December 27, 1918; Bath, September 25, 1919; London, November 29, [1919], January 14, [1920], and January 26, 1920.
1. Cf. GR to RF, London, December 4 and 15, 1919.
2. Cf. GR to HJGF, London, July 20 and August 10, 1920.
3. Cf. RF to HF, London, n.d.

title page and one for use as frontispiece and on the dust
jacket; when they were done, Firbank approved them over
lunch with Sevier at the Café Royal, and by July 9 Richards
and Firbank were discussing colors for the pictures.[4]

❧ V ☙

With everything in order for the book, including a "lucky"
date for publication, Firbank left England. He believed the
past winter had threatened his health; so he was determined
not to spend another in a cold climate. By August 2, 1920, he
was in Paris. Returning to Paris was always a pleasure, and he
was happy to be there this time, his first visit since the war. He
ran about all day to shops and favorite haunts and then rested
in the Luxembourg Gardens. The next day he left for Marseille, where he planned to take a ship for either Corsica or
Algeria. When he got to Marseille on the morning of August
4, he found every berth on the boats to Corsica booked for
the month ahead. The fare to Algeria, five hundred francs, he
thought too expensive; so he decided to try Arles, Aigues-
Mortes, Angoulême, and Avignon for a few days each,
choose one which was pleasant and inexpensive, and settle in
for the winter. By the next day he had changed his mind; he
could not face the provincial French towns, and whatever the
cost he meant to go to Algiers—but not until September. The
heat and lack of hotel facilities made it intolerable in August.
He could not stay in Marseille either until September. He had

4. Cf. GR to RF, June 7, 1920, July 9 and 13, 1920; RF to HJGF,
[London, July 1920].

enjoyed a drive in a hired victoria along the *corniche,* where he stopped to sea-bathe; but however amusing and beautiful it might be, the dirt, the glare, and the expense made Marseille unbearable. On August 7 Firbank went to Cassis, taking a collapsible rubber bath with him in case of need. The Hotel Cendreon was small and primitive but busy; so he eventually found rooms in the village. The beauty of the sea and the mountains enchanted him, and he took pleasure in Cassis's white wine drunk at the Café Liautaud and in the walk from La Ciotat along the cliffs, which Grant Richards had recommended. Early in September, Firbank moved on to Aix. And from Aix, although he had planned to visit Nîmes, Aigues-Mortes, Arles, and Avignon, he returned directly to Marseille on September 7 in order to have his laundry done before sailing that same week for Algeria.[1]

On September 12 Firbank reached the Excelsior Hotel, Algiers, bringing with him from Marseille the proofs of *The Princess Zoubaroff.* This time he did not make corrections at once. He was full of plans—to stay in Algiers one week and then go to Biskra, to Constantine, to Tunis, to Sicily, to Capri (where he was offered Augustus John's villa). But in Algiers everything was novel and everything delighted him. He remarked on the heat, the low cost of living, sea-bathing, excursions into old Algiers, the mosques, the hazy sea, the jasmine on the night air, a village in the Atlas Mountains. He was happy to see no more than a dozen English people, but he reported the presence of the composer of *Samson and Delilah,* Saint-Saëns. He managed to correct the galleys for *The Princess Zoubaroff* by the end of the month. When he did, he sent one set of proofs to Evan Morgan, because of the pro-

1. Cf. RF to HJGF, Paris, August 2, 1920, and [August 3, 1920]; Marseille, August 4, 5, and 6, 1920; Cassis, August 8, 1920; Aix-en-Provence, September 6, 1920; GR to RF, London, August 20, 1920.

posed dedication, and another set to Grant Richards.[2]

At that time, Firbank was still in Algeria and he remained there until early November. Indeed, he set up a small bank account in Algiers before leaving that city on October 4 for a fifteen-hour ride in a crowded train to Constantine. His impression of the country through which he traveled was one of a terrifying and brutal wasteland. Constantine itself he liked, and he described his experiences to Baba, telling her about the charm of the Arab quarter (despite its smell), the flowers and many birds he saw as he walked in the town, a visit to a cinema house to see Theda Bara as Cleopatra (despite the fleas), the vast stretch of sand behind his hotel, the sad music of a snake charmer. From Constantine he went on to the ruined city of Timgad by way of Batna and, after a few "perfect" days at Timgad, went again by way of Batna to Biskra. He admired Biskra's beauty and strangeness, with the camel caravans riding in from the desert, but he feared the savage dogs which roamed its streets. From Biskra, Firbank made an excursion to Touggourt and then, after a quarrel with Biskra's Hôtel du Sahara over prices, returned again to Constantine in order to transfer money from Algiers. On November 3, 1920, following a train ride of more than sixteen hours and difficulties with his trunk at the frontier, he reached Tunis.[3]

His plan was to stay very briefly in Tunis. Firbank was obsessed with movement. He rarely arrived anywhere without preparing to depart at once for one or two other places. When he got to Algiers, he had meant to go promptly to Capri, Sicily, Biskra, Constantine. Once in Constantine, he was

2. RF to HJGF, Algiers, September 13, [1920], September 26 and 28, 1920, n.d., October 1, 1920; GR to RF, London, September 29, 1920; GR to Peacock & Goddard, London, November 13, 1920.
3. RF to HJGF, Algeria, October 1, 4, and 30, 1920; Constantine, October 5, 7, and 9, 1920; Batna, n.d. and October 15, 1920; Biskra, October 16 and 20, 1920; Tunis, November 3, 1920.

ready to go on to Biskra. And now in Tunis, because he found his hotel, the Tunisia Palace, fashionable and vulgar, he considered going on to Rome, where he was sure to have sympathetic surroundings.

Then, as he had done in Algiers and Constantine, Firbank began to find Tunis to his taste, and he settled down to write his next book. He had commenced thinking about it immediately after his arrival in Algiers. On October 1 he mentioned it first in a letter to Baba and said he wanted to go to Bou-Saada, a village in the desert accessible only by vermin-infested motor cars; the scenery, he said, was sure to be helpful. He spoke, too, of going to Tunis to construct the book. Then, on October 4, he asked his mother to send him a Koran in the Everyman edition. In the same letter he reported having sent back to his solicitor an agreement for the sale of some fields on the Welsh estate for use as a cemetery; but his thoughts were on his book. Three days later, writing from Constantine, Firbank said that when he reached Tunis he would have "enough notes to make a story of." He described what he intended to do:

> I want to rewrite Odette in an Arab setting—a child seeking Allah—I shall try & make the descriptions of scenery beautiful & keep the whole thing as simple as possible. I shall call the story "Santal," which is the name of a perfume of the East.[4]

By October 22, with the English version of the Koran in hand, he had developed his notes and his ideas enough to suggest to Grant Richards that *Santal* be announced in *The Princess Zoubaroff*. And on October 30, 1920, in a letter from

4. RF to HJGF, Constantine, October 7, 1920; cf. RF to HJGF, Algiers, October 1 and 4, 1920.

Constantine, Firbank told Baba that he had started writing
Santal. By November 9, more comfortable than he had anticipated at the Tunisia Palace with its friendly Arabs and Palm
Court, where there was an orchestra at tea time, he had made
enough progress to declare that he meant to dedicate the new
book to Helen Carew and to tell his mother that he would very
likely devote the next six months to *Santal*.[5]

On that day, Tuesday, November 9, Firbank believed that
The Princess Zoubaroff had been published on Monday. It
was one of the days he had designated as "lucky" before leaving London in August, and Grant Richards had written on
October 27 to say that he hoped the book would be ready by
the eighth. On November 3, he had written again saying the
book might be delayed until the "next lucky day," November
13, but that, "thank heaven," the artist Michel Sevier had
seen an early copy of *The Princess Zoubaroff* and approved
the reproduction of his drawings. Then, the following day,
November 4, 1920, Richards wrote again in great agitation:
Evan Morgan had very strongly objected to being made the
recipient of the dedication. Richards went on to say that in a
visit to the St. Martin's Street office Morgan had behaved with
such truculence that Sevier, who was present at the interview,
expressed surprise at Richards's "forbearance." Richards continued, "I think Mr Morgan is rather a donkey: he talked
about 'highly placed personages' at St James's Palace on
whom he was in waiting, and generally tried to ride about
three horses at once."

What had happened was that when Sevier received his advance copy on November 3 (three hundred copies were bound

5. Cf. RF to HJGF, Biskra, October 20, 1920; [Constantine, October 30,
1920]; Tunis, October 9 and 14, 1920; GR to RF, London, October 27,
1920.

by that date), he showed it to several friends, among them Evan Morgan. With Sevier, Morgan then went to the publisher's office and stated his unwillingness to receive the dedication. Richards explained that the way in which the book was printed and bound made unusual technical difficulties if the dedication were to be removed and, in any case, he could do nothing without instructions from Firbank. Richards lent Morgan a copy of the book in the hope that when he had read it he would withdraw his objections. The book was returned through Morgan's London solicitors, Peacock & Goddard, whose accompanying letter, dated November 4, 1920, emphasized their client's resentment at being "associated with the book in any way especially having regard to its general tone towards the Catholic Church of which he is a member." The letter further stated that if the book appeared with the dedication, Morgan would "take such steps as he may be advised to protect his interests and to make his views on the subject perfectly clear to the public and his friends." Morgan, some twenty years later, blamed "certain mischief-making people such as the late Colonel Sneed" for calling the attention of his "Pappa" to the dedication. His account of the affair ran,

It had long been a standing joke that I should be called "Cardinal Morgan"—it was much about this time that I myself had taken to considering becoming a Roman Catholic and I had been busying myself with ritual and Church practices. Unfortunately the dedication was brought to the notice of my family . . . I was sent posthaste to Grant Richards to tell them that unless the book was published without the dedication my father would take steps against the author and publisher. Just about this time I was about to be posted equerry to Lord Aberdeen, then Viceroy of Ireland and for

some obscure reason it was assumed that this dedication in
the most faultless prose would be a deterrent to my gaining
this exalted post, one which I may say I never acquired.[6]

Whatever the reason for Evan Morgan's attitude, Grant
Richards was forced to move the publication date of *The
Princess Zoubaroff* forward. Meanwhile he wrote to Peacock
& Goddard pleading Morgan's earlier willingness to accept
the dedication. He spoke also of Firbank's absence from England and of the technical difficulties which might well cause
an expense of "something in the neighbourhood of fifty
pounds."[7] Morgan finally agreed to receive the dedication if
his name were omitted and only his initials included. This was
a concession which solved nothing in respect to the printing
and binding of the book.

Richards's harried letters did not reach Firbank until November 11 because they were misfiled by a clerk of the Poste
Restante. On November 9 he was so certain his play had been
published the day before that he wrote to his mother to say
how eager he was to have it staged. He needed only financial
backing, he said, to get it produced with Lillah McCarthy in
the title role. When he finally had Richards's letter of November 4, the first one to give details of Morgan's behavior, Firbank acted at once, according to his own statement: "I wired
that on no account would I dedicate a book to a fool & that
the first edition must be canceled . . . Morgan had had five
weeks to make up his mind."[8] After thinking it over, Firbank
sent a second, more cautious telegram stating his aversion to
more expense. But Richards took the matter up with the bind-

6. Evan Morgan to Richard Buckle, Newport, Monmouthshire, July 25,
1940.
7. GR to Peacock & Goddard, London, November 6, 1920.
8. RF to HJGF, Tunis, November 29, 1920; cf. RF to HJGF, Tunis,
November 7 and 9, 1920.

ers and found that another leaf could be substituted at a reasonable cost for the one containing the dedication. He notified Peacock & Goddard on November 13 and prepared to bring out *The Princess Zoubaroff* on November 26, another of Firbank's days of good omen.[9] When it appeared, Richards received a letter which Morgan had written from Madrid on December 2 to thank him and Firbank for "being so obliging."

Firbank was distressed by Evan Morgan's breach of friendship. When he first heard about it, he pretended indifference to any attack which might come from Morgan, even legal action, since it would provide publicity for the book. At first, too, he was inclined to lay these events at the door of the Sitwells; he was sure they had influenced Morgan, whom, Firbank said, he had always considered "*a little fool.*" The situation, however, was painful: it rankled. Within a few days, Firbank repeated his estimate of Morgan and told Baba that his writing must invariably "bring discomfort to fools, since it is aggressive, witty, & unrelenting." Here was Ronald Firbank's real evaluation of himself as an artist; but he rarely stated it even to his mother, and this time his outburst was provoked by Morgan. At the end of December, Firbank declared that it was "a relief not to have a cad's name on the first page" of his play.[1] For quite a while thereafter he hardly mentioned Morgan in his letters, and he appeared to regain his sunny outlook. But for more than two years he declined to communicate with Evan Morgan. During the latter part of that period Firbank was writing a novel, *The Flower Beneath the Foot,* in which he satirized Morgan in the person of the Honorable Eddie Monteith, son of Lord Intriguer. Firbank's aversion to intimate relationships and his suspicion of others'

9. Cf. GR to RF, London, November 12, 16, and 23, 1920.
1. RF to HJGF, Tunis, November 29, 1920; cf. RF to HJGF, Tunis, November 11 and 14, 1920.

motives, first developed during the years in Oxford, were intensified by the experience with Morgan. Firbank had already speculated on having more enemies than friends in London.[2] For the few years left to him, he gave his affection to no one outside his family, and his sexual encounters were casual ones.

However much this incident contributed to Firbank's appraisal of life as a nightmare, his days went on as usual. Before Christmas he urged Baba to choose a rose tree or ferns for her gift and send the bill to him. He wrote a similar letter to Heather, explaining that all he could find in Tunis was one of "those spangled Eastern scarfs, etc." that, although attractive in Tunis, could "only look pitiful in London."[3] He encouraged his sister to get on with a translation of *Odette* into German, which she had started two years before. He gave attention to his affairs in England. He signed leases and other documents sent by his solicitor and had them notarized. He authorized the expenditure of £1,000 to repair a road on the Welsh estate and castigated his estate agent for his mismanagement of the transaction. He lamented but took no active part in a proposal to commit his uncle Annesley Garrett, who was in a state of senility; Firbank objected strongly to his relations' callous and cruel behavior to Uncle Annesley.[4]

Meanwhile, Firbank was worried about the reception of *The Princess Zoubaroff*. On December 11, 1920, Richards wrote that he had so far seen only two notices, one in *The Times Literary Supplement* and the other in the *Daily Express,* a brief comment by Louis MacQuilland. Since neither

2. Cf. RF to HJGF, Tunis, November 21, 1920.
3. RF to HF, Tunis, December 17, 1920; cf. RF to HJGF, Tunis, December 17, 1920.
4. Cf. RF to HF, Tunis, November 12, 1920; RF to HJGF, November 16 and 29, 1920, December 23, 1920, January 26, 1921, February 15, 18, 25, and 26, 1921, March 6, 1921.

had anything "quotable," advertising had to wait; it was still waiting on December 21, although *The Tatler* and the London *Times* had had reviews. It was all unfortunate, since few bookshops had ordered copies. Eventually, in late January 1921, Richards wrote to say that he had two or three comments, including one from *The Spectator,* which might be used to encourage sales. But whatever was done, *The Princess Zoubaroff* was unlikely to sell. Its characterization is thin, its dialogue forced, its material without focus; and as drama, which it purported to be, it is entirely too static. It lacked in every aspect the inevitability of a piece of literature. Briefly Firbank had hopes for it when Helen Carew wrote that Lord Berners liked it, but by mid-January he accepted the fact that it was a failure with no one to promote it. His consolation was that perhaps those few who ordinarily liked his books would find some pleasure in reading *The Princess Zoubaroff* too.[5]

Despite his dread of poor trains and fleas, Firbank went south early in January 1921, going first to Sousse and Sfax on the way to Gabès. There he found the oasis, except for the dogs, a veritable Eden. At Kairouan, the real destination of his excursion, he visited and revisited the mosques, and he spent more than one morning on the tower of a muezzin's minaret in the full sun, lazily observing the life below him. Throughout this journey of ten days along the African coast of the Mediterranean, Firbank was sharply aware of the thinness of civilization, which he saw at best as no more than a veneer. He remarked on it at both Gabès and Kairouan and, as he told his mother, it was apparent even in Tunis.[6]

Firbank remained in Tunis until mid-March 1921. His room at the Tunisia Palace was a quiet one overlooking a

5. Cf. RF to HJGF, Tunis, December 27, 1920; Kairouan, January 13, 1921; GR to RF, London, January 26, 1921.
6. Cf. RF to HJGF, Gabes, January 8, [1921]; Kairouan, January 13, 1921; Tunis, December 14, 17, 27, and 30, 1920.

convent garden. It was cheap, and he took his meals outside
the hotel in the interest of further economy. Once, at a restaurant, he was present when two angry people exchanged shots,
narrowly missing him. As a rule, however, his existence was
uneventful. He went repeatedly by tram to Carthage, where
he visited the Greek theater and the Coliseum, the site of the
martyrdom of St. Catherine and St. Perpetua. Then, like Cer-
vantes before and Gide after him, Firbank discovered Sidi
bou Saïd, the village perched on a cliff beyond Carthage and
across the lake, and for a while he went there daily. In Tunis
there was the opera: *Madame Butterfly,* Massenet's *Hérodi-
ade, La Bohème, Tosca.* He wrote to his mother about the
British in Tunis, a Captain and Mrs. Campbell, with whom he
lunched; Sir Philip and Lady Brocklehurst, whom he observed
at the hotel (Sir Philip was an old Trinity Hall colleague);
and the nameless ones who danced at tea time at the Majestic
Hotel. He read a great deal, remarking on all kinds of books,
from the memoirs of Herbert Beerbohm Tree and Isabelle
Eberhardt's *Pages d'Islam* to Maurice Rostand's *Cerceuille de
Cristal* and Edmond Cazal's *Life of St. Thérèse.* But he declared that the mosques and bazaars of Tunis were more interesting than books.[7]

Then Tunis began to pall. By December, when he had been
there five or six weeks, the novelty was gone. He began to
think about England, Malta, Sicily. He complained of the
cold nights and his lack of an overcoat; he had only his
"Aquascutum" with him, really inadequate for the weather.
In January he complained that his hotel was unheated, hot
water a rarity, and service impossible. In January, too, his
socks began to go, and until new socks arrived from England

7. Cf. RF to HJGF, Tunis, November 7, 9, 11, 21, 25, and 29, 1920;
December 3, 6, and 14, 1920; January 16, 1921; February 11 and 14, 1921;
RF to HF, Tunis, February 18, 1921.

he was forced to darn his old ones every week. By the first of the year, Firbank had been away from England five months, all because his health demanded it. Besides, life was cheaper everywhere else. He thought again of Malta, and he mentioned Amalfi and southern France in his letters. Yet he was weary of hotels and hotel living. Worse than that was the difficulty of writing in hotels.[8]

Nevertheless, he was composing *Santal*. In early December 1920, when he began to talk of Malta and Palermo, he realized that he would probably stay on in Tunis until the first section at least was done. On December 19, he told his mother that he had completed that part. In January he said he had got some "useful things" from the journey to Gabès and Kairouan and thus had added "a few beautiful touches." At the end of the month, well after his return from southern Tunisia, as he sat engulfed in the scent of both violets and orange blossoms, Firbank said that his book would be finished in ten weeks. By February 26 he had started the last chapter, and on March 6, 1921, Firbank told his mother that he had finished *Santal* that morning. He was happy to have remained in Tunis long enough to do it; he believed that thereby he had "caught and fixed" some of the "fascination of the East" in his book.[9]

8. Cf. RF to HJGF, December 3, 8, 14, and 19, 1920; January 16, 20, and 21, 1921; February 11, 1921.
9. RF to HJGF, Tunis, March 9, 1921; cf. RF to HJGF, Tunis, December 3 and 17, 1920, January 28, 1921, February 26, 1921, March 6, 1921; Kairouan, January 12, 1921; Palermo, March 12, 1921.

❧ VI ❧

Once Firbank felt free, he lost no time in leaving Tunis. By March 11, five days after the completion of *Santal,* he was at Palermo and in a flurry of restless activity. He went at once to the opera and by March 14 had heard both *La Bohème* and *Francesca da Rimini.* He walked the streets to observe the candles and bouquets of violets set before statues of the Madonna as Easter drew near. He revisited the places he had remembered since 1910, including Monreale. He compared the prices of Italy with those of Tunisia and found Italy's lower, but the Italians unreliable.

He went off to Girgenti and Syracuse and Taormina and, after an "endless" journey via Messina and Calabria, arrived in Naples and its Grand Hotel de Londres the day before Easter. He had expected to find his annuity checks there, but Lady Firbank had changed his instructions so that the checks had gone to Palermo, and he needed money. Still, Naples was interesting, and on the night of his arrival he heard *The Barber of Seville*—or a part of it; he was too tired to stay to the end. On Easter he went to mass at the Cathedral with its "wonderful" candles and music. And that night he heard Margaret Sheridan, Melba's pupil, sing *Madame Butterfly.* Without having got his checks or a letter from Baba, Firbank went on to Capri, where he sailed around the island. He considered Corfu, but the cost of getting there and the fact that Greece must inevitably follow from Corfu and in Greece all foreigners were suspected as spies deterred him. After Capri came Castellamare, with its orange gardens by the sea, Sorrento, and Amalfi. On April 8 Firbank reached Rome, where, because of a scarcity of accommodations, he spent the night in the billiard room of the Hotel Inghilterra.[1]

Firbank was agitated, of course, about where to go next, directly to Paris or to Paris by way of Florence, Bologna, and Venice. In either case, he assured Baba, before moving on to New York or Bucharest, he meant to spend a few weeks in London. There were a number of things requiring his attention. He needed new clothes and those he had needed to be put in order. More important was the question of his publisher. He wrote to Lady Firbank from Rome on April 9, 1921, that he was "furious" with Grant Richards for "neglecting to push" *The Princess Zoubaroff*. Richards, on March 17, had sent reviews of the book to Firbank at Tunis so that he might select quotations from them for use in advertisements. But by March 17 Firbank was in Sicily and now, on April 9, in Rome, the reviews had not yet caught up with him. Firbank believed they were lost, and he discredited Richards's statement, "Of course we are doing all we can for your play, but it is beyond the powers of any publisher to *make* a book sell."[2] He said about Richards, "He has simply collared my money & put the play on the shelf."[3] Firbank was convinced that Richards must not publish *Santal*. In order to make another, more advantageous connection with a publisher, Firbank thought he should be in London. He was dissatisfied, too, with his estate manager and the amount of income he produced. To improve that situation also he ought to be in London. But as soon as he had taken care of these matters Firbank planned to

1. Cf. RF to HJGF, Tunis, March 9, 1921; Palermo, March 12 and 14, 1921; Taormina, March 23, 1921; Naples, March 27, 1921; Capri, April 1, 1921; Sorrento, April 6, 1921; Rome, April 9, 1921.
2. GR to RF, London, April 9, 1921.
3. RF to HJGF, Rome, April 9, 1921.

leave London, very likely for New York, and write a new book.

This new book, which would be called *The Flower Beneath the Foot*, started to take shape in the autumn of 1920, when Firbank was in Algiers and had hardly commenced writing *Santal*. His preface to the American edition, written in the early summer of 1924, told about the book's beginning in Firbank's application of two phrases: one, "her Dreaminess, the Queen," to an unknown woman seen late at night in a restaurant of Algiers, and the other, "His Weariness, the Prince," to an Arab boy asleep beside the warm sea. As Firbank moved about Algeria—Constantine, Timgad, Biskra— he saw "his Weariness, or his simulacrum" over and over, all princes, all weary, and all "wonderful boys." His Weariness recalled her Dreaminess; and around these, "figures & objects composed themselves." Firbank's first reference to the book was in a letter written from Tunis on November 9, 1920, to Baba, when he told her that he had "a wonderful plan for a novel which ought to be a surprise for all the people who have disbelieved in me." Thereafter during his stay in Tunisia, while he was at work on *Santal*, he mentioned *The Flower* only in connection with the problem of finding a suitable place in which to write it. Then, when *Santal* was completed and Firbank was in Palermo, the next book occupied him seriously. As he told his mother in a letter from Palermo dated March 12, 1921, he was "busy making notes"; that is, he was setting down in a series of five notebooks[4] phrases and sentences which served him in creating his characters and dialogue for *The Flower*. By the time he reached Rome he was almost done with his note making; but despite his recurrent worry as to where to go for a "sympathetic" environment in which to write, he "warehoused" his notebooks and for a

4. (Jack H. Samuels).

while did nothing about his book or his problems.

Firbank settled down in Rome for a stay of several weeks. First he took a room at 57 via Firenze, a private home. Next he arranged through Miss Wilson at the English Library to have a Russian princess, nameless and in exile, type *Santal*. He was gleeful about that; it appealed at once to his snobbery and a sense of the incongruity of the ways in which lives are lived. His practical affairs arranged, Firbank went about his pleasures. He visited the pension where he had lived in 1909 and 1910 and reported that after more than ten years the Bedini family was dead but the maid who opened the door greeted him by name. Firbank was so sure he went unnoticed that that sort of recognition always surprised and gratified him. Here in Rome it added to his enjoyment of the city's diversions. He went three consecutive nights, April 11, 12, and 13, to a "delicious" Viennese operetta, *Die Schöne Mama,* with music so "adorable" he and all Rome could have gone endlessly. In the way of other music, he had his choice of German operas, a fact which he thought reflected the unpopularity of the French and English and the popularity of the Germans. It was a part, he said, of the unsettled state of Italy, where thousands of socialists paraded the streets singing and brandishing knives and sticks. But Firbank kept out of the way with visits to the lakes of Nemi and Albano, southeast of Rome, or to the Villa Borghese, where he sat under the pine trees. His own future, he was certain, was secure anyway. The Countess Amelia, a fortuneteller decorated by the Italian government, had assured him that his future would be brilliant and, if he survived the twenty-third day of April and of May, he would live to the age of seventy-two.[5]

Nevertheless, he was not entirely at ease. The fate of *The Princess Zoubaroff* nagged at him. The reviews sent from

5. Cf. RF to HJGF, Rome, April 12, 14, 21, and 24, 1921.

London in mid-March failed to reach him until the beginning
of May. Without them, advertising had been futile; but when
they came he immediately extracted favorable comments and
sent them with careful instructions to Richards for use in various papers—*The Morning Post, Times Literary Supplement,
Nation, London Mercury.* Firbank had hopes, still, that Lillah
McCarthy might produce *The Princess* and act in it; but it
was now unsettled and, like all life, too "enigmatic" for his
peace of mind. There was, as well, the question of *Santal.* By
April 21 it was typed, and he reread it with approval. He
declared that it was superior to anything else he had written—
the "truest," he said—and that it would last as long as an
Eastern rug. He was sure he must find a new publisher. But
that conviction did not last long, and he concluded that it
would be a mistake, as he told Baba, "to leave Richards with
a story as slight as Santal." He feared that without Richards
the book might be "passed by unnoticed."[6]

When he reached that conclusion Firbank had already left
Rome. He went first to Florence, where without much interest
he encountered Osbert Sitwell. Then he spent several days in
Venice revisiting St. Mark's and the Lido. He wrote to
Heather from Venice, saying how sorry he was that the "Bath-
ing season" had not begun, since the sea "looked so blue &
inviting." He told her that "the only advantage of Venice in
Spring is there are hardly any mosquitoes!"[7] Firbank moved
on to Milan and a look at the "frescoes" of Leonardo. By
May 22 he arrived in Paris, having come on the same train as
King Alfonso of Spain and Queen Amelia of Portugal.

The next few days in Paris were filled to overflowing. Firbank attended the ballet at the Gaieté-Lyrique and he went to

6. RF to HJGF, Venice, May 12, 1921; cf. RF to HJGF, Rome, April
21, 1921, May 1, 1921; GR to RF, London, May 6, 1921.
7. RF to HF, Venice, May 14, 1921.

several motion pictures and to the Vaudeville, where Spinelli and Max Dearly were playing. After a performance of the Guitrys in *Le Grand-Duc,* Firbank went backstage to renew his acquaintance with Mme Jeanne Granier and came away with ecstatic appreciation of her. His youth and his joy in the theater were revived. He also investigated a flat in Versailles which he could hire from its owner, M. Dufourq, and there start his next book.[8] It was a flat wedged against the barracks at the top of the rue des Réservoirs, number 4, and directly across from the entrance to the palace. He had made no decision about it when he reluctantly left Paris for London on the morning of May 26.

Arriving that evening, after standing most of the way on a crowded train, Firbank had much to do in London. He went at once to his club, the Junior Constitutional, and the next day moved into the Jermyn Court Hotel. Although he liked the view of Piccadilly Circus from his window, the hotel was unsatisfactory—too expensive (15s. daily for bed and breakfast) and not adequately clean. So Firbank took a flat at 2 West Chapel Street, and by May 31 he was busily rearranging furniture.

That same day, however, he wrote a letter to Dufourq accepting the summer rental of the Versailles flat for a period of three months commencing in July, provided linens and a servant went with it. Firbank thought he was getting a bargain in the flat, since he had miscalculated the rent at £3 10s. a week. Dufourq quickly disabused him: it was almost double that. Firbank might have stayed on with a reasonable rent at 2 West Chapel Street, but he was determined not to remain in London. On the evening of his arrival, May 26, he had told his mother that he had never returned to England with less

8. Cf. RF to HJGF, Venice, May 12, 1921; Milan, May 20, 1921; Paris, May 23, 1921; London, May 26, 1921.

enthusiasm. The "unsettled" state of the country, naturally most apparent in its major city, disturbed him. Besides, it brought to mind wasted dreams and affections. In any case Firbank was now a confirmed tourist, a transient; it was a status which demanded almost nothing personal from him and left him free to do his work. Remarking only that Versailles would be better than London for himself and his book, he reconfirmed by a letter dated June 3 his willingness to take the flat at Versailles despite the greater cost.

Firbank was eager now to resume his usual life in London. He had already prepared for it by inserting a notice of his arrival from an extended "tour in the East" in the social columns of *The Morning Post*, a practice he would follow on all subsequent returns to London.[9] He began to appear nightly at the Eiffel Tower Restaurant. He saw old friends and acquaintances: John Wells, the artist; Lady Angela Forbes, who suggested that they write a book together; and Augustus John. Once he dined with John, Curtis Moffat, and his wife, Iris Tree. Throughout dinner Iris Tree, deadpan, recited hymns, including a favorite of the Salvation Army which ended numerous stanzas with "the Gates of Sin, the Gates of Sin." When the Ballet Russe moved into the Prince's Theatre for the month of June, Firbank was a regular member of the audience. From time to time he went the short distance by train to Richmond, where he visited Baba and Heather at Denbigh Cottage.[1] He ordered new clothes and went for fittings. He began negotiations with the Tate Gallery whereby he would lend them his portrait by Alvaro Guevara. The picture had to be adjudged a work of art by the Tate before it

9. *The Morning Post,* June 2, 1921, p. 7; cf. Sitwell: "Ronald Firbank," *Noble Essences,* p. 82.
1. Cf. RF to HJGF, London, May 26, 1921, May 31, [1921], June 3, 1921.

could be accepted, a procedure completed later that summer.[2]

The month went rapidly enough while Firbank saw to the publication of *Santal*. A few days before June 3 he took the typescript to Richards, who, on that date, wrote to say that although he had not yet read all of *Santal,* he had "read enough" to see that he would ask for "one or two slight alterations." He found some of the dialogue, especially several Arab expressions, "shocking." Firbank made the changes which Richards wanted, and on June 6 they reached an agreement for an edition of three hundred large-paper copies for which Firbank would pay the cost plus 33⅓ per cent. A top limit for production costs was set at £40. Actually, with advertising added, the book cost almost £100, of which Lady Firbank paid £20. Firbank decided to omit illustrations and divert their cost to hand-made paper for both text and covers, the paper for the covers to be violet (this was changed to rose) with a crescent moon marked on the front and back. He was happy in the thought that the appearance of the book would be exotic and attractive. The matter of the dedication, however, caused him some concern. After the *contretemps* with Evan Morgan and *The Princess Zoubaroff,* Firbank was reluctant to have any dedication, but he had committed himself to Helen Carew when he had written less than half of *Santal*. Now Mrs. Carew suggested that the dedication read only "To Helen" with her name in Greek, and she wrote it for him, "To εἰσένη." When he instructed Richards to send proofs to Mrs. Carew, Firbank was finished with arrangements for *Santal* and free to leave England again.[3]

2. Cf. RF to HJGF, Versailles, July 10, 1921.
3. Cf. GR to RF, London, June 3, 1921, and July 9, 1921; RF to HJGF, London, [June 1921]; Tunis, November 9 and 21, 1920; Venice, May 18, 1921; Helen Carew to RF, Hove, June 22, [1921] (Fales).

❦ VII ❧

By July 3, Firbank was established in M. Dufourq's flat at 4 rue des Reservoirs, Versailles. Versailles was hot, but his own rooms he described as "delightful, so pretty & ever so French!" He went on in a letter to Heather: "All the doors in the sitting rooms are of glass lined with primrose coloured silk, & the walls are white & most of the furniture is old."[1] The only drawback was a servant who watched his every move through those glass-paned doors. But he got used to her. He paid his rent to M. Dufourq, resplendent in his blue uniform, who stopped by to collect it on his way to maneuvers at St. Cyr, and Firbank settled down to his own affairs.[2]

Almost at once he began to advance a scheme to secure funds for the production of *The Princess Zoubaroff* with Lillah McCarthy, the project he had supported for some months. His idea now was that the art entrepreneur Sir Joseph Duveen should finance the production. Firbank had no exact figures as to the cost of production and secured none before October, when Miss McCarthy—Lady Keeble—gave him an estimate for the inclusion of his play in a twelve-weeks' season of repertory. But without waiting for figures he suggested to Lady Firbank in July that she approach Duveen and ask him to provide £1,000. She did so, and apparently he agreed to consider the matter. While he considered, a procedure which went on indefinitely, Firbank's hopes rose and fell regu-

1. RF, ALS to HF, Versailles, July 16, 1921.
2. Cf. RF to HJGF, Versailles, July 3, 1921, and [July 7, 1921].

larly. In September he was still awaiting word from Duveen, but at the same time he realized how great a distraction from his next book the play's staging would be. Furthermore, he said he disliked subjecting actors and actresses to the sneers and smears of critics who were incompetent to understand his work. Firbank was preparing himself for disappointment. Nevertheless, he sent a copy of the play to Edith Evans with an eye to including her in the cast; he said later that she had been fascinated by the piece. He also thought of a presentation of *The Princess* in a drawing room rather than in the theater. In October, Duveen and Firbank met in Paris. Duveen gave him advice—that he should be in London with his public—and offered to introduce Firbank to Lady Cunard, whom Sir Joseph described as a most important woman. Firbank said that when he left Duveen he still did not know the older man's intentions; but he stopped talking about a production of *The Princess Zoubaroff*.[3]

Firbank gave much attention to *Santal* throughout his stay in Versailles. There were problems with the cover, the color of the crescent moons, and where to place them on the cover. He sent two telegrams asking to hurry the proofs. After he had read them, they were lost in the mails between Paris and London, and he had to send a duplicate set. The appearance of the dedicatory page displeased Firbank, so that Richards had a second block engraved in accordance with the author's request. Firbank wanted the book published in July, but his own delays forced postponement until autumn. He selected September 8 as a day of good omen, although he wanted advance copies before that date. When he had one on August 20, he suggested changes in the cover, already complete and beyond change. After the book appeared and he had sent cop-

3. Cf. RF to HJGF, Versailles, July 10 and 17, 1921, September 18 and 28, 1921, October 3 and 9, 1921.

ies to his friends, including his physician Dr. Head and Sir
Philip Brocklehurst, the acquaintance seen in Tunis, Firbank
began to fret about reviews and sales. At the beginning of
October Richards sent him enough reviews to warrant advertising, and Ronald copied out the excerpts he liked and authorized Richards to spend £10 for advertising. Indeed, the
reviews were favorable enough for Richards to tell Firbank he
"ought to be satisfied with the criticisms" which had appeared.
Richards went on: "I think they will do a great deal for your
literary reputation. . . . It is very seldom that a book so slight
in bulk is reviewed so well and so seriously. I congratulate
you—and myself—"[4]

Firbank, who had complained bitterly of poor reviews or
none at all for his earlier books, had little satisfaction in the
reception of *Santal*. Both the Glasgow *Evening News* and the
London *Observer* compared him with Pierre Loti ("a more
reticent Pierre Loti," the *Observer* said), and the Southport
Guardian spoke of him as a "discriminating artist." But because the notices preferred *Santal* to his longer and more
important works and indicated no understanding of them,
Firbank was scornful of the reviews; he dismissed them as
"treacle." *Santal* is the story of the orphaned Cherif's search
for Allah, a search which leads only to illusion and ends as
the Arab boy, dying of thirst, prays, "Lord Allah! Show compassion to thy child Cherif." Only a few months before, in
Rome, Firbank had been enthusiastic about *Santal*, convinced
of its truth and permanence. He knew, however, that its simplicity placed it within everyone's understanding. He had
come to see it as merely a *tour de force*, a North African pas-

4. GR to RF, London, October 18, 1921. Cf. GR to RF, London, July
9, 16, and 19, 1921; August 16, 18, and 25, 1921; September 30, 1921;
October 6, 1921. RF to HJGF, Versailles, September 4, 18, and 28, 1921;
October 3 and 21, 1921. [RF], holograph excerpts from reviews of *Santal*,
2 pp. (MJB).

time, depending on few of the technical achievements with which he had struggled in four novels. That may be why he had been, as he confessed later, "unutterably" bored by the composition of *Santal*. Had he known about it, he would no doubt have agreed with Lord Berners's remark that *Santal* was "not up to the standard of the kind of thing one expected" from Firbank.[5]

Certainly by mid-September, when Firbank belittled the reviews of *Santal*, he was entirely aware of his own resources in technique and language. By that time he had been steadily at work on the composition of *The Flower Beneath the Foot* for almost three months, that is, since his arrival the first part of July at 4 rue des Reservoirs. It was a difficult novel, composed on several levels. On one, it was a *roman à clef*. Firbank clarified that aspect for his mother:

"Princess Elsie" = Princess Mary. "Mrs Chilleywater" = Mrs Harold Nicolson. "Eddy" = Evan Morgan—& of course "King Geo" & "Queen Glory" are the king & queen. The English ambassadress is founded on Mrs Roscoe & Lady Nicolson . . . The lady journalist must be "Eve" of the Tatler or any other of the prattling busybodies that write for the magazines.[6]

Needless to say, the chief target of this satire was Evan Morgan, depicted here in the person of "Eddie," the Honorable Eddie Monteith, an amateur archaeologist digging at a "faubourg of Sodom." He dies in the course of the novel from "the shock received by meeting a jackal while composing a sonnet." Morgan was often in Firbank's thoughts during these months in Versailles. In more than one letter to his

5. Lord Berners to Jocelyn Brooke, Berkshire, November 19, 1948 (Berg).
6. RF to HJGF, Bordighera, January 14, 1923. Eve in fact was a man named Eves.

mother Firbank referred to Morgan: that he had published a
novel;[7] that the poet and art critic Thomas Earp, whom Firbank met unexpectedly in Paris, had said it was a dull novel;
that if *The Princess Zoubaroff* were staged, sending tickets to
Morgan for the first night would be amusing.[8]

Obviously the character Eddie and the other identifications
are thrusts at a society from which Firbank felt excluded because it was indifferent to him. Unhappily that fact mattered
to Ronald, but it is unimportant in a consideration of *The
Flower,* since the novel exists on another, far more complex
level. It creates its own court in the Kingdom of Pisuerga,
complete with a royal household, during a state visit from the
rulers of the Land of Dates. Within this environment Laura
de Nazianzi reluctantly enters a nunnery when the prince and
heir of Pisuerga deserts her for a marriage of state with the
English Princess Elsie. The book closes as Laura watches his
marriage procession over the convent wall and, in the agony
of her memories and her deprivation, "beat her hands, until
they streamed with blood, against the broken glass ends upon
the wall" and spoke the prince's name again and again. Of
course, this abridgment oversimplifies the novel. *The Flower
Beneath the Foot* is not a love story, but as usual with Firbank's novels a commentary on a number of things: courts,
England and the English, human passion, the religious life.
The comment is not explicit. It is made by technique, that is,
by a manipulation of setting, characters, and situations so
that, in a sense, they perform technically as do the images of
poetry. Wallace Stevens in *The Necessary Angel* spoke of an
image in poetry as a "restatement of the subject of the image
in the terms of an attitude." In *The Flower* it is not the characters or their setting which perform the functions of images;

7. *Trial by Ordeal,* published in London by John Lane.
8. Cf. RF to HJGF, Versailles, [September 22 and 25, 1921].

it is their relationships and shifts in relationships, as well as the expectations these arouse and disappoint. That is to say, Firbank's comment depends on contraries. Unless the preface to the American edition is as fictitious as the novel itself, than the entire novel derived not only from the application of titles to an unknown woman in an Algerian "supper-restaurant" and to the beautiful boys of North Africa, but also from the contraries suggested in the preface: the Nile-green color of a court dress visualized "at Touggourt in mid-Sahara" and a "soul-trip" of two ladies of questionable sex habits inspired by "two shed rose-leaves in a Moorish fountain," which the preface said were "clinging, tender, courageous little rose-leaves" and "curious ones as well." Indeed, Firbank maintained that the whole was "as much a country-buttercup as a cattleya-orchid." The suggestion of opposites in the preface is confirmed by Firbank's telling his mother that *The Flower Beneath the Foot* was "vulgar cynical & 'horrid,' but of course beautiful here & there for those that can see."[9] Firbank was accustomed to comment technically rather than specifically. By such means in most of his fiction he had remarked on the tragedy and tragicomedy of humanity's transgressions in the name of religion. But it is a more fully developed method in *The Flower Beneath the Foot,* so that the remarkable ending is only one aspect of a statement remarkably controlled by technique. As Firbank said to Van Vechten about *The Flower:* "its parfum is what concerns me most, & if it is exotic & elusive & bafflingly embaumé, the gardener, (poor dear), will be glad."[1]

9. RF to HJGF, Fiesole, March 20, [1922].
1. RF to CVV, Bordighera, January 17, 1923. Cf. James Hafley: "Ronald Firbank," *Arizona Quarterly,* XII (Summer 1956), 164; V. S. Pritchett: "Firbank," *Books in General* (London, 1953), p. 229; Evelyn Waugh: "Ronald Firbank," *Life and Letters,* II (March 1929), 191–2; Edmund Wilson: *Axel's Castle* (New York, 1931), p. 132 *et passim.*

Firbank was preoccupied with *The Flower* while he was at Versailles and for some months afterward. Within two weeks of his arrival there he was already so involved with the book that, as he reported to Baba, he had not been to Paris once. He kept at it steadily, spending so many solitary days that by August he was happy to accept the English chaplain's invitation to sit in his garden evenings after eight in order to avoid being entirely alone. With exactly this concentration, he worked on *The Flower* until late spring 1922.

That does not mean that Firbank had no distractions. He gave attention to financial matters, going at least twice late in the summer to a bank in Paris. At one time he had only £3 to his credit, but he wrote frequent letters toward collecting interest due him on £2,000 and toward stabilizing his affairs so that, at the end of his stay in Versailles, Ronald could tell Lady Firbank that he had an annual income of between £700 and £800, an amount with more than five times the buying power of the same sum today. Whatever its worth, it is not necessarily the income he had. He was inclined to belittle his financial resources, to live more modestly in England than he did on the Continent, to plead scarcity of funds. The only certainty is that he had no less than £700 a year. Some of that, a few pounds, he occasionally spent as a respite from his unceasing composition on odds and ends in the antique shops of Versailles. That summer, too, he made a new friend in Miss Frances X. Fleming-Jones. She was stopping at the Trianon Palace Hotel with a gentleman named David Sears, who was usually too ill to leave his room. Miss Fleming-Jones called him her "malade."[2] In 1921 she was fifty-five, a fact which, contrary to the practice of most ladies whom Firbank knew (including Baba), she "proclaimed." She was a small woman,

2. Cf. Frances X. Fleming-Jones to RF, Paris, December 6, 1922; Bessinger-Coligny, Switzerland, September 5, 1924 (MJB).

exquisitely dressed, and at that time she had fine jewelry, her own motor car (both of which she sold after the invalid's death),[3] and a lively interest in music and painting. Firbank saw her frequently, going to her hotel for tea and dinner. He dined or lunched as well with an acquaintance from his university days, J. S. Purvis, also stopping at the Trianon Palace. He had visits from Thomas Earp, who came to Versailles at Firbank's invitation, and from Curtis Moffat and Nancy Cunard, who arrived unexpectedly in late September. Firbank persisted in calling Nancy by her castoff married name, Fairbairn; he described her as a charming woman with a hard and cruel face. In October, near the end of his stay, he had a call from Nina Hamnett, who brought with her Princess Eugène Murat and her daughter. Nina had told her companions that there would be "lots of drinks" and brilliant talk on Ronald's part. But the guests were disappointed, as Miss Hamnett tells it: "We got there about 3.30 R was sober & had an attack of shyness he rushed to a writing desk & produced a stuffed bird of paradise which he pushed into the astonished Princesses's hands."[4] The Princess may have startled Firbank as much as he astonished her. A woman in her early sixties with a passion for life and firm opinions about it, she talked so steadily and so rapidly on occasion that her listeners had no notion what she was saying. René Gimpel described her as having shiny, intensely black hair "parted down the middle of her scalp" and covering her head "like a roof of well-twisted thatch"; falling to her cheeks were "horizontal curls resembling miniature stove pipes."[5] Firbank's habit of observing the unself-

3. Interview with Mrs. Stanley Fuller, 1966.
4. Nina Hamnett, Document, n.d. (written at the request of Richard Buckle); cf. RF to HJGF, Versailles, July 10 and 15, 1921; n.d.; September 4 and 28, 1921; October 3, 21, and 31, 1921.
5. René Gimpel: *Diary of an Art Dealer* (New York, 1966), p. 237; cf. p. 276.

conscious movements of women, as recounted by Sewell
Stokes, had a worthy object in the Princess.[6] Firbank accepted her invitation to lunch with Nina Hamnett, Nancy
Cunard, and others whom Princess Murat considered interesting. On the appointed day, a Sunday, according to Miss
Hamnett, they waited and waited. When they were "just eating dessert R turned up & a very old frère. R refused to eat
drink or speak." It is not surprising that she added, "My feelings can be imagined."[7]

When he left Versailles on November 2, Firbank visited
Paris and then Lausanne, Geneva (where he heard two wonderful concerts by Ansermet, who had been associated with
the Ballet Russe for some years), and Vevey before settling
into a châlet at Montreux on November 19 for the winter and
getting back to his book.[8] The Châlet Bon Port, Montreux,
was a mistake. Firbank's decision to spend the winter in
Switzerland was precipitate. As late as September 28 he had
no plans beyond Versailles and even on October 9 knew only
that he would not go back to England for the rest of the year.
On October 24 he talked of Rome or Palermo or Cairo as his
next destination, but on November 8, from Lausanne, he
wrote to Lady Firbank that he had hired a villa at Montreux
for three months from the seventeenth. For it he had agreed
to pay £11 11s. a week. He intended to go to Vienna, he said,
after Montreux. The châlet was not available on November
17 as its owners, a family named Liddel, had promised. Firbank spent the few days after his arrival in Montreux at the

6. Cf. Sewell Stokes: "Reminiscences of Ronald Firbank," Tape No. TLO
25131 transmitted by BBC Third Programme, February 24, 1957.
7. Nina Hamnett, Document, London, n.d. (written at the request of
Richard Buckle).
8. Cf. RF to HJGF, Lausanne, November 8, 1921; Geneva, November 10
and 11, 1921; Vevey, [November 15, 1921].

Grand Hotel Excelsior and then on November 19 moved to the chalet. It was a beautiful place. Its sitting room, exotic with elaborate *chinoiserie,* fine silks, and an inside garden of ferns and rare chrysanthemums, had a view of both lake and mountains. But because the house was flimsy in construction, it was almost impossible to heat. His health suffered from the cold and the fact that he was in despair over his work. Before moving into the Châlet Bon Port, Firbank had consulted a Dr. de Mouter about his nerves. They were not helped by the fact that he had great difficulty in writing. He blamed it on the Liddels, who lived in a neighboring villa. "Even when they are not chattering on the other side of the wall (they are four, with two servants, gardeners, dogs etc)," he told his mother, "you feel all the time they are *there* & it is impossible to write until they are gone."⁹ By early December he had begun to count the days until his lease would end and to think about Vienna and Venice, Trieste and Florence. Then, in mid-December, forced to stay in bed two days, he was too ill to work. The crowning blow was the discovery of mice in the châlet.¹

As soon as his agreement with the Liddels was terminated, on February 18, 1922, Firbank moved on to Florence and then to Fiesole, where he hired the Villa I Lecci at 15 via Benedeto da Maiano. He was pleased with the rent—"something like 12/6 a day"—and the large rooms, but there was much to find fault with. The villa stood "high on the hillside exposed to the sun" so that the heat at midday was trying. The distance from Florence was a drawback. There were no

9. RF to HJGF, November 25, 1921. Cf. RF to HJGF, Versailles, September 28, 1921; October 9 and 24, 1921; Montreux, November 17, 18, and 20, 1921.
1. Cf. RF to HJGF, Montreux, November 29, 1921; December [3], 12, and 18, 1921.

linens, pots, or pans, all of which had to be hired. Worst of all were the servants, a gardener and his wife, who were firmly established in the basement and inclined to regard the tenant as an intruder. The wife, Firbank told Heather, was "hardly trained enough for 'English' ideas," and he promptly had "quite a scene with her." But his complaints were less bitter than they had been in Montreux, and he settled into a routine, an uneasy and solitary existence. It was one which, as he told Heather, he had come to by many stages.[2]

Firbank thought it right for his book. Although he yearned above all places for the ineffable utopia which he associated with Vienna, he was sure Florence—or Fiesole—was better for his book. On February 25, 1922, he wrote to Baba from Florence, "How different my book would have been had I gone to Vienna, for of course one's surroundings tell. Probably it would have been more brilliant & flippant, but not so good as the steady work I hope to do here."

In his isolation he worked as he had predicted, steadily. Apart from his difficulties with the two servants there were almost no distractions. In March, when Princess Mary and Henry, Viscount Lascelles, came to Fiesole for a part of their honeymoon in a villa which Firbank said "one sees . . . from here quite well," he spent many hours peering at his neighbors. Four days after their arrival, he wrote to Heather about them:

> Princess Mary is here & the roads all guarded with sentries & thick with dust! She arrived Saturday evening, but quite late in the afternoon the villa did not seem half ready for her, as they were beating the carpets out of the windows & everything looked neglected in the extreme. Weeds flourish beneath the windows in sumptuous crops! And nobody can

2. Cf. RF to HF, Fiesole, March 13, 1922.

have lived there for a very long time. . . . all day yesterday
many beautiful motor cars were plying between Fiesole &
Florence.[3]

He made occasional sorties down to Florence, where, according to Harold Acton, he "endeared" himself to the waiters at
Betti's with his generous tips. With some exaggeration Acton
described Firbank at Betti's:

> Having carefully ordered fruit that was out of season, he
> would sit and contemplate it like an El Greco saint in ec-
> stasy. Muscat grapes in mid-winter he would dangle against
> the light, eyeing the clusters caressingly as he sipped glass
> after glass of wine. At the food he merely picked and jabbed
> as if it repelled him.[4]

On one of his sorties he managed, if possible, to intensify
Reggie Turner's dislike of him. Firbank had known Turner
since 1907, when they had met at Vyvyan Holland's twenty-
first birthday party. Seeing Turner one day as he was walking
down the via Tornabuoni, as Acton tells it, Firbank "rushed
upon him from a flower shop and covered him from head to
foot with lilies."[5] On one of these visits to Florence, Firbank
met Ada Leverson, Oscar Wilde's Sphinx, who had written
admiringly to Grant Richards about *Vainglory* and *Inclinations*. She was driving with one or more of the Sitwells, who
had also come down to Florence from their Tuscan strong-
hold, Montegufoni. Of course Firbank was suspicious of the
Sitwells, but he permitted them to introduce Mrs. Leverson.
She wrote about it to Richards: "I was shown R. Firbank the

3. RF to HF, Fiesole, March 13, 1922. Cf. James Pope-Hennessy: *Queen
Mary* (London, 1959), pp. 519 ff.
4. Harold Acton: *Memoirs of an Aesthete* (London, 1948), p. 105.
5. Ibid.

other day we met him when we were driving—& he said he
hoped I was not disappointed in him! I was not."[6]

Except for this "jerky acquaintance" with Florence, Firbank stayed at Fiesole and kept his thoughts on his book. In
March he asked Grant Richards to announce it as being "in
preparation," but the name he had given it, "A Record of the
Early Life of St. Laura De Nazianzi and The Times in Which
She Lived," seemed "repellent" to Richards; he suggested
making that a subtitle to Firbank's alternative one, *The
Flower Beneath the Foot*. By May 4 he had begun to pack,
since he expected momentarily to complete his book. He was
in Fiesole and it was Tuesday, May 23, 1922, however, when
he told his mother that he had finished the book the day before; he added that he thought it "very radiant."[7]

ꙮ VIII ꙮ

By the time Ronald Firbank completed his stay at Fiesole, the
end of May, his attitude toward his literary reputation was
changing. That was due to an unexpected American response
to his work. He had long wanted his books to appear in the
United States. As early as 1916 he had written on August 6
from Torquay to Grant Richards about the proofs of *Odette,*
"Yesterday the wind bore off with them seawards. This must
be a *favourable omen* for America!" The first American in
quiry had come from G. P. Putnam's Sons, who asked to

6. Ada Leverson to GR, Florence, May 1922 (Illinois); cf. Violet
Wyndham: *The Sphinx and Her Circle* (London, 1963), p. 87.
7. Cf. GR to RF, London, March 15 and 29, 1922; RF to CVV, Florence,
May 4, 1922.

consider *Inclinations* and *Caprice,* but then decided not to issue either title. In July 1921, Firbank instructed Richards to send a complete set of his novels to the American publisher Thomas Seltzer. Walter Peacock of that firm had indicated an interest, but the matter went undecided for months. Richards wrote again and again to Thomas Seltzer and to his English representative Douglas Goldring without getting a reply. At last, in a letter dated April 10, 1922, Seltzer declared they could see no possibility of a sale large enough to justify publication. In 1922 Firbank's novels were still under consideration by Alfred A. Knopf, but Richards thought that demand was too small to warrant an American publisher's buying an edition or making separate publication.[1]

Even while Richards was reaching this conclusion, Firbank was on the verge of an American success. Early in 1922, Stuart Rose, a young man interested in books and writing, was browsing in the Holliday Bookshop, then at 10 West Forty-seventh Street, New York, when he discovered Firbank. Rose picked up a book because he liked its dust wrapper, one designed by Augustus John. The book was *Valmouth.* Rose read it with rising excitement, and he carried word of his find to a dinner party given by the Alfred Knopfs for J. C. Squire. Other guests, older and better informed than Rose—Carl Van Vechten and George Jean Nathan for example—said they knew almost nothing about Firbank. Thomas Beer recalled that some years before during a stay in London he had once seen Firbank plain and heard him described as a great exquisite. But none of them, including the Englishman Squire, was familiar with Firbank's novels. Carl Van Vechten, on the basis of Rose's recommendation, proceeded to read *Val-*

1. Cf. GF to RF, London, October 31, 1917, December 30, 1921, March 15, 1922, April 19, 1922; Grant Richards Ltd. to Thomas Seltzer, London, July 16, 1921, December 30, 1921; GR to Douglas Goldring, London, January 7, 1922.

mouth, and when he had finished it determined to make America aware of Ronald Firbank.[2]

As a consequence, Firbank received this letter, dated March 12, 1922, from Van Vechten:

Dear Mr. Ronald Firbank,

I am very sorry to be obliged to inform you that I think there is some danger of your becoming the rage in America. J. C. Squire queried at a recent dinner party declared he had never heard of you, with the result that everybody present rushed into bookshops the next morning to demand your complete works. I have done what I can to stem the rising tide by writing a paper about you, a copy of which I shall, of course, send you when it appears. But more must be done. Can't you write me some facts about yourself, *so that* I can publish them injudiciously, *so that* people may be kept misinformed about your incredibly delightful books to the last possible moment.

Firbank replied at once with the explanation that his books were "a cult" in England, the reason Squire had never heard of them. Firbank said, too, that nothing would give him more happiness than having his books known in America. The facts which Van Vechten requested were another matter. Although Firbank eventually wrote with honesty and sincerity to Van Vechten, the immediate reaction to this letter which "brought excitement & surprise" was a coy one. Here was another opportunity, his last one, as it happened, to project an artificial personality as he had done long ago with R. St. Clair Talboys and more recently with Evan Morgan. The facts about himself which Firbank supplied read, "Well I usually write with purple ink . . . I am older than this, but only admit to nine-

2. Interview with Stuart Rose, 1958; cf. MJB: "Ronald Firbank in New York," *Bulletin of The New York Public Library,* LXIII (May 1959), [247]–59.

teen."[3] Firbank was reluctant to commit himself until he had asked Richards about Van Vechten. Richards was reassuring with the information that Van Vechten was a "fairly well-known and very modern American critic"; but he cautioned Firbank against expecting too much, that it seemed unlikely there would be "any large sale in America for advanced, modern work."[4]

Meanwhile Firbank received a copy of the April number of *The Double Dealer*, a prestigious periodical issued from New Orleans. In it was the article by Carl Van Vechten, who had started his campaign. The article began by stating that the world ought to know something of Ronald Firbank. It went on to describe his novels as unsuitable for public libraries or reviews by writers of the establishment such as Brander Matthews and William Lyon Phelps and to describe Firbank as an "Aubrey Beardsley in a Rolls Royce" a "Sacher-Masoch in Mayfair," and a "Jean Cocteau at the Savoy."[5] Baba was so pleased that she wrote to an editor of *The Double Dealer,* John McClure, to compliment Americans on their capacity to appreciate her son's "literary brilliancy" and to ask McClure to seize every opportunity to make Ronald's books known. "Seeming so light!" she wrote, "there is a wealth of thought, and often great beauty for those who grasp and understand."[6] By that time, Firbank knew that he was the subject of another of Van Vechten's essays, to appear in the May issue of *The Reviewer*, a magazine published in Richmond, Virginia.[7] But he, too, was delighted with the article in *The Double Dealer,* so delighted that he wrote to Van Vechten, "My success in

3. RF to CVV, Fiesole, March 29, [1922].
4. GR to RF, London, April 29, 1922.
5. CVV: "Ronald Firbank," *The Doubler Dealer*, III (April 1922), 185–
7. Cf. GR to RF, London, April 27, 1922.
6. HJGF to Editor of *Double Dealer*, Richmond, Surrey, May 2, 1922 (Berg).
7. Cf. CVV to RF, New York, April 14, 1922, and May 20, 1922.

America overjoys me—any new experience . . . You will
understand."[8] He called Van Vechten his first intelligent
critic. He agreed to Richards's quoting from *The Double
Dealer,* and from time to time Firbank showed the essay to
anyone who would look. Sewell Stokes saw it in London,
when Firbank declared it was "enough to give one wings for a
week."[9] Walter Shaw, an American who did some art criticism and worked occasionally with Man Ray, recalled Firbank in Paris that June, "his hands fluttering about," producing the article from his pocket and then, in an attack of
shyness saying suddenly, "Let's talk French!"[1]

IX

Before Firbank reached Paris early in June 1922, he first
made the short journey from Florence to Venice. Then came
the stay in Paris of a week or more. He rushed around Paris
looking for a copy of *Ulysses* by a man, he explained to Baba,
reported to be even more corruptive than himself. He found
the book, of course, at Sylvia Beach's shop, Shakespeare and
Company; and to his joy he also found nearly all his own
books there. He sought out Nina Hamnett at the Dôme, where
they had brandy and champagne instead of dinner. They went
together to the Jockey with its "wild swoops of tenebrous

8. RF to CVV, Paris, June 10, 1922.
9. Sewell Stokes: "Reminiscences of Ronald Firbank," Tape No. TLO
25131 transmitted by BBC Third Programme, February 24, 1957. Cf. RF
to HJGF, Fiesole, May 7, [1922]; Helen Carew to RF, Hove, May 21, 1922;
GR to RF, London, May 11, 1922; Sewell Stokes: "A Recent Genius,"
Pilloried! (London, [1928], p. 223.
1. Nancy Cunard to MJB, Mallorca, July 24, 1958.

colours all over the walls and ceiling" and its bottles of "splendid coloured water here and there—apothecary style." This was the Montparnasse creation of the American painter Hilaire Hiler, who sat at the piano nightly, " 'vamping till ready' on and on and on."[1] Nina Hamnett remembered taking Firbank, extremely drunk after two bottles of champagne, back to the Lutétia Hotel from the Jockey. From Paris he wrote to Van Vechten, who was increasingly curious about Firbank and eager to have a picture, "A 'likeness' is seldom satisfactory, since 'looks' vary with moods, etc. I am sometimes told I am a reincarnated Egyptian, or Greek, & although, alas, I can remember very little about it, it is pleasant to think of having lived in some more attractive Age than one's own!"[2]

When Firbank returned to London on June 11 and took up residence at 49a Pall Mall, he had several projects in mind. For one thing, he went to Newport with a representative of his estate agent, Field Garner of Bond Street, London, to inspect his Welsh properties. The sale of more land was in question.[3] Of immediate concern, too, was the publication of *The Flower Beneath the Foot*. Before going to Wales, he took the book to Richards. By June 27 Richards had read it and, as he said, enjoyed it. Two days later he and Firbank reached a verbal agreement, confirmed the following day by letter, whereby Richards was to produce an edition of one thousand copies, binding only five hundred, at a cost to Firbank approximated at £115 plus the publisher's commission of 33⅓ per cent. Richards agreed also to improve the quality of the cloth used for binding so that it would resemble the cloth used

1. Nancy Cunard to MJB, Mallorca, [1958]. Cf. RF to HJGF, Paris, June 1922; Nina Hamnett, Document, London, n.d. (written at request of Richard Buckle).
2. RF to CVV, Paris, June 10, 1922.
3. RF to Messrs. Field Garner, Bordighera, November 20, 1922 (MJB).

for Charles Whibley's *Book of Scoundrels*. Although John
Wells designed a dust jacket, his was discarded in favor of one
by Charles Nevinson. Richards made all arrangements with
Nevinson.[4] Publication was set for October.

For illustrations, Firbank insisted on using two portraits of
himself. At first he intended to have only one, a portrait
drawn by Wyndham Lewis in early July. That was another of
his projects for the summer in London, and he took great
interest in the sittings. Lewis's account of them tells how difficult Firbank was to get onto the model's throne and how
even more difficult to keep there. He kept leaping off the
throne and rushing to see what Lewis had drawn. Finally
Lewis set him on the corner of a table and made him stay
within reach of a kick.[5] Firbank's account is shorter and
different in detail. He wrote that to his horror mice scampered
about the studio throughout the sittings and that Lewis kept
praising his subject's appearance, repeatedly calling him an
Adonis.[6] In any case, Lewis made two drawings. One pleased
Lewis because it emphasizes every aspect of decadence and
sickness in Firbank's face. It is a graphic but cruel likeness.
That Firbank ever saw it is questionable. The other pleased
Lewis and Firbank; it is the one which appears on the title
page of *The Flower*. The second portrait in the book was
drawn spontaneously by Augustus John late in July, "at 2
a.m. in the Café Royal"[7] Because Firbank thought it "brilliant," he decided to include it also. Richards protested. "The
John drawing," he told Firbank, "is beautiful. It will make an

4. Cf. GR to RF, London, June 27 and 30, 1922; GR to C. R. W. Nevinson,
London, July 1, 1922; Nina Hamnett, Document, London, n.d. (written at
request of Richard Buckle); RF to CVV, London, July 29, 1922.
5. Cf. Wyndham Lewis: *Blasting and Bombardiering* (London, 1937),
pp. 226–8; GR to RF, London, July 7 and 14, 1922.
6. Holograph note in a notebook for *Concerning the Eccentricities of Cardinal Pirelli* (Berg).
7. RF to CVV, Bordighera, January 17, 1923.

admirable wrapper and frontispiece—so admirable that I im-
plore you to hold it over for the next book. It would be a great
pity to put it in this one." He told Firbank further that the
presence of both portraits would be awkward and "people
would not like having two in the same book."[8] Firbank readily admitted that the Lewis portrait was "wildly obscure," the
John drawing "rather 'gypsy,'" and the two together "exces-
sive"; but he refused to omit either, whatever Richards
thought.

Firbank was no longer inclined to take Richards's advice.
His dissatisfaction with the publisher, expressed to Lady Firbank before *Santal* appeared, was growing. Besides, he was
intoxicated with Van Vechten's story of his success in America. In May, beginning his letter with "Dear gay genius," Van
Vechten had written to Firbank, "To say that you are a sensation in New York is to speak modestly. I think you are at least
as famous in New York as Anatole France. Certainly more
than Beerbohm."[9] In late June, Firbank received Van Vechten's second essay, "Satirist or Decadent," which appeared in
the May *Reviewer*.[1] It had been sent with newspaper clippings which Van Vechten's two articles on Firbank had
evoked. They took long enough to arrive for Van Vechten to
conjecture that they had "perished in passage—like consti-
pated rabbits."[2] But they caught up with Firbank in London.
Earlier newspaper excerpts, received in Venice, had made
him feel, he said, "quite like a bottle of prohibition whiskey, &
not atall like the *Veuve Cliquot* (1886), special cavee"[3] that
he was. But he found the clippings, Van Vechten's article, all
the notice paid him in America "wing-giving very." And he

8. GR to RF, London, July 25, 1922.
9. CVV to RF, New York, May 20, 1922. See above, pp. 218–20.
1. Pp. 458–9.
2. CVV to RF, New York, May 20, 1922.
3. RF to CVV, Venice, June 4, 1922.

refused to let Richards clip his wings; *The Flower Beneath the Foot* must have both portraits as well as Nevinson's dust jacket.

With these arrangements complete and the month for publication of *The Flower* settled, Firbank could get on with his next novel. He probably mentioned it first in July when he wrote to his mother from London to say that his next would be "a negro novel with a brilliant background of sunlight, sea, and as tropical" as he could make it. To prepare for it he wanted to return to Jamaica. He asked Baba to apply to the Elder Dempster Line in his behalf and request the reduced "college fare" which they allowed students out of season. Always ready to do what he asked, Baba wrote the necessary letters, but Elder Dempster refused to allow him to go on a student rate. He was forced to take a fully paid passage on the *Orcoma*, a ship which took him from Liverpool along the coast of Spain and Portugal and landed him on Saturday, August 26, 1922, not at Jamaica but at Havana, Cuba. With its graceful, golden-hued people, its white buildings, and broad streets edged with palms, Havana delighted him. But he had hardly settled into Havana's Ritz Hotel before he was preparing to go on to Jamaica. In July, still in London, he had written to Van Vechten and suggested a visit to New York after Havana. He had romantic notions about New York, anyway, that it must be "very fascinating & nerve-shattering with the remains of exquisite Bars that one could visit with regret & emotion."[4] But Van Vechten could not face in New York in August what he had heard about Firbank; so he discredited Firbank's fanciful picture and discouraged his visit, saying November or March would be better times for him to come. Firbank replied that he questioned having the "chastity requisite for America . . . especially in March" and

4. RF to CVV, London, June 29, 1922.

in any case it might be "dangerous" for them to meet. "Let us keep one another," he told Van Vechten, "as last illusions."⁵ And so, instead of New York—or Jamaica yet—Firbank went to Santiago de Cuba. He was, as he put it, "butterflying about." But there was little to do in Santiago except "swim in the Caribbean sea—in spite of the sharks." He was restless and bored, as he indicated in a letter to Van Vechten written on September 11, a Monday, from the Hotel Casa Granda, "I go on Tuesday to Jamaica, & count the minutes as Santiago seems very dull. I expect to drive through the Blue Mountains, & catch a Banana-boat back again to Kingston."

Yet from Santiago, Firbank told his mother that he had "found" his book. He confirmed that fact in another letter to her, one from Kingston, Jamaica, dated September 19, 1922. "Cuba," he declared, "gave me all I needed for another novel."⁶ And on the corner of a letter from Van Vechten dated August 30, 1922, which Firbank received in Cuba, he scribbled,

In Preparation

A novel of

The East Indies.

The actual composition of the novel, however, had to wait. Once back in London at the beginning of October, Firbank

5. RF to CVV, Santiago de Cuba September 11, 1922; interview with Carl Van Vechten, 1953. Cf. RF to CVV, Havana, [August 29, 1922]; CVV to RF, New York, August 30, 1922.
6. This is the time to deal with the persistent legend that Firbank went to Haiti for this novel, *Prancing Nigger* or *Sorrow in Sunlight*, prefacing his departure with the statement, "Tomorrow I go to Haiti. They say the President is a *Perfect Dear*." (Sitwell: "Ronald Firbank," *Noble Essences*, pp. 81–2; cf. Fletcher: *Ronald Firbank A Memoir*, p. 73.) Firbank may have made that statement. I have not seen it. He often thought of going innumerable places from wherever he might be and then thought better of it the next day. To my knowledge there is no evidence of any kind that Firbank went to Haiti. Certainly Cuna-Cuna of *Prancing Nigger* is a modified Havana as it was as late as 1936.

was forced to revise *The Flower Beneath the Foot*. Richards
had postponed printing because he feared that certain passages in the book were libelous and that if action were
brought damages "might run into big figures." He wrote Firbank to that effect on September 23 and delayed until the
author was back in London and could make his own changes.
In the course of revising, Richards and Firbank disagreed
about punctuation, vocabulary, and spelling. Richards urged
consistency in punctuation, he questioned Firbank's use of
"depreciated" instead of "deprecated," and declared himself
"doubtful about 'organicly.' "[7] They also disagreed about another publication date for *The Flower*. Richards wanted it
brought out as soon as possible, preferably late in November.
Fearing it would be regarded as a "Christmas book," Firbank
wanted to delay until January. He had his way, and in November he wrote to Van Vechten that *The Flower*, "timed for
early New Year," would "race the first white lilac."[8]

X

By November 8 at the latest Firbank was at work on his next
book, called then "Drama in Sunlight." In a letter of that date
he told Van Vechten that he had already begun his "Negro
novel." He had arrived in Bordighera, that somnolent resort
on the Italian Riviera, a week or more earlier and gone to the
Hotel Bristol. At the end of November he moved to the Villa

7. GR to RF, London, November 11, 1922. Cf. GR to RF, London, October
13 and 16, 1922; GR to HJGF, London, November 2, 1922.
8. RF to CVV, Bordighera, November 8, 1922; cf. GR to RF, London,
October 13, 1922.

Sans Souci, which he hired with the thought of spending the winter. But he was at the Hotel Bristol when he started the composition of the novel.

Because of his work and because of the continuing problems with *The Flower,* Firbank paid little attention to Van Vechten's request for a short piece suitable for the periodical *The Reviewer.* Van Vechten was sorry that he had discouraged Firbank's projected visit to New York. Firbank might be conspicuous, but in late August and early September few of Van Vechten's friends would have been in the city to see him. When Firbank completed his "wanderings in Jamaica & the Caribbean Seas" and returned to Europe, the opportunity was past. On October 25, from New York, Van Vechten sent a lame apology, that New York had been "especially unamusing," that he had had no Jamaican address for Firbank and so could not cable him to come at once when "New York suddenly became very brilliant." In that letter, too, Van Vechten said that he had posted a copy of *The Reviewer* and asked Firbank for something to publish there. He went on to explain about the editor (actually there were two editors, Emily Clark and Mary Street), "an amusing woman who looks like a Toulouse-Lautrec portrait of the Grand Duchess Anastasie— quite more curious than anything ever seen at Palmyrès." He assured Firbank that everyone gave her "things for nothing" and that she would be "only less happy" than her readers to have a piece from him. Firbank replied from Bordighera on December 2 that he would love to write for *The Reviewer* and suggested possibilities: a "little thing called 'Filtered Water,'" which was too pure to send, a libretto for an "'all British' musical comedy" though its "Valse-refrain business had still to be considered," or a "Prose-poem on 'Violets' dealing, as they say, with those of Oxford, Naples, & Athens—not to forget *Parma.*" Writing before "a bowl full of French Mig-

nonette," which he was sure accounted for his frivolity, he
added, "Once long ago I used to idolize Edna May (how
charming in the 'Belle of New York,' & the 'Girl from Up
There') & my style, as I grow old, seems to be becoming more
& more like that of Mrs Leslie Carter, or Mrs Fiske."

Firbank was increasingly conscious of growing old. On
December 2, 1922, when he wrote that letter to Van Vechten,
Firbank was approaching his thirty-seventh birthday. Yet he
was fearful of aging and extremely self-conscious about the
appearance of age. He referred to his "fast-greying hair." He
was most annoyed at the "crude Way" the John drawing was
reproduced in *The Flower*. On the day of its publication,
January 17, 1923, he complained about it. "It was never very
flattering," he said, "but now!" That was in a letter to Van
Vechten in which Firbank offered to send a photograph "with
becoming lights à la Baron de Meyer" so that it could be plain
"what a darling" he was. He was still complaining about the
"horrid John picture" in February. Part of this commotion
derived from vanity; he wanted Van Vechten to think him
handsome. Much of it, though, reflected his real concern with
age. He was close to the attitude which he caused a character
in *Prancing Nigger* to express: "My dear, Age is the one disaster." When he had a photograph of Florine Stettheimer's
portrait of Van Vechten, Firbank declared himself terrified.
His letter to Van Vechten read, "You have not a wrinkle. I
might be your Father, Your Grandfather. . . . I had always
figured you as 'elderly', & with a beard—I feel too shaken to
write any more just yet."[1] He could add only that Van Vechten
had some resemblance to that youthful ideal of the twenties,
the Prince of Wales.

Firbank's anxiety was intensified by his rapidly deteriorat-
ing health. From Bordighera on Christmas Eve he told Baba

1. RF to CVV, Bordighera, March 1, 1923.

that if his health did not improve he would soon be forced to live outside Europe and its climate. Exertion or agitation brought on asthmatic attacks. In February 1923 he was ill enough to require bed-rest for more than two weeks, and eventually he went the short distance to Monte Carlo for a brief convalescence. While he was there he attended a dinner party given by Grant Richards. Firbank described it to Heather as an enjoyable "outing" with "all the amusing clever people." Among them were "Blazo Ibenez of the '4 Horsemen of the Apoclypse' fame, & Mrs Langtry," whom he liked "enormously." At another table sat Miss Fleming-Jones with a party, and all in all Firbank had an "amusing evening."[2] Because illness was frightening, it reassured him to go to the party. He could boast to Van Vechten that he was "already gadding about again à la Sainte Thérèse."[3] In May he complained to his mother of difficulty with breathing when he climbed stairs or walked fast or when the wind blew from the East. He was increasingly ill and tired, a condition aggravated by misgivings about his work.[4]

His presence at Richards's dinner party at Monte Carlo did not imply that Firbank felt less anxious about his literary career or more kindly toward Richards. Firbank was disturbed at the cost of producing *The Flower,* which by December had risen from the estimated cost of £115 to £200. Profits from sales in America of earlier books, about £130, were applied toward *The Flower* and, when the balance came due on December 29, 1922, Firbank asked to postpone payment until April, with the hope that sales would provide the amount involved, £66. Before this request reached England, he had heard from Richards reminding him of his obligations. Fir-

2. RF to HF, Bordighera, February 27, 1923; cf. RF to HJGF, Monte Carlo, February 24, 1923.
3. RF to CVV, Monte Carlo, February 24, 1923.
4. Cf. RF to HJGF, Bordighera, May 28, [1923].

bank said Richards's letter was "like a shark." Eventually
Richards agreed to the delay, extending the due date not to
April but to the following October, a more reasonable one if
profits accrued from sales were to be utilized for payment.
His answer was slow in coming, however, and there was confusion about dates and addresses. The advance copy of *The
Flower* was also slow in getting to him, partly because he had
told Richards that on January 26, 1923, he would go to Florence and instead he stayed at Bordighera. When he saw the
book, he complained about its appearance, especially the dust
jacket and, of course, the reproduction of the John portrait.[5]

Firbank worried about advertising, which was dependent
on reviews. From Havana, well before publication, he had
asked Sewell Stokes to "say something" about *The Flower* in
the *Sunday Times*. Then in December he had told his mother
that he fully expected to be ill-treated by reviewers and maintained that he was indifferent to anything said about him. But
when Richards's office sent no reviews, he was so distressed
that Baba inquired about them only to find they were again
delayed because of uncertainty as to his address. This Firbank
may have straightened out with a note to Richards which
read, "Oh how I'm sulking! Yes this address will find me for
the next 3 months."[6] When Firbank finally got the reviews, he
was thoroughly irritated, although he wrote to Heather, "The
abominable & spiteful reviews in many of the British papers
do not matter one straw to me or the people I cater for! The
only annoyance is, it would please the relations & a few jealous fools!"[7] Approval of *The Flower* from Helen Carew

5. Cf. RF to HJGF, Bordighera, December 9, [1922], December 30, 1922,
January 4, 1923; GR to RF, January 1, 4, 10, 20, and 26, 1923.
6. Bordighera, n.d. (Holograph draft on reverse of letter from CVV to RF
dated December 22, [1922]; cf. RF to Sewell Stokes, Havana, September
1, 1922; RF to HJGF, Bordighera, December 1922.
7. RF to HF, Bordighera, February 27, 1923.

("The best thing you have yet given us. The delicacy of its style and touch pleases me enormously . . .") and Carl Van Vechten ("The perfume of The Flower is all that you could desire—") hardly comforted Firbank.[8] There were, in fact, a number of good notices. The Birmingham *Post* said that he wrote "brilliantly," and both the *New Statesman* and the Manchester *Guardian* spoke of the wit in the book. "It has grace & vividness & wit," the *New Statesman* declared. Firbank carefully copied these and other quotable passages and instructed that they be used for advertising in the exact order he designated.[9]

Despite his poor health and the agitation which further debilitated him, Firbank concentrated on his new book. Without effacing its identity, he was converting Havana into the city of Cuna-Cuna. To it from Mediaville—or Santiago de Cuba— he brought the Mouth family (Mr. and Mrs. Ahmadou Mouth and their children Charlie, Edna, and Miami, beloved of the fisher-boy Bamboo) and recounted their adventures and misadventures in Cuna-Cuna. Firbank here, as in most of his work, had something to say about the moral vacuum of the times and society he knew. In this book he altered the equivalents by which he usually composed his statement; that is, instead of measuring human behavior against the divine design implicit in its earthly manifestations, the Church and Christianity, in this book Firbank set up a "civil-savage" juxtaposition. The Mouth family's flight from Mediaville, with its primitive, natural life, to the city of Cuna-Cuna, following their dream (Mrs. Mouth's heart-felt cry was for a "villa with a watercloset"), brought only corruption. The natural life of Mediaville led to natural joy. The artificial one of Cuna-Cuna

---

8. Helen Carew to RF, Hove, January 27, [1923] (Fales); CVV to RF, New York, February 4, 1923.
9. Cf. RF to George Wiggins, Bordighera, March 6 and 17, 1923; holograph copies of excerpts from reviews, 2 pp. (MJB).

meant degradation and sorrow. It is all recounted, as E. M. Forster declared, with "an opulence as of gathered fruit and enamelled skies"[1] so as to be unquestionably illusion. But it is an illusion which holds the truth. While Balzac may have found that he conveyed the fantastic most convincingly by drawing on the real, Firbank reversed the process. He conveyed the real by presenting the fantastic. The book went so well that by late December Firbank could declare that if he were left undisturbed, it might easily be the most beautiful of all. Nancy Cunard and a friend found him in the midst of his work when they visited him "one dripping January day." After several inquiries along "this or that alley that would soon be filled with happy mimosa, transformed into a feathery little pleasaunce," they found the right house. Nancy's account of the visit runs,

> I remember a drenched magnolia and some draughty, unhappy stairs and damp rooms as that particular background. He seemed glad to see us. He was working a lot, fairly well, liked Bordighera and did not mind the seasonal discomfort. The lunch that followed, full of agreeable talk and cheering wine, lasted till nearly tea-time and there was a glow to it that made us forget January. He was a very good talker—this came out yet better that day *à trois*—with individual ideas about art and writing and sudden offshoots now and again, into fancy. We left him amid the dank palm-trees, and he impressed me that day as spiritually at ease and full of vitality, mainly perhaps because he was working hard.[2]

To ensure better working conditions, Firbank moved at the end of that month, January, to a "more secluded" residence

1. "Ronald Firbank," *Abinger Harvest* (London, 1946), p. 115.
2. Cunard: "Thoughts About Ronald Firbank," p. 4 (MJB).

located high up the hill overlooking the town and the sea, the Villa Olivetti. There he lived quietly with a housekeeper, reading such things as David Garnett's *Lady into Fox*, a gift from Nancy Cunard, and taking occasional walks into the village, where he observed everything and everyone, including "an attractive looking Fasciste" who was Bordighera's ironmonger.[3] In this environment the book steadily grew, so that by April 23, 1923, he had written a rough draft of at least eleven of fourteen chapters.

On that date he agreed to send the eleventh chapter, which he described as the " 'Earthquake' chapter—seen through the eyes of a very darling of a nigger," to Van Vechten for publication in *The Reviewer*. After his first appeal, dated October 25, 1922, and Firbank's nonsensical reply of December 2, Van Vechten had pleaded for a contribution in letter after letter. On March 20, 1923, Firbank admitted that he could produce nothing suitable, though he declared that he had recently started a "conte called 'The Story of Percy Eton & Evie Cutbush,' but 'Evie' grew too terrible & Percy took to his heels."[4] Van Vechten was especially eager to get something from Ronald for the April number of *The Reviewer*, but that issue was complete when Firbank suggested the chapter from his current work. Even then he was not entirely definite. "I do not know," he wrote to Van Vechten, "how it would detach itself, & must look at it again—"[5] Because he could find no typist in Bordighera, the contribution was not mailed until mid-July from London. It appeared in the October number of

3. RF to CVV, Bordighera, April 28, 1923. Cf. RF to HJGF, Bordighera, [December 24, 1922]; RF to CVV, Bordighera, January 17, 1923; RF to HF, Bordighera, February 27, 1923.
4. RF to CVV, Bordighera, March 20, 1923. Cf. CVV to RF, New York, March 6, 1922, December 22, [1922], February 4, 1923. See above, p. 227.
5. RF to CVV, New York, [April 23, 1923].

The Reviewer with the title "A Broken Orchid (From Sorrow in Sunlight)."[6]

In April, when he wrote to offer the section from his novel, Firbank still had much to do to complete it. He decided, that month, to stay on in Bordighera until the end of June. By that time he was certain to have written his book. With waning strength—he complained that his work left him too tired for anything else—he kept at it until on June 17, 1923, he could write from the Villa Olivetti to tell Baba that he had finished that morning:

> It is too soon & I am too tired of it to judge it—But as a bit of colour & atmosphere it is the best of all my others & some of the figures negroes & Spanish South Americans are as wonderful as their setting! It is an amazing affair altogether & some no doubt will be horrified by it while others will be carried away by its vivid unusualness & the crude touches left purposely unshaded.

As he said to Van Vechten two days later, the book was then called "A Drama in Sunlight."[7]

By then, June 19, 1923, Firbank was preparing to go to London "in time," as he wrote to Van Vechten, "for a Duse matinée on the 26th." His real business in London was to arrange for another publisher. His vexation with Grant Richards over the past eighteen months had deepened into such anger that publication with him was now impossible. The quarrel revolved around the poor sale of Firbank's books. He had been disappointed by sales since the publication of *Vainglory* in 1915. His misgivings had been great enough in 1921,

6. Pp. 15–19. Cf. RF to CVV, Bordighera, May 26, 1923; London, July 16, 1923.
7. Cf. RF to HJGF, Bordighera, [April 1, 1923] and April 17, [1923]; RF to CVV, Bordighera, April 23, 1923; RF to GR, Bordighera, June, 19, 1923.

when he was at work on *Santal,* to make him consider breaking off with Richards at that time. Then came the correspondence with Van Vechten and further dissatisfaction. At first
Firbank was only bemused by American awareness of him.
From Fiesole on May 3, 1922, he wrote to Van Vechten, "It
is very mysterious & strange, & I had really no idea my books
were so restless and had found their way over to the United
States & were wandering about all alone in New York like a
family of orphans in their deep black jackets." Soon he began
to have reports of an enormous success in New York. One
letter from Van Vechten dated May 20, 1922, ran, "All the
world is reading you, quoting you, buying you, admiring you.
You are almost a 'best seller.' One shop cannot keep you in
stock at all. They are sold as fast as they come in." Another
letter written four days later said, "Your books are now selling here like copies of a new detective yarn by Maurice Le
blanc. The demand is *terrific.*"

Firbank had long been convinced that his books deserved
far more recognition than they got in England. During the
past year, bolstered by Carl Van Vechten's admiration, he
had bravely begun to assert the fact. Sewell Stokes had met
Firbank for the first time while he was in London in the
summer of 1922, just before he went to Havana. Nevinson
had introduced them at the Café Royal on an occasion when
Dikran Kouyoumdjian, that small, elegant Armenian who
called himself Michael Arlen, was also present. Both Arlen
and Firbank proclaimed Firbank's superiority as a writer, and
Firbank openly wondered at Arlen's success. In fact, that
summer, when Firbank had had enough brandy, he lost his
usual reserve about his ability. He attended more than one of
the parties held in Nevinson's garden in Hampstead. As a
rule, Firbank arrived unnoticed and remained invisible behind a tree until the party was well in progress. Then when he

was eventually found, he laughed "inside himself" both at being unseen and at being finally observed. But as soon as he had had enough to drink, his shyness and his reticence fell away; and he boldly declared his excellence as both person and writer. He did so with drunken dignity until someone questioned or seemed to question his estimate; then Firbank grew abusive.[8] Had he not had profound faith in his writing, he could hardly have continued it, book after book, in the face of the indifference he had known for almost ten years. He wanted to believe Van Vechten's exaggerated account of his American sales.

They made his lack of sales in England all the more puzzling. In the light of Van Vechten's letters, Baba asked Richards to explain her son's continued loss on his books. His reply was an analysis of the fate of all *avant-garde* artists. It began by saying that Firbank wrote "those books to please himself" rather than the public or the critics and that critics are always "slow to praise work of an entirely new kind." Richards went on, "No man who has put his own individuality into his work has leapt immediately into success." He named as examples Samuel Butler, George Meredith, Joseph Conrad, T. Sturge Moore. John Davidson; and Richards concluded, "Your son's work, everybody says, is esoteric: he makes no concessions."[9] Perhaps Firbank reacted arrogantly but honestly when Baba reported all this. "The more I think about my literary efforts in the light of others," he told her, "the less do I feel that I owe them any concession, either to happiness inspiration or money."[1] But Richards's letter soothed Lady Firbank and her son briefly.

In early May Ronald was still expecting large returns from

8. Interview with Sewell Stokes, 1967; cf. Sewell Stokes to MJB, London, January 22, 1967.
9. GR to HJGF, London, [May 1923].
1. RF to HJGF, Bordighera, May 12, [1923].

The Flower Beneath the Foot. Although the early sales had not been very promising, he knew it was superior to anything he had written before. When he asked about the sales soon after publication, Richards answered that London booksellers had not done well with his books and turned a "deaf ear" to the assurance that *The Flower* would "turn the scale." By May 18, 1923, out of an edition of one thousand, only 456 copies had been sold. Before he had that information, Firbank, convinced of the merit of *The Flower,* believed that he must have several hundred pounds to his credit, and he wrote to Richards to inquire. Richards's reply, according to Firbank, had the "atmosphere of a dog with a stolen bone which its trying to hide."[2] Firbank blamed Richards for not pushing the book and declared that only the commission, based on production costs rather than sales, interested him.

Firbank's vexation turned to anger when, on June 7, 1923, he received Richards's statement of account for the latter half of 1922. An accompanying letter explained that the cost of producing *The Flower* had been charged to his account but none of the proceeds from sales in 1923 had been credited so that the author's account was "practically" in balance, only 3s. 6d. being due. Firbank was furious. He wrote to his mother about Richards that the statement had kept him "awake a whole night from indignation at his effrontery!! . . . it appears that he sold in the last year £225 of my books & that I still owe him 3/6!"[3]

Firbank had asked for the statement in January. When it had not come by May, he decided that he must request an audit of his account and transfer his balance to another publisher. He

2. RF to HJGF, Bordighera, May 23, [1923]. Cf. GR to RF, London, January 26, 1923, May 18, 1923; George Wiggins to RF, London, March 1, 1923.
3. RF to HJGF, Bordighera, June 7, [1923]. Cf. GR to RF, London, May 21, 1923.

was too impatient and suspicious to hear Richards's explanation. Richards protested that publishers render accounts five or six months after the termination of a given period, that he had followed that practice throughout their association. There is much to be said against Richards as a businessman. By 1923 he had had two bankruptcies, and he was slow in paying his bills, especially in 1922 and 1923, when depressed conditions were everywhere. His life was more luxurious than his means warranted, and he went too often to Monte Carlo. Nevertheless his statements of account with Firbank as compiled under George Wiggins's supervision were accurate.

Firbank's bitterness at what he termed the "sordid & unattractive side of authorship," his financial relationship with Richards, was sharpened by discussion of it with Van Vechten. He, too, expected Richards to publish a book of his in England, *The Blind Bow-Boy,* and he asked Firbank about Richards's "sending anybody anything." Firbank's response was ardent: "He has never me." He added that he had "never seen back *one* farthing piece" of the six or seven hundred pounds spent to produce his books. "Nine long years, sir," he wrote, "since I took him Vainglory & never a cent! . . . However it is only (today) April 22nd, 1923 & Vainglory was published early in 1914, & so there is always Hope. . . . it seems that 'the returns' from one book barely cover 'the outgoings' of the next—& so it goes on." A few days later, fearful that Van Vechten might think him " 'impatient & mercenary,' " Firbank wrote again to say that perhaps he had been unfair to Richards, that he ought to have waited his "decade 'silent' as they say in Novels" before complaining. But, he went on, he had "never made yet a sou" in his life and he hated being "deprived of a new sensation." In a more serious mood Firbank said that all his "happiness in writing (ex-

cept from the actual writing itself)" had come from Van
Vechten.[4]

Now, with Richards's statement in hand, Firbank determined to find another publisher. On June 8 he wrote to the
London literary agent Eric Pinker asking for an appointment
at the end of the month. The day after he finished his book,
that is, on June 18, he drafted a careful letter questioning
Richards's entire statement. After giving facts and figures, Firbank wrote, "I cannot but be puzzled by your statement shew-
ing 'the balance due to Publisher at the end of 1922 to be
3/6!' " The letter continued, "I find since 1914 I have spent
not far short of £1000 on the production of my books & it is
not unreasonable in 1923 to be expecting some return!" Firbank ended by saying that his novels in New York were
"fetching big prices," that Blanche Knopf of 220 West 42nd
Street listed *Valmouth* at $7 and *Odette* at $3.50, and that he
had received nothing for his work "over a span of soon ten
years."[5]

That was almost Firbank's last act before leaving Bordighera. Once back in London, he pursued his differences with
Richards. On June 25, a Monday, immediately after he
reached London, Firbank went to the publisher's office in St.
Martin's Street, repeated his objections to the crucial financial statement, and maintained that his letter of June 18 had
been ignored. Until this meeting, Richards had not realized
the extent of Firbank's hostility. Confronted with Firbank's anger, Richards replied the next day with a memoran-

4. RF to CVV, Bordighera, [April 22, 1923], April 28, 1923, May 26,
1923. *Vainglory* was published in April 1915.
5. For the complete text of the letter see MJB: *Bibliography of Ronald
Firbank* (London, 1963), p. 41. Cf. GR to RF, January 10, 1923, May 18
and 31, 1923; RF to HJGF, May 9 and 20, 1923, June 17, 1923. Grant
Richards's account books are at the library of the University of Illinois.

dum from George Wiggins which took up Firbank's complaints, one by one. Firbank was still not satisfied. He engaged
W. B. Peat and Company to audit Richards's accounts. By
July 5, 1923, that firm had obtained permission to examine the
publisher's record. Seeking further satisfaction, Firbank
placed the matter in the hands of the Society of Authors,
which began attempts no later than August 2, 1923, to collect
what was due to Firbank. That went on until May 31, 1924,
when Richards paid £54, a sum derived largely from the sale
of *The Flower,* to close Firbank's account to the end of 1923.[6]

Firbank was left in the summer of 1923 with an uncom-
mitted manuscript and no publisher. Either through his own
efforts or those of the literary agent Pinker, Firbank offered
his book to C. S. Evans of Heinemann's, describing it as "pur-
posely a little 'primitive,' rather like a Gauguin in painting—
extremely Gay."[7] Evans agreed to consider the book, but no
immediate decision was forthcoming. Firbank was forced to
wait for one throughout the summer.

While he waited, Firbank managed to keep busy. Although
he called it "obscure," he got off his "Earthquake Chapter" to
Van Vechten for publication in *The Reviewer.* In the same
post he sent two photographs to Van Vechten, who hung
them up in his bathroom, "somewhere between Gaby Deslys
and Mary Garden."[8] Ronald studied and declared "marvellous" the "variations of the 'chorus'" of the song *Yes, We
Have No Bananas,* sent him by Van Vechten.[9] He revisited

6. Cf. GR to RF, London, July 6, 1923; GR to W. B. Peat and Company,
London, July 21, 1923; GR to Society of Authors, London, December
31, 1923, April 2, 1924, May 23 and 29, 1924, etc.; Society of Authors
to GR, August 2, 8, and 10, 1923, March 31, 1924, May 22 and 29,
1924, etc.
7. GR: *Author Hunting,* p. 205.
8. CVV to RF, New York, September 19, 1923; cf. RF to CVV, London,
June 16 and 19, 1923.
9. Cf. RF to CVV, London, July 19, 1923; CVV to RF, New York, July 4,
1923.

the Café Royal and the Eiffel Tower. Alan Harris was at the Percy Street restaurant late one night in July when only his own supper party and, at another table, Firbank and a young man were in the dining room. Harris's account of the incident which occurred that night runs,

> The young man had gone out (by the side door into the hotel passage) to get his coat, when Stulik [the Eiffel Tower's proprietor] being rather drunk, got very matey (& slightly scurrilous) and insisted on introducing Firbank to our party. All I remember F's doing or saying was to point rather languidly to the place opposite him where the young man had been sitting—and at this point the young man had come back & was standing in the doorway (the side door that leads into the hotel passage), and waiting for Firbank to get up, but F did not see him—and said: "A charming young man, a delightful young man, but so common, so *dreadfully* common!"[1]

Firbank had grown less discreet about his homosexuality. He disliked it, if his novels are an indication. When he first faced his inversion, he may have tried to brazen it out. His boastful letters of 1904 to Talboys and his deliberate cultivation of Alfred Douglas make that a plausible conjecture. But he soon learned—certainly by the time he left Cambridge—to conceal his homosexuality. He came to dislike it as well. Firbank did not, as Gide and Douglas did, write lyrically of homosexuality. In his books it is either comic, as in *Inclinations* and *The Flower Beneath the Foot,* or calamitous, as in *The Eccentricities of Cardinal Pirelli.* But as with Gide and Wilde, the *"wonderful"* and obliging boys of North Africa had broken down his reticence so that, after his stay in Algiers and Tunis, he was less circumspect. His illness and his fear of

1. Alan Harris to Richard Buckle, London, July 24, 1940.

illness sharpened his desires. That summer of 1923, according
to Nina Hamnett, was the one in which he confided to her that
he had found the "most beautiful creature about 16" with
"eyes like a gazelle" digging up a road in London. Firbank
took a taxi each morning at six to "look at it."[2]

Yet Firbank was careful that nothing happen in England to
distress Baba. Certainly his association with Hunter Stagg
amounted to one thing in London and something else in
Paris. Stagg, an American who was literary editor of *The
Reviewer,* was traveling abroad in the summer of 1923 with
his friend Montgomery Evans. Stagg carried with him an introduction to Firbank dated June 24, 1923, on Carl Van
Vechten's visiting card. They met first at the Café Royal,
where Stagg presented the introduction to a "slender creature"
pointed out to him as Firbank. That was on July 13, a Friday.
The next Monday, Stagg stayed up until two in the morning
answering an "intriguing letter" from Firbank. Some time
that week Evans, a young man from New Orleans and a de-
votee of the diabolist, cultist, and charlatan Alistair Crowley,
went to the Continent, while Stagg remained in London until
about July 27. On that day he wrote a letter to Evans saying
that he had dined two times with Firbank. The letter ran in
part, "He [Firbank] came to call!—but all about that you shall
hear later. Now I shall only say that I am still chaste—and
you'd be sure of it without an affadavit if you saw the fantastic
creature!"[3] By the time Evans and Stagg met again in Paris,
the situation had changed. On August 11, Stagg had a note
asking him to "look up" Firbank at his hotel, the Palais d'Or-
say, and Stagg was eager to do so. He confessed to Evans that
he needed money which he hoped to borrow from Firbank

2. Nina Hamnett, Document, London, n.d. (written at request of Richard
Buckle).
3. (Philip Kaplan Collection, University Libraries, Southern Illinois
University).

and that he felt almost as though he would be "willing to allow R. F. certain privileges." Stagg did not know it, but there could be no question of money between him and Firbank any more than there had been between Evan Morgan and Firbank. The charming but "common" boy of the episode at the Eiffel Tower was another matter; class differences were involved. Besides, any attempt to cajole Firbank where money was concerned was risky. It may be that Hunter Stagg's aim was obvious enough to prompt Firbank to take the initiative in Paris and end the "chaste" relationship. They spent at least three nights at Firbank's hotel, they drank a "great deal," Stagg "allowed Firbank's love making to go a great way," and he got no money at all. After their first night together, Stagg was depressed and angry with himself, but he accepted an invitation for dinner which Firbank extended to both Americans the next day. The record of the evening as set down in Montgomery Evans's diary begins,

> To the Palais d'Orsay and after a little wait, Ronald came down, a slender wavering figure with a very sensitive face, a fine sensitive profile, soft deep blue eyes, and fine hands with which he articulated in a feminine fashion, or rather worse. His voice is low, almost a whisper. His ideas are fleeting, contradictory, & impossible to remember. . . . He explained his voice as due to talking to so few people. . . . He liked places out of season, & has had few male friends. I feel that he loves people.[4]

Firbank bought drinks, martinis, and then took his guests by taxi to a restaurant in the rue du Bac, which Evans described as "very seductively decorated" and with an orchestra playing "softly." They had two bottles of Veuve Cliquot with dinner,

4. Diary of Montgomery Evans, August 12, 1923 (Philip Kaplan Collection, University Libraries, Southern Illinois University).

and the host bought cigarettes. Evans "objected in words to the glances" evoked by "Ronald's blubbering gestures." He stated in his diary that he felt sincere pity for Firbank and even more disgust. But Firbank had the last word. He remarked that of his books, only *Santal,* an inferior one in his view, was likely to please Evans. Of course, Firbank had already evaded Stagg's hints for a loan. Yet after dinner, Stagg and Firbank delivered Evans to his hotel and went off together. Two days later, when he had another appointment to meet Firbank, this time at Weber's, Evans "sat and drank bocks for 2 hours, but Ronald did not appear."[5] Firbank's only remark about Stagg in his next letter to Van Vechten was, "I met your friend Hunter both in London & in Paris, & so much liked him."[6]

✤ XI ✤

Firbank had come to Paris en route to Spain in search of his next book. He told his mother, writing from Paris on August 12, that when he returned to England in September he expected to have notes for another novel. Without one on which to work he felt aimless and empty. As he said to his sister later that year, "it is only in forgetting oneself that one can be happy."[1] Besides, since *The Princess Zoubaroff,* he had planned and composed his books outside England. His presence there was not necessary either as far as "Drama in Sun-

5. Ibid., August 15, 1923.
6. RF to CVV, Madrid, August 20, 1923.
1. RF to HF, Rome, December 30, 1923.

light," the West Indian novel, was concerned. Heinemann had decided not to publish, and Firbank had asked Elkin Mathews, the firm which had brought out his first book in 1905, to read this one. They were doing so when he left London about August 10. After a stay of less than a week in Paris, he went to Madrid. That city, "notwithstanding a quite *sweltering* heat," he found once more to be "quite a pleasure."[2] On August 20 he moved on to Seville for a stay of almost three weeks. There, as he had done in Havana, Firbank found a new book.

He enjoyed Seville with its wide boulevards, its fountains sparkling in the soft, flower-filled nights, and its easy acceptance of several cultures. He like the Alcazar with its fine gardens and the unexpected glimpse of a tiled patio in the Barrio de Santa Cruz. He told Van Vechten in a letter written from the Grand Hotel, "Seville, in August, is marvellous, though naturally, an Andalusian summer is far from cool. Beyond the Alcázares, I like best the orange-gardens with their piano organs & the songs à la Raquel Mellar."[3]

Firbank took time from his wandering through Seville on foot or by horse-drawn carriage and his somnolent hours in the orange gardens to attend to his literary life. He learned during his stay in Seville that Elkin Mathews were willing to produce his West Indian novel if he were willing to pay the costs and a commission. They were suggesting an arrangement such as he had had with them in 1905 and with Grant Richards since 1914. Before August 30 Firbank replied to Elkin Mathews, asking for their estimate of costs.

By that date, too, the new novel had started to take form. Earlier that week, on August 26, a Sunday, Firbank wrote to Van Vechten about Seville's Archbishop Ilundain y Esteban:

2. RF to HF, Madrid, August 20, 1923.
3. RF to CVV, Seville, August 26, 1923.

Your Archbishop, dear Carl, lives in a rose colored palace
beneath the Giralda-tower, & a few yards only divides him
from the discreet gardens of the Alcázares, he looks out (if
ever he does look out, for all his sunshutters are drawn, &, in
fact, over *some* of the windows heavy mats of India-matting
are hanging) on to a large, but untidy Patio, full of moaping
palms, & drooping bananas—& such bananas too—that
seem to bitterly resent the Giralda's giddy flights: Needless
to say I have not seen the great man, nor shall I ever, but he
has suggested to my fancy a really amusing book.[4]

The book was to be *Concerning the Eccentricities of Cardinal Pirelli*. By August 30, as he told Baba, he was longing to
commence it; he knew it would take a long time to write.

Firbank did not start to write the new book, however, for
almost three months. He stayed on in the south of Europe
until late September. Early that month he went from Seville to
Lisbon, where he spent some two weeks, stopping at the
Avenida Palace Hotel. In Lisbon he began to formulate still
another novel, an "American novel," which he declared he
"pined" to begin, though he was certain the "Seville Cardinal," the fictitious Prince of the Church conceived in Seville,
would "hold" him longer than he cared to think.[5] He was still
making notes for the Spanish book and allowing it to shape
itself slowly as he lingered in Lisbon. Despite its heat and the

4. The phrase "Your Archbishop, dear Carl" derives from a prank by Van
Vechten which began with one of Firbank's habitual jokes. As he had once
called Evan Morgan "Cardinal Morgan" and even earlier, with R. St.
Clair Talboys, referred to himself as an ambassador, Firbank had played
the game with Van Vechten of being an official of the Church. Van
Vechten carried out the joke by directing a parcel to Firbank under a
church title. After being delivered to the Archbishop's Palace, where the
addressee was unknown, the parcel was returned to Van Vechten. He then
told the story to Firbank, speaking with proprietary interest of the Archbishop of Seville. Cf. CVV to RF, New York, July 4, 1923; RF to CVV,
July 19, 1923. See above, pp. 35, 189.
5. Cf. RF to CVV, Lisbon, September 8, 1923.

fact that, as he told Van Vechten, it "was better in memory," he still found Lisbon "beautiful in its way" and some of its restaurants "delightful."[6]

In the third week of September, Firbank returned to London preparatory to going to Rome for the winter. He intended to collect his warm clothes and make final arrangements with Elkin Mathews before his departure for Italy. This was all taken care of by September 28. On that date he wrote from the Grosvenor Hotel to Van Vechten, commenting on his differences with Richards and recounting how the Society of Authors was attempting to "deal" with him. "The poor man disgorges with quite comic reluctance!" Firbank said. He wrote also about his book "Drama in Sunlight," "You will be amused that I am returning to Elkin Mathews for my new novel—after twenty years it is rhythmic."

Everything was in order for publication when, on October 1, 1923, the day before Firbank's scheduled departure for Rome, a letter dated September 19 came from Van Vechten. The letter began, "It may be possible that I have secured you an American publisher." Stuart Rose, Firbank's first American discoverer, had completed an impulsive enlistment in the Chilean army, returned to New York, and gone to work in a "prominent position" with Brentano's, whom Van Vechten identified as George Bernard Shaw's publisher. Rose and Van Vechten together were responsible for Brentano's willingness to consider Firbank's work; Van Vechten delivered the news. He wrote:

> Hunter Stagg tells me that you and Richards have drifted apart. If this is true and you have not yet made other arrangements, the best plan, as I see it, would be to publish your next book in America instead of England. Your principal

6. Ibid.

sales and your biggest reputation is here. In case you have
made arrangements in England the American publication
should be as nearly simultaneous as possible. Of course, you
will incur no expense, in this, and Brentano's will pay you
good royalties.

As if this offer were not enough, Van Vechten said that if the
book did well Brentano's would bring out Firbank's earlier
novels, and he ended with "Go to it, kid!"

The letter galvanized Firbank. He rushed to Elkin Mathews and succeeded in getting them to return the typescript of
"Drama in Sunlight." He sent it to Rose the same day. Then,
"in agitation & haste," he wrote to Van Vechten, "Dear Carl
what an angel you have always been to me." He continued by
saying how sorry he was that the novel was "not longer
(some 22000 words)," but he assured Van Vechten of its
quality. "It is of my very best," Firbank wrote, "& I rate it
higher than any of the others."[7]

Although American publication was not yet settled and
would not be until November, Firbank's literary life, which in
effect was his whole life, was changed irrevocably. Hence-
forward he was a professional writer occupied with prefaces,
copyrights, and royalties. He was to know for a little while the
sweet taste of success. But like W. H. Auden's mariner watching Icarus fall from the sky, Firbank was now completely
unaware of the momentousness of his American possibilities,
and he sailed serenely on with his plans. The day after all the
activity with his typescript, he left London for Rome.

There, while he anxiously awaited Brentano's decision, he
renewed his acquaintance with Lord Berners, the Sitwells,
Harold Nicolson, and others of what he called "the collony,"
including his old friend Evan Morgan. Nancy Cunard re-

7. RF to CVV, London, October 1, 1923.

membered seeing Morgan in Rome that year, dressed as "some sort of papal chamberlain" in what looked "somewhat like a British Admiral's uniform—the hat particularly."[8] Not only Evan Morgan but the whole group as well fascinated and frustrated Firbank. He belonged with them, and he did not belong. They brought back vividly his anger and pain at Morgan's refusal of the dedication of *The Princess Zoubaroff* and his disillusionment with the Sitwells in Oxford. Indeed he told his mother that Rome might as well be Oxford as far as "the collony go." He listened attentively to the maliciously funny accounts of them which he had daily from the artist Geoffrey Lovelace. Firbank described the whole lot as "jealous and spiteful." He was certain that his satire of the English in *The Flower Beneath the Foot* had not been exaggerated, but he refused none of their invitations.

As might be expected, Firbank "naturally took offence" at them. In this instance, the cause was neither suspicion nor misunderstanding, but a specific event. He told Baba that when he lunched with Berners at his home in Rome, they both "deplored" a plaster cast of a Psyche in one of Berners's sitting rooms. The next day, at another luncheon party, Berners again termed the cast a "horror" and wondered what to do with it. One of the Sitwells promptly suggested, "Send it to Ronald." His letter to Baba reads:

> This amused everybody, & on the broken crown of the Psyche the whole luncheon party autographed their names thus
> "Homage to Ronald Firbank from Berners, Edith Sitwell, Sacheverell Sitwell, Geoffrey Lovelace (the little artist), Aldous Huxley, Harold Nicolson, Vita Sackville-West (his

8. Nancy Cunard to MJB, Lamothe-Fénelon, Lot, July 27, 1963. Evan Morgan was made Privy Chamberlain of the Sword and Cape by Pope Benedict XV and continued in the same office under Pope Pius XI.

wife, the Mrs Chilleywater of 'the Flower'), W. T. Walton
& Evan."9

They then sent the inscribed plaster cast to Firbank. Although
he thought the sight of Berners's butler delivering it in a cab
laughable, Firbank was vexed, and he wrote a tart note to say
so.

Meanwhile he was busy in a number of ways. In a letter of
November 1 to Carl Van Vechten, Firbank noted that there
was still no news from Stuart Rose and Brentano's and reaffirmed his eagerness for a favorable decision. "How delightful," he wrote, "if I can come out with Brentano first; he
seems more cosmopolitan & enterprising than the majority of
our publishers are!" The letter had news of his activities, too.
Firbank was going to Capri for a few days. It was, of course,
the Capri of Norman Douglas's *South Wind,* and Firbank
expected it to be an amusing place. Furthermore, after weeks
of "house-hunting," which left him "too worn out to write,"
he had succeeded in hiring Prince Orsini's flat, complete with
a servant, in the Palazzo Orsini, Via Monte Savello 30, for
the "next half-year."

When Firbank returned from Capri to Rome, it was to that
address, one partially occupying the ancient remains of the
Teatro di Marcello and marked at its entrance by the Orsini
bear. There he had a letter which Van Vechten had written
from New York on October 30, 1923. It told him that Brentano's was sending a contract that same day and before long
the royalty checks which Firbank wanted would "begin to
arrive." They had reached the decision to bring out not only
the West Indian novel (Van Vechten said he thought it one of
Firbank's best) but also several of his other novels already

9. RF to HJGF, October 28, [1923]; cf. RF to HJGF, Rome, October 25,
[1923].

out of print. The letter said, too, that after reading the "delightful opus," Van Vechten had suggested as a title for it "Prancing Nigger," a title which he assured Firbank would "beyond a doubt" sell "at least a thousand more copies." The plan was to produce the book in a format as like the English books as possible with a frontispiece by Robert Locher and an introduction by Van Vechten. Firbank declared the news was "like the 'Announce faite à Marie.'" He declared himself speechless with pleasure and "Prancing Nigger" as a title, "delicious." He told Van Vechten, "It never occurred to me, & any success the novel has will be due to you." The postscript to Firbank's letter read, "I am going round to pray now in the Pantheon."[1] Well he might. American publication, dreamed of at least since 1916, when he watched his proofs of *Odette* blown seaward at Torquay and thought it a good omen for America, was now assured.[2]

That was in mid-November 1923. The next few months Firbank devoted with renewed vigor to his life as an author. By December 1, 1923, he had at last started the book for which he had made notes during the past August and September, the Spanish novel. On that date, in a letter to Van Vechten, Firbank wrote from Rome that he had begun it and said it was "to be called 'Concerning the Eccentricities of Cardinal Pirelli.'" In February he wrote again, "I am still busy with the Spanish novel, alas! it cuts deeper than Chocolate (*which* I abhor)." He was consoled for his lack of progress, however, by the fact that the novel "promised to be really good."[3]

There were still matters to settle with Grant Richards. In January 24, Firbank asked Richards for a statement for the six months ending December 31, 1923. Richards promised to

---

1. RF to CVV, Rome, November 17, 1923.
2. See above, p. 216.
3. RF to CVV, Rome, February 13, 1924.

send it when his accounts had been analyzed, but to the Society of Authors. The month before, December, Firbank had refused Richards's offer to explore again the possibility of American publication for Firbank's books.[4]

To refuse Richards's unwanted and unnecessary help was a satisfaction, but Firbank was puzzled over Brentano's failure to send a contract for *Prancing Nigger*. In December he expressed his concern to Van Vechten and then said that perhaps he was too impatient. Again in February, this time to Stuart Rose, Firbank remarked that he had no contract, but he supposed he would have one soon.

He was less involved with the production of *Prancing Nigger* than he had been with the novels published in England. Brentano's approved Locher's frontispiece and Van Vechten's introduction. Van Vechten read proof (somewhat carelessly). Firbank participated only by hoping that the introduction said nothing "dreadful" about him and that his "somewhat wilful punctuation" had been retained. Indeed, he was so uninformed about the book's progress that he wanted to add a dedication well after it had gone to press.[5] By mid-February 1924, not surprisingly, he sent Van Vechten a "line" to say how much he longed to see the book. It was not ready, however, much before March 15, 1924,[6] and copies were dispatched to Firbank that same month.

4. Cf. GR to RF, London, January 29, 1924, December 21, 1923; GR to Lowell Brentano, London, February 16, 1924.
5. Cf. RF to Stuart Rose, Rome, February 10, 1924; RF to CVV, Rome, December 1, 1923, February 13, 1924.
6. *Prancing Nigger* was first announced in the Boston *Evening Transcript* on March 15, 1924.

☙ XII ❧

Before the books reached Firbank, disaster struck. On March 25, 1924, at Denbigh Cottage, Richmond, Surrey, Baba died. Notified that cancer made her condition hopeless, Firbank rushed from Rome to be at her bedside and to see that she was cremated as she had asked and the ashes, in an earthenware urn, placed with those of her mother and between her "other darlings."[1] Ronald stood at this ceremony on a cold wet day looking so ill that he was admired for his bravery in being there at all. In the previous year he had acknowledged to Heather that, though it was "a good deal in this world of pain & woe" to have no "definite tragedies to face—fear, & pain & sordid horror," he often indulged in synthetic sorrow, the "*happyness* of despair" he called it. That was a parallel to his admission that he made "his own gloom" and could "turn it on anywhere," even in "quite ravishing places."[2] But Baba's death made real his protest that "life at best is an Ordeal." In the midst of his grief and the many duties resulting from his mother's death, he was indignant at the "incredible off-handedness of the relations" and distressed at being barred from a conference between Heather and her solicitor. In a letter written to Van Vechten four days after Baba's death, Firbank tried to relieve his pain at the whole circumstance by disengaging himself and putting it into a literary context. "London is odious and so cold," he wrote, "& full of one's

1. Cf. HJGF to RF, London, March 25, 1913 (Berg).
2. RF to HF, Rome, December 30, 1923; RF to CVV, Rome, September 25, 1924.

relations, who scowl & frown on poor Ronald. He is dreadfully unhappy & depressed & would give worlds to be in Cuna-Cuna by 'the Violet Sea—.' "³ But the "sort of numbness, a comic tollerance" about which he had boasted to Heather in December, did not serve him in March. The loneliness and isolation cultivated for the sake of his work⁴ were now a spiritual separation. He had not, as Jonathan Swift had in the death of his mother, lost the last barrier between himself and death; Ronald Firbank had lost the barrier between himself and life.

Overcome by fear and pain after he returned to Rome in early April, Firbank suffered a psychic and physical collapse. Days of despair followed. He had lapsed into what Evan Morgan named "a sort of melancolia." At first he would see no one, and the only food he had was brought from a little neighborhood restaurant and placed on his doorstep. When darkness came, he went out furtively, snatched in the food, and locked the door behind him. According to Morgan, Ronald was "neither at this moment sure of death as a means of release nor life as a means of enjoyment."⁵ During this period he wrote briefly to assure Heather that she might remain in Denbigh at least for the next year. He managed, too, to thank Van Vechten for his "charming" introduction to *Prancing Nigger* and promised to write about it more fully when he had regained his "leisure mind." Then he began to go frequently with Morgan to the Crypt of St. Peter's, where he spent long hours on his knees.⁶ Gerald Wellesley, Berners, Morgan tried

3. RF to CVV, London, March 29, [1924]. Cf. RF to HF, Rome, [April 23, 1924].
4. Cf. RF to HF, Fiesole, March 13, 1922.
5. Evan Morgan to Richard Buckle, Newport, Monmouthshire, July 25, 1940.
6. Cf. RF to HF, Rome, April 11, [1924]; RF to CVV, Rome, April 16, 1924; Evan Morgan to Richard Buckle, Newport, Monmouthshire, July 25, 1940.

to help him. On April 23, he wrote with bitterness and pride to Heather that he was at last able "to put some perspective between the distressing few weeks" which had passed, especially those in London. He censured her behavior and the "relations," proclaimed his amusement and relief at "everybody's indifference" to him, and ended by saying that the situation in London had nevertheless been distasteful.

Eventually Firbank's conviction delivered him. As late as the end of June, he declared that his laugh, which Augustus John had likened to "a clock suddenly running down" and Sewell Stokes had called the "most wicked laugh in London," was becoming "rarer and rarer."[7] But because Firbank believed firmly that he had an obligation not to "evade life," he began to force himself back into his usual habits. He had calls from Nancy and Victor Cunard; he went to tea with Berners and the Duchess of Sermonetta; and he took an interest in meeting "chez Berners" Prince Phillip of Hesse, just returned from Vienna to Rome—all, as he assured his sister, "delightful people." He started to plan for the coming months, to think of "passing the summer between Naples & Florence & really getting down to the Andalusian romance!"[8] He arranged instead to stay in his flat in the Palazzo Orsini until June 10, with the option on it for the rest of the summer, though he feared it might be too hot for writing.

7. Cf. RF to Sewell Stokes, Rome, June 22, 1924; Stokes: "A Recent Genius," *Pilloried!*, p. 223.
8. RF to CVV, Rome, April 16, 1924; cf. RF to HF, Rome, July 19, 1924, [April 23, 1924]; Lord Berners to RF, Rome, n.d. (MJB).

❧ XIII ❧

It was the writing which revitalized Firbank. Some time in late April he heard from Van Vechten that the first impression (he called it an edition), 3,000 copies, of *Prancing Nigger* was almost exhausted and a second impression being printed. Firbank had made polite remarks about the book, but he had been so upset by the undue number of printer's errors in *Prancing Nigger,* which he said its "rather common" dust jacket did not help, that he had not sent out his usual gift copies. Now he quickly corrected the text of the book and posted it to Stuart Rose, hoping to avoid the same errors in the new printing.[1] The corrections failed to reach New York in time, but the fact that the book had "caught on" helped him to face his grief. As he said to Heather, his success would have "delighted" Baba. To hear of the sales was personally gratifying and, as Van Vechten put it, to be "so much more famous in America," a country he had never visited, than in England was highly amusing. Firbank read with satisfaction reviews written by such critics as Joseph Wood Krutch, Ben Ray Redman, Herschel Brickell, and Edmund Wilson. Only one, the Brooklyn *Eagle*'s, seriously disturbed him. It read, "Silly. Bevo-naughtiness. Highly praised by Carl Van Vechten." Firbank told Van Vechten, "I would not for the world that you should suffer annoyance atall through me." He went on to question Van Vechten about the *Eagle*'s "rough and

1. Cf. CVV to RF, New York, April [1924]; RF to HF, Rome, July 10, 1924; RF to Stuart Rose, Rome, May 17, 1924.

crude style of criticism" and then explained that while he might "thrive on 'Yayhs!'" it became "unpleasant when one is not alone. And that is just the point."[2] But the other reviews considered *Prancing Nigger* seriously and nearly all were excellent. They quite justified what Ronald had told his sister in late April, when he told her also that his unfinished book was "under offer" in America: "It is all very encouraging, & something to live for; which after all is the great thing—an object."[3]

Firbank had much cause for literary contentment and more than one object in the next few months. In May he had several rewarding offers. The London office of Brentano's solicited *Prancing Nigger* for English publication, and Brentano's, New York, activated their plan to publish an American edition of Firbank's works. Albert and Charles Boni also offered to bring out an American edition, but Firbank decided to continue with Brentano's. "One publisher," he said, was "better than gadding, as Saint Theresa did."[4] He quickly suggested that Brentano's have the "English handling" of all his books. Meanwhile he approved Brentano's proposal to commence the American edition of his novels with *The Flower Beneath the Foot,* since the English stock was so depleted that there need be "no anxiety," he was certain, "of its springing up, unseasonably, like wild flowers after rain."[5] He also agreed to write a preface. By July 10, 1924, he had posted to Stuart Rose proofs read but never used for the English edition and the Nevinson drawing, which had ornamented the dust jacket, for reproduction as frontispiece "as it was originally

2. RF to CVV, Rome, May 22, 1924. Cf. CVV to RF, New York, April [1924]; RF to HF, Rome, [April 23, 1924].
3. RF to HF, Rome, [April 23, 1924].
4. RF to CVV, Rome, May 26, [1924]. Cf. RF to HF, Rome, April 27, 1924; RF to Stuart Rose, Rome, May 17, 1924; Stuart Rose to RF, New York, May 3, 1924 (private collection).
5. RF to CVV, Rome, May 26, [1924].

intended to be." In the same mail Firbank sent the preface; he had tried to make it "as logical & simple as possible" so as to explain his "methods such as they are." Although he said it might be omitted if Rose or Van Vechten thought it too "temperamental," he believed the preface must "help the book enormously by removing the prejudice" about his "supposed depravity & lack of design."[6] A few days later Firbank asked Rose to change one word of the preface, "fabric," to "evolve," explaining that in Rome's July weather "le mot juste" came "reluctantly—if atall!"[7] During this time Firbank also completed arrangements with Brentano's, London, to publish *Prancing Nigger* in a limited edition under an earlier title, "Sorrow in Sunlight." He wrote apologetically to Van Vechten on June 27, 1924, about changing the title Van Vechten had given the American edition: "In England people love the sun since they so seldom see it." Firbank went on to say that Nevinson would design the wrapper, though, since he never left Hampstead, Firbank doubted that the artist could tell an elm tree from a palm.

To give his success tangible form, he received his first check from Brentano's on July 13, 1924. Firbank thanked Rose at once and later wrote to tell Van Vechten how delighted he was with Brentano's generosity. "As you know," Firbank wrote, "with the St Martin Street edition there was not much 'swanny cloak' for the author! And not a quill (of any moult) was ever shed for me!"[8] When Firbank had Brentano's accounts in October showing $695 or about £150

6. RF to Stuart Rose, Rome, n.d. In a letter to HF dated July 10, 1924, RF wrote, "I have just got off the preface for the New York version of The Flower beneth the Foot." Cf. RF to Stuart Rose, Rome, May 17, 1924.
7. RF to Stuart Rose, Rome, [July 13, 1924].
8. RF to CVV, Rome, September 25, 1924. Cf. RF to Stuart Rose, Rome, [July 13, 1924].

earned on *Prancing Nigger,* he concluded that at last "the ball" was "set rolling."[9]

All these things, as he himself said, were "most inspiriting after so long," and he took wry satisfaction in being "unobtainable" except by way of New York just as the London public was "rallying." But they came too late for real enjoyment. In June, Philip Moeller, armed with Van Vechten's note which identified him as "one of the first dramatists" and the author of *Madame Sand,* knocked on Firbank's door, up two flights of stairs in the Palazzo Orsini. Moeller's report of the visit, addressed to Van Vechten, is made up about equally of preconceptions and observation. It runs in part:

> I have never seen anyone seem to droop so in fifteen different ways and still stay standing. He said you had been so charming. I told him you were a sort of high priest of the cult and he squirmed like a very sly lizard, in a sort of oncoming and, at the same time, reticent delight. He graciously asked me to dine with him to-night. Of course, I was delighted, and begged him to work out whether or no the mood was really auspicious. . . . I understood that maybe the moment wasn't a very blessed one. . . . when he gurgled in a syncopation of tiny gasps that it was "all perfectly wonderful." . . .
>
> And then, with a glance of despair about him, he suddenly ejaculated:
>
> "But there aren't any flowers! None! None! Perhaps it doesn't matter. . . . It's all too dreadful! Nothing matters. . . . Yes, it will be charming to-night. Where shall we go? . . . To-night then."
>
> Then I said again:
>
> "I shall be delighted." . . .

9. RF to HF, Rome, October 3, 1924.

He seems to be delightful, but my only impression so far is that if he suddenly stood still, I don't think he would be there.[1]

They dined together, or at least Moeller dined and Firbank ate peaches and drank a "bottle or two" of champagne; and at the end of the month Firbank thanked Van Vechten for sending Moeller to call. But he wrote to his sister about Moeller, "I feel alarmed by his sudden advent into my life & of these new friends that my books are bringing me. I feel often far too tired & their sympathy comes too late to make a *personal* success of my literary one—!"[2]

Firbank's fatigue indicated that his health was declining rapidly. Maurice Sandoz, who first saw Firbank at about this time, was shocked by his emaciated face and reminded by his thinness once of an animated silhouette and then of the leather figures manipulated in Javanese shadow theaters. Even his walk, disjointed and jumpy and jerky, was upsetting.[3] It was partly his exhaustion which kept Firbank in Rome. Although its narrow streets seemed "meant for summer," he was unenthusiastic about remaining there. Yet, going from city to city on the Continent, as he had done only a year earlier, appeared burdensome, and London, "oppressive" on the one hand and "like a constant bank-holiday" on the other.

Now he went only from flat to flat. As he had once written to Baba about the possibilities of Paris and Palermo, he now wrote to Heather about the flats available to him: a very spacious one in the Palazzo Orsini which Prince Orsini occupied and which he suggested they share, "shutting off half of it"; a

1. Quoted in Fletcher: *Ronald Firbank A Memoir,* pp. 82–4; cf. CVV to RF, New York, May 19, 1924.
2. RF to HF, Rome, June 6, 1924; cf. RF to CVV, Rome, June 27, 1924.
3. Cf. Maurice Sandoz: "Ronald Firbank," *The Crystal Salt Cellar* (London, 1954), pp. 78–88.

charming flat in the Piazza di Spagna owned by an attaché of the French embassy; and a large apartment in the Palazzo Antici Mattei at 4 Piazza Paganica, near the famous "tortoise fountain." He chose that one, and on June 10, moved from the Palazzo Orsini to the Palazzo Antici Mattei.

The flat had several disadvantages. Firbank described it as "a jumble of magnificence & poverty, & with 'reception rooms' thirty feet high! which would suit my book on Spain, although I shrink from the gloom & sadness."[4] He lived there with a servant who, it was understood, was to prepare his meals and "do" his rooms without ever being visible to him. That arrangement did not always work, since he often complained that the servant "worried & annoyed him." Another problem at the Palazzo Mattei, according to Mr. Sandoz, was a single goldfish which "resembled a carrot in a jar of pickles." When Sandoz called on Firbank at the Palazzo Mattei, Firbank talked about the expense of feeding the fish. It refused to eat anything except real pearls; even artificial ones it spat out. Sandoz says that at the end of his visit, as he took his leave, he slipped on something round and hard which lay on the floor near the fishbowl. It proved to be an artificial pearl.[5]

Still, the flat was a "divine setting" for his own Cardinal Pirelli, a fact so advantageous that when he told Van Vechten about being "chez the Cardinal Mattei," Firbank added, "Please God I do not do something very wicked!"[6] Since commencing it some time before December 1923, Firbank had worked at his novel throughout his stay in Rome. He mentioned it often and reported on its progress to his friends in America and to his sister. On May 17, in response to Stuart

4. RF to HF, Rome, June 16, 1924.
5. Cf. RF to HF, Rome, June 6, 1924, August 19, 1924; Nancy Cunard to MJB, London, January 3, 1954; RF to Sewell Stokes, Rome, June 22, 1924; Sandoz: "Ronald Firbank," *The Crystal Salt Cellar*, pp. 83–5.
6. RF to CVV, Rome, June 27, 1924.

Rose's inquiry about publishing the "new novel about Spain" in New York, Firbank wrote that it might be finished toward the end of that year, 1924. He explained, "It will be very short & very elabourate & condensed." On May 26 Firbank wrote to Van Vechten that the novel moved "but slowly though unruffled & surely." In early June he told Heather that he hoped to have finished his book by November; and on July 10 he said he had four chapters still to write, that each usually required a month. But the heat of Rome was so intense that the composition of his novel, he said, needed determination. By July 19 the weather had got worse, and he was unable to continue. In mid-August he managed some work, though he looked forward wearily to the time when his book would be done and he might be released from a daily routine. At the end of August a "quite terrific thunder storm burst over Rome" and many windows in the flat were "blown to by the wind so violently that they were shattered into the street."[7] Although the "tension in the air" had given him neuralgia, the heat then subsided and he could resume work once more; he decided to stay in Rome at least another month. At the end of September he still hoped to complete the book in November, when he might "fly to Egypt for a little or follow the sun somewhere until the Spring again."[8] But he had not completed the book by mid-November; on the sixteenth of the month, after Lord Berners and Victor Cunard had come to tea, he wrote to Heather that now he intended to "settle down & see nobody" until the book was finished.

Tea with Berners and Cunard was not the only interruption. Neither were dinners with them nor a chat with Evan Morgan, encountered "dressed as a priest & with a paper bag

7. RF to HF, Rome, August 28, 1924; cf. RF to HF, Rome, August 19, 1924.
8. RF to CVV, Rome, September 25, 1924.

containing he said his lunch"; nor the crowded jubilee cele-
brations inaugurated by the Pope at Christmas that year with
"very fine music" and St. Peter's, "a most magnificent sight."[9]
He gave much attention to Heather. He wrote long letters to
her in an attempt to help her decide on a satisfactory way of
life now that she no longer had Baba as an excuse or a reason
for evading life. That he could not spend the winter with her
in the English climate Ronald made quite clear. He patiently
discussed the relative merits of Heather's taking rooms at a
farm at £4 4s. a week and "vegetating," going to live with a
Mrs. Hardcastle, or joining the Fräulein of her childhood,
now in Russia, where he feared so much "would jar." He
urged Heather to travel, however, warning her against the
effect of solitude if she stayed alone at Denbigh Cottage. He
suggested that when his book was done they might spend together a few months' holiday which he proposed to "take from
books." There are so many lovely places, he assured her,
where they might live quietly at little cost in winter. He reminded Heather that he had been twenty years among
"strangers" and that with a little self-control and a few
friends, he preferred living abroad to living in England.
"There is much more to be got from life abroad," Ronald told
her, "than in England on a little money."[1] When Heather
insisted on remaining in England at Denbigh Cottage, Firbank offered to meet at least half "the rates & taxes," and
possibly all. But he pointed out that Heather could hardly
afford to waste her youth any longer if she wanted to make
anything of it. "Drifting, if you can bear it & are resigned," he
told her, "is probably less painful than grappling with the
cruelty of the world, but I do not think we are here to drift";

9. RF to HF, Rome, November 7, 1924, December 28, 1924.
1. RF to HF, Rome, July 30, 1924. Cf. RF to HF, June 6, 1924, July 19,
1924, August 11, 1924.

and he pleaded with her to "form" her own ambitions.[2] He
was preaching to Heather the moral determination which produced his novels.

His own and Heather's problems, apart from her indecisive-
ness, were compounded by two facts. The ninety-nine-year
lease on Denbigh Cottage for which Firbank had contracted
was not yet entirely paid for, and most of the furnishings
of the house, Baba's property, had to be sold in order to
meet two legacies, one to Lady Firbank's maid Hallett and the
other to her grandson Tommy. The prospect of the sale disturbed Ronald. "It will be really wonderful," he wrote to
Heather, "if out of all the contents of Coopers & particularly
of the aftermath—Curzon Street, there remains a chair &
table. On reflection it is not atall astonishing for Baba was the
soul of generosity." More distressing to him than the disap-
pearance of the beautiful things he was accustomed to and
loved was his conviction that such a sale was not "darling
Baba's intention."[3] She had told him she had set aside £200 to
take care of her bequests and had even offered to lend it to
him so that he could pay the art dealer Colnaghi for a canvas
by the English painter John Downing purchased in 1922 or
1923. But he could do nothing to settle Baba's affairs or
Heather's except write letters to the solicitor Emory and await
replies until Knight Frank & Rutley's probate was accepted.[4]

Other interruptions to the composition of *Cardinal Pirelli*
were literary; as Firbank wrote from Rome in late August, he
had more "literary work" than he could manage. Proofs of
Sorrow in Sunlight occupied him in late August. On the
twenty-seventh of that month he also received a copy of Van
Vechten's *The Tattooed Countess* for review. That Firbank

2. RF to HF, Rome, July 19, 1924.
3. RF to HF, Rome, November 9, 1924; cf. RF to HF, Rome, January 16,
1925.
4. Cf. RF to HF, Rome, July 10 and 19, 1924.

wrote the review is unlikely; if he did, where it was published is unknown. He had a letter dated October 3 from Stuart Rose asking permission to dramatize *Prancing Nigger*. Rose and Thurston Macaulay, who was connected with New York's Cherry Lane Theatre, had elaborate plans for a comedy adaptation in ten scenes with music by George Gershwin and a mobile stage set designed by Mordecai Gorelik. It was to be called "A Jazz Fantasy." Apparently the time was propitious for such an enterprise. Van Vechten himself thought of writing a "serious jazz opera, without spoken dialogue, all for Negroes" with music by Gershwin.[5] Nevertheless, nothing came of Macaulay's and Rose's treatment of *Prancing Nigger* after both Philip Moeller and William Brady decided that production would be too costly. But Firbank authorized the dramatization and followed its progress with interest, even sending a message to Gershwin by way of Rose and declaring that the staging of the piece would be an excuse for him to visit New York.[6] In November Firbank had a letter from Montgomery Evans (Hunter Stagg's former traveling companion), then in Prague, asking permission for Emerick Reeck of Frankfurt, who sometimes published under the pseudonym Hyazinth Lehmann, to translate *Prancing Nigger* into German. Firbank gave permission at once, but nothing came of that either.[7]

No later than the fifteenth of November, Firbank had word of the publication of the American edition of *The Flower Beneath the Foot* with his preface. He had not seen a copy of

5. CVV to Hugh Walpole, New York, October 18, 1924 (The New York Public Library).
6. Cf. RF to HF, Rome, August 27, 1924, September 9, 1924; RF to Stuart Rose, Rome, December 16, 1924, March 13, 1925; Stuart Rose to RF, New York, October 3, 1924 (whereabouts unknown); New York *Telegram*, February 6, 1925.
7. Cf. Montgomery Evans to RF, Prague, October 30, 1924 (private collection); Max Niedermayer to MJB, Wiesbaden, 1962.

the book or read a review by mid-December, but remember-
ing the Brooklyn *Eagle*'s critique of *Prancing Nigger,* Firbank
was nervous about *The Flower*'s reception and fearful in the
midst of his success that it might cause unpleasantness to the
"champion" of his books, Van Vechten. To him Firbank
wrote from Rome on December 16, 1924, "There are sure to
be hoots, but in Italy I shall not hear them! Dear Carl I owe
you endless things & my distress would be acute if arrows
meant for me went astray— . . . I am dead & indifferent for
myself & abuse amuses me & stimulates me." He then promised to send his photograph "as San Sebastian, all darts, &
reading the Brooklyn *Eagle*." Even at the very peak of his
success, distrust and anxiety had their "sovran shrine." Furthermore, he was upset by the printer's errors in *The Flower*
when he got a copy early in 1925. He was even more unhappy
with the publication of *Sorrow in Sunlight,* which appeared in
England in the latter part of November. Because Brentano's,
London, failed to publicize the book, Firbank talked about
their "gauche mishandling" of it and the "furtive way" in
which it had come out.[8]

Meanwhile Firbank had moved once more, an event which
meant real interruption of his work. Knowing that his rental
of the flat in the Palazzo Mattei was due to terminate October
10, he thought from time to time of going to Florence to write
the last chapter of *The Cardinal* or to Rapallo and staying
there until spring. But as he told Nancy Cunard, "a fatigue
had set in against travelling." He extended his lease at the
Palazzo Mattei at a higher cost for another month, that is,
until November 10. Before that date Berners, who was leaving Italy for England, offered his residence to Firbank; but
because the offer involved keeping on Berners's butler, Fir-

8. RF to CVV, London, May 23, 1925; cf. RF to Stuart Rose, Rome,
February 16, 1925.

bank refused. After much "house-hunting," in which he had help from Berners, Firbank moved with his own servant into "a cupboard of a flat" on the fifth floor of 36 via Porta Pinciana. At the gate of the Villa Borghese and the Pincio— what Firbank called "the nicest & most brilliant part" of the city, as well as "the healthiest & highest part . . . —as also the most fashionable"—it overlooked the park and all Rome. He described his "too divine" view to Heather: "I see from here to the mountains round Tivoli above the parasol pine-trees in the Borghese gardens, & St Peters & the whole of Rome are at my feet!"⁹ The only drawback to this fifth-floor flat (it had a lift), apart from the weekly rental of £10 10s., was a lack of fireplaces. There was central heating, but all the rooms, with their stone floors, were cold; that was especially true of the study.

Firbank followed Nancy Cunard's practice of wearing two dressing gowns at the same time, and in that flat he completed *Concerning the Eccentricities of Cardinal Pirelli*. As he had told Heather he would, he settled down to the novel within a week of moving to the Pincio. Thus he was ready to begin the last chapter shortly before December 16, 1924. He wrote to Rose on that day to say that he had started the final part and to describe the novel again as "very 'elabourate' " and much more complex than *Prancing Nigger*. He also told Van Vechten on the sixteenth that "Enfantments of Cardinals are slower than Niggers," but he expected to be free "to 'enjoy' the world again" in a few weeks. Not until February 4, 1925, however, could he say to Heather, "I am glad to tell you that my book is finished at last."

In Firbank's mind there was no problem about the publi-

9. RF to HF, Rome, November 16, 1924. Cf. RF to HF, Rome, August 11, [1924], October 3, 1924, November 7, [1924]; RF to CVV, Rome, December 16, 1924; Nancy Cunard to RF, Paris, [1925] (MJB).

cation of *Cardinal Pirelli*. He thought that Brentano's, New York, would bring it out, at least in America. He had been encouraged to think so in a number of letters from both Rose and Van Vechten. Two weeks after it was completed, he promised to send it to Rose from London when it was typed.[1] As for the English publication, that must wait until he returned to England and could attend to it. Once, when younger and less ill, he would have rushed away from Rome almost the minute he wrote the final word of his book. Now he did no more than decide that he would not allow *Cardinal Pirelli* to come out with the London branch of Brentano's; *Sorrow in Sunlight* had not been advertised adequately. "It allows the author no fun!" he explained. "I adore annoying my relations, & miss [their] rude remarks."[2]

Even with *Cardinal Pirelli* finished and its publication in America a matter of course as far as Firbank knew, his enjoyment of the world was meager. In April he was happy to welcome Berners back to Rome and to anticipate Nancy Cunard's arrival and a quiet dinner with her. But the amount of work on hand left little time for pleasure. Even the "American novel," first conceived in Lisbon in the autumn of 1923,[3] had to wait until he had satisfied other commitments. Well before *Cardinal Pirelli* was completed he had agreed to provide a preface for Brentano's next reprint of one of his novels, this time *Caprice*.[4] As soon as the Spanish book was done, he had got at the preface and on February 16, 1925, posted it to Rose with the admonition that he must not "feel constrained to use it." His next task was the revision of *Vainglory*, also for Brentano's, New York. His practice in revising,

1. Cf. RF to Stuart Rose, Rome, February 16, 1925.
2. RF to CVV, London, May 23, 1925.
3. See above, p. 246.
4. Cf. RF to HF, Rome, April 17, 1925, February 4, 1925; RF to Stuart Rose, Rome, December 16, 1924.

as it had been in 1916 with *Odette*,[5] was to mark changes directly in a copy of the book, in this case one bound especially for him in white vellum with gilt lettering. In this revision he saw an opportunity to retaliate for all the fancied wrongs done him by the Sitwells, especially Sacheverell. Throughout his copy of *Vainglory* Ronald changed the first name of the futile poet, the character called Winsome Brookes (patterned on Rupert Brooke), to Sacheverell. Firbank eventually reconsidered, and to emphasize that he did not want the change wrote on the end paper of his work copy, "N.B. 'Sacheverell' = retain 'winsome' throughout—Retain name Winsome NOT Sacheverell as alternate."[6] All other changes, largely verbal and often unimportant, were kept. These were extensive enough to occupy Firbank until March 13, 1925, when, still in Rome, he wrote to Rose that *Vainglory* was "revised & greatly improved." At once he began to compose a new version of the fourth chapter of the second part of *Inclinations,* the "dinner party" chapter which had displeased him since he had hurried with the book in January 1916.[7]

During much of the time he was engaged with these literary matters, Firbank was also engaged in a quarrel with Heather. It arose, possibly justifiably, from his irritation at his sister's helplessness and extravagance, but he persisted in it with cruel determination. In October 1924 he had assisted her in the payment of an overdue bill of £40 owed to her dressmaker, Lucile. He had allowed her to remain at Denbigh Cottage after Baba's death although the cottage which he had leased for Baba was not fully paid for and he had no intention of completing the payments for Heather's benefit. But there

5. See above, p. 148.
6. The revised copy is the property of Donald G. Wing.
7. See above, pp. 145–6.

Heather stayed with two servants while she considered various possibilities, and he urged economy on her and insisted that it could be practiced better by living outside England. After nearly a year of this, Ronald's patience was exhausted. In the same letter announcing that he had finished *Cardinal Pirelli*, he wrote to Heather:

> Now as you do not seem to be able to live economically at Denbigh Cottage (You are living at present there at the rate of more than £1000 a year, has it occurred to you?) I feel hardly encouraged to postpone the letting, or the selling of it another year, which I should be obliged to do if I let the Spring & Summer pass now. Even if you could manage to run it efficiently on your Annuity, which should go towards "Jones" the greengrocer as well as to "Lucile" the dressmaker —it seems a little *stupid* to *have* to point out! ! ?

He continued with an account of his plan to replace the valuable furniture by "a few pounds outlay at Maples & Harrods," to turn the place into an "artist cottage," and to let it "modern furnished on 'spec.' " He promised he would not put the cottage in the hands of an agent until after Easter, which fell on April 12 that year.[8] Instead of a reply from Heather, Firbank had a letter from her maid Hallett (once Baba's maid) telling how "worried & distressed" Heather was "at having to leave the Cottage & not knowing what to do for the best." Hallett's letter went on,

> I think, Sir, if I may say so, you should return & help her to make some sort of plan; she is far from strong & suffers every few weeks internally so much that she is absolutely obliged to rest in bed—& she is not able to turn out of Denbigh Cottage unless there is a fixed plan to go on— . . . I do hope Sir, you will try & help her."

8. RF to HF, Rome, February 4, 1925.

Hallett then apologized for writing. She had given up domestic service a few days before, but after fifteen years with the Firbanks she felt she could not "leave Miss Heather" without asking Ronald to "return to London & try & comfort her a little."⁹ Ronald thanked Hallett for her letter, stated that he expected to remain in Italy until the winter was over, and wished her well in her "new life." The same day he wrote an equally noncommittal letter to Heather. In March he wrote again, saying, "Your year to make plans at Denbigh Cottage has caused me *many* reflexions . . . 'Your letters are all omissions'! As Mrs Malaprop says."¹

Without waiting for his Easter deadline, Heather moved out of Denbigh Cottage after notifying her brother by cable a week before she left. She went to her London club, the Ladies Carlton Club, and promptly regretted her action. On April 13, 1925, she wrote to Ronald, "I am very sorry that in a moment of temper, owing to your letter which you should never have written to me I left the cottage." She spoke of her small income and the high cost of living; she said that unless she went "far away, to some isolated place" she knew of no "decent flat," however small, "under 6 or 7 g^s a week." She asked to hire Denbigh Cottage at £100 a year, unfurnished, "plus rates & taxes." Heather closed her letter by saying, "That such misunderstandings should come ever between us is too sad, & if not too late!—let us forgive and forget—Will you?"² Firbank's answer is dated April 17, 1925. He declared that he was astonished that Heather had found anything in his letters "to take umbrage at." From his expensive and very fashionable flat in Rome he talked of his distaste for

9. A. E. Hallett to RF, Kington Magna, Gillingham, Dorset, February 16, 1925 (Berg).
1. RF to HF, Rome, [March 1925]. Cf. RF to HF, Rome, February 23, 1925; RF to A. E. Hallett, Rome, February 23, 1925 (Berg).
2. HF to RF, London, April 13, [1925] (Berg).

hotel and club life and of how his books were marred by the
"constant annoyance" of such life. He remarked that England
was much too costly. His implication was that if he could
sacrifice his novels for the sake of the economy of living out
of England, she should be willing to sacrifice her preference
for living in it, especially now that, judging by the papers,
England was becoming more and more odious. He urged her,
"Find a friend with whom you have things in common &
travel, as people do, & will do, & have always done even on
moderate incomes such as ours." Then he informed Heather
that he preferred to "let the cottage to one outside the family
or even sell it altogether." This time Heather wrote in desperation, unable to believe he was insensible to her "extremely
difficult position." She said that she had "no other alternative
than to beg" for his help "& without delay." Because she
could stay at her club only two weeks and because she was
"feeling desperate & ill—with no roof" over her head, she had
taken a flat, "or rather attic," for six months at 21 Davies
Street, Berkeley Square, at "6½ gˢ a week" and paid three
months' rent in advance. It was more than she could afford,
and, hoping to sublet the flat, she asked again to return to
Denbigh Cottage. She wrote, "My health seems broken and
because of that, even were I financially able—to travel as you
suggest is absolutely out of the question. What I need is *rest*—
mental & physical after the incessant strain & grief I have
gone through." She begged his forgiveness for her having left
the cottage and asked him to reflect that it was his "only
sister" asking for the "favour" of being allowed to go back.
"It is not a question of the family—," Heather wrote, "but
merely one between an only brother & an only sister. Besides,
for Baba's dear memory, don't refuse me."[3] Ronald ignored
her appeal. He was adamant until the next month, after his

3. HF to RF, London, April 22, [1925].

return to England. Then he and Heather met in the offices of the solicitors Field Roscoe, mingled their tears and their kisses, and were friends once more.

Perhaps Heather learned economy. Some years later, when she stayed at a hotel in Hove where the rate included meals, she invariably ordered two chickens or two steaks so as to have one for herself and one for her chauffeur, with whom she dined in her hotel apartment. Since only one is usually provided under such a hotel arrangement, the management naturally protested, and that attempt to save came to an end. When her chauffeur ran her car into a ditch and Heather's arm was broken in the accident, she gave him £100 and sent him off, thereby ending an intimacy of several years' duration. That was more than likely an economical move too; he pleaded earnestly with her to take him back, saying he had counted on her support in his old age.[4] In her own old age Heather began to hoard bank notes, placing them between the leaves of periodicals stacked in her rooms. In this way she accumulated a large sum, which was found after her death in the 1950's. In 1925, however, Ronald saw her need and agreed to help her financially; but he sold Denbigh Cottage.[5]

XIV

Firbank's return to England was made at the end of April, before he had completed the "dinner party" chapter for *Inclinations*. He went back to London, where he took a flat at 78

4. Numerous letters from her chauffeur to Heather Firbank have disappeared. They were once among her effects.
5. RF to HF, Arcachon, August 25, 1925.

Brook Street and attempted to pick up his usual London life.
Most of his friends were scattered, married, settled down, and
busy with everyday affairs. In June, Vyvyan Holland made an
effort to re-establish their old friendship. He wrote a note
asking Firbank to visit him at his flat in Sloane Square. "I
have got so many things I want to show you, and so many
things to talk over," Holland wrote. "I really *do* want to see
you. I haven't seen you since October 24, 1918; and as I don't
keep a diary I think my memory should touch you."[1] They
met and talked, but without satisfaction; the years had taken
them in dissimilar ways. Firbank, of course, frequented the
Café Royal and the Eiffel Tower Restaurant. Hunter Stagg,
again in Europe, saw him there. In a letter written from London on July 19, 1925, he described the "Eiffel Tower group"
to Montgomery Evans as "Greenwich Villagy" and named in
it Thomas Earp ("several cuts above the others"), Robert
McAlmon, Sisley Huddleston, a Paris correspondent for the
Times, and the artist Nevinson. Stagg added, "At the Tower,
too, by the way, I saw Ronald . . . and reacted differently. I
don't know if I can bear seeing him again. However I shall
try; maybe it was because he was very drunk."[2]

Firbank was often drunk, and he was very ill. His cough
was deep and rasping, and he breathed with difficulty. Consul-
tation with a doctor, Edward P. Furber of Welbeck Street,
Cavendish Square, made clear that his lungs were seriously
affected. According to one report, Furber's pronouncement
was so disquieting that Firbank, after hearing it, got drunk
enough to cry aloud in the midst of the dubious gaiety of the
Café Royal, "I don't want to die!"[3]

No doubt this confrontation with death accounts for the use

1. (Fales).
2. (Philip Kaplan Collection, University Libraries, Southern Illinois University).
3. Fletcher: *Ronald Firbank A Memoir,* p. 85.

of two absurdly youthful portraits as illustrations for *Concern-ing the Eccentricities of Cardinal Pirelli*. To arrange for the novel's English publication was one reason for Firbank's stay in London that summer. He had hardly posted the typescript to Rose for American production when he decided that he "might do worse than *return*" to Grant Richards for the English edi-tion.[4] First, Firbank called on Richards in his office in St. Martin's Street. Then, on May 27, 1925, he sent as a gift to Richards copies of *Sorrow in Sunlight* and the American edi-tion of *The Flower Beneath the Foot;* with these books went the typescript of *Cardinal Pirelli*. Two days later, in response to the author's request for an immediate decision, Richards accepted the book, and he and Firbank entered into a con-tract. Firbank agreed to pay the cost of producing an edition of one thousand copies plus 25 per cent and to accept pro-ceeds of sales less 15 per cent. At Firbank's suggestion, Rich-ards asked William Rothenstein to design a frontispiece. When Rothenstein refused the commission on the grounds of his "ripe years," a portrait drawn by John in 1915 was repro-duced for the frontispiece and one made by Charles Shannon still earlier was used on the dust jacket. Death haunted neither portrait; in them Firbank had his youth again. And the entire transaction called back happier times. Although no date for publication was named, the book progressed well, with com-plete proofs in Firbank's hands by June 29. These he read and returned to Richards in July.[5]

Perhaps a week before he received the last proofs, perhaps on June 22, 1925, Firbank learned that Brentano's, New York, would not publish *Cardinal Pirelli*. He did not mention this rejection to Grant Richards then or later. In answer to

4. RF to CVV, London, May 23, 1925.
5. Cf. RF to GR, London, May 27, 1925; Cairo, November 22, 1925; RF to CVV, London, June 22, 1925; GR to RF, London, May 27 and 29, 1925, June 29, 1925; GR: *Author Hunting*, pp. 205–6.

Richards's question as to when the American edition was "likely to appear," a question put in August with the intent of bringing out the English one first, Firbank said only, "There is no *immediate* American edition."[6] But in a letter dated June 22, 1925, he told Van Vechten that the book had "shocked" Brentano's. Indeed, their decision had been based on "religious and moral grounds." The firm feared that the "outspokenness of the book regarding the life of the Cardinal and particularly church matters" would alienate its bookstore clientele.[7]

Yet, a judgment of Ronald Firbank's ability as a writer must rest on *The Flower Beneath the Foot, Prancing Nigger,* and above all on *The Eccentricities of Cardinal Pirelli.* This statement does not ignore the decline in power which would be sadly apparent in his last book, *The New Rythum.*[8] There is little in that, an incomplete work with parts still in the author's notebooks, to compare with his three most polished novels. Of these three, and indeed of all Firbank's novels, *Cardinal Pirelli* is the capstone. In its way it is a masterpiece of morality and technique.

It is a temptation to look on the book as autobiography and to believe that Firbank intended for himself the epitaph which he wrote for Pirelli:

> Now that the ache of life, with its fevers, passions, doubts, its routine, vulgarity, and boredom was over, his serene, unclouded face was a marvelment to behold. Very great distinction and sweetness was visible there, together with much nobility, and love, all magnified and commingled.[9]

6. RF to GR, Arcachon, August 22, 1925. Cf. GR to RF, London, August 20, 1925.
7. C. J. Herold to RF, New York, June 18, 1925 (present whereabouts unknown).
8. See below, pp. 289–90.
9. *Concerning the Eccentricities of Cardinal Pirelli* (London, 1926), pp. 149–50.

Firbank, like Pirelli, regarded the onslaught of age as a threat. Also like Pirelli, the child was an examplar of the unattainable to Firbank. He had told Baba after a visit in 1920 to Cézanne's studio that he had seen there a drawing of a child to whom he could pray.[1] The poet Walter Lowenfels has talked of *Leaves of Grass* as an attempt by Walt Whitman to put himself "freely, fully, and truly on record," not so much as he was but as he wanted to appear.[2] In his compulsion to seem wicked, a feeling which recurred throughout his life, might not Firbank have presented in Pirelli a perverse apotheosis of himself and then, as he was almost ready to do with his own artificial temperament, stripped the Cardinal of his gaudy trappings?

Although the book carries Firbank's deepest and most mature convictions, it is in fact a wholly imaginative creation inspirited by the "rose colored palace" of the Archbishop of Seville and the "giddy flight" of the "Giralda-tower."[3] *Cardinal Pirelli* has no story. Indeed, it has only two pieces of action. The book opens before the baptismal font as Pirelli in the full panoply of his office is administering the sacrament to a puppy, a young police dog named Crack. It ends when the naked Cardinal, on the night before his departure for Rome and the Pope's discipline as a consequence of the baptism, falls dead chasing the boy Chicklet around the great empty Cathedral of Clemenza, the "Cage of God."

These two actions are not elements of a plot in the sense of cause and effect. Having no plot, Firbank could keep time sequence to a minimum and organize his book spatially. That is, a series of set-pieces, of cinematic frames, effects the novel's progress. The spatial concept is emphasized by frag-

1. Cf. RF to HJGF, Aix-en-Provence, September 6, 1920.
2. Cf. Walter Lowenfels to MJB, Peekskill, New York, July 17, 1967. The quotation is from Whitman's preface of 1888.
3. See above, p. 246.

mented dialogue, so that everything, as Flaubert said it
should, seems to sound at the same time. Typically, Firbank
found a party suitable for such framing. *Vainglory, Caprice,
Valmouth,* and *Prancing Nigger* have parties. In *Cardinal
Pirelli* there is the "Tertulia (that mutual exchange of familiar
or intellectual ideas)" at Dun Eden Palace, "an evening . . .
in honor of the convalescence of several great ladies, from an
attack of 'Boheara,' the new and fashionable epidemic." The
Cardinal, "like a red geranium," is present, "surrendering his
hand with suave dignity" to the lips of young men "all
mouchoir and waist."[4]

Compositions in which the Cardinal appears alternate
loosely with those in which he does not. The first piece of
action, the baptism of the dog Crack, occurs within a portrait
of clergy and fashionable society before the font. Another is
the celebration "with considerable fanfaronade and social
eclat" of " 'Foundation' Day" at the College of Noble Damo-
sels in the Calle Santa Fe.[5] But the essential vignettes are two
of the cathedral sacristy, which is described as "quite the live-
liest spot in the city" after "the tobacco-factory and the
railway-station":

> In the interim of an Office it would be besieged by the laity,
> often to the point of scrimmage: aristocrats and mendicants,
> relatives of acolytes—each had some truck or other in the
> long lofty room. Here the secretary of the chapter . . . might
> be consulted gratis, preferably before the supreme heat of
> the day. . . . He was, with tactful courtesy, at the disposal of
> anyone soliciting information as to "vacant dates," or
> "hours available," for some impromptu function. Indul-

4. *Cardinal Pirelli,* pp. 49–62. Cf. *Vainglory* (London, 1915), pp. 18–48
and 154–75; *Caprice,* pp. 75–86 and 111–17; *Valmouth,* pp. 127–56;
Prancing Nigger (New York, 1924), pp. 23–31 and 91–106.
5. *Cardinal Pirelli,* pp. 75–90; cf. pp. 7–14.

gences, novenas, terms for special masses—with flowers and
music? Or just plain; the expense, it varied![6]

From this description Firbank developed two broad, teem-
ing scenes. The first occurs on "the morning of the Feast of
San Antolin of Panticosa" with many waiting at the secre-
tarial bureau and outside the vestry door, where "aficionados
of the cult liked best to foregather." There Doña Consolacion,
the laundress of the basilica, and Tomas, the beadle, discuss
her "knack" with a "frilly" and her temperament. They are
silenced by the entry from the vestry of a file of monsignori;
and the silence, in turn, is broken by the sound of "passing
mule bells along the street." Meanwhile the celebrant of a
maiden mass in his first cope is showing his tonsure to his
brothers and sisters. When his grandmother, "moved to tears
and laughter," declares he will be a Pope one day, Mother
Garcia of the Company of Jesus, who has "looked in" with a
bouquet of sunflowers and a basket of eggs from market, dis-
agrees. " 'Not he, the big, burly bull,' " she says with a "melli-
fluent chuckle." Mother Garcia, the laundress, and the beadle
then remark on the element of luck in careers until they see
coming from the muniment room the "sleek silhouette" of a
Monsignor known not to be "averse to a little stimulant in the
bright middle of the morning." Doña Consolacion turns her
head as she murmurs, " 'He has the evil Eye, dear . . . !' "
Then, as the maiden mass gets under way, the women vanish
from the sacristy. The secretary, at his bureau, "without the
presence of *las mujeres,*" finds the atmosphere a little heavy.
But since it is a day of obligation, "a fair sprinkling of boys,
youthful chapter hands," whom he sometimes calls the "lesser
delights," relieve the place of its "austerity." A request for
permission to view the orangery in the cloisters interrupts his

6. Pp. 26–7.

"siestose fancies" briefly. And all the while the boys await
their participation in a service. The second scene also begins
with the secretary of the chapter, Don Moscosco, "seated before his usual bureau" and at the "disposal of the public" on
another feast day, that of St. Firmin. The sacristy, "thronged
with mantons and monsignori," resembles a "vast shifting
parterre of garden flowers." for Don Moscosco " 'business'
indeed had seldom been livelier"; under enormous pressure he
goes on with his plans for various masses of intent, assessing
their value and adding five per cent where they seem less than
chaste.[7] These carefully composed and varnished pictures
degrade an institution of idealism. The Church here is not a
metaphysical concept, and the money-changer is an official of
the temple.

All the vignettes of *Cardinal Pirelli,* taken together, create
a pattern of reflexive meaning. It is as though Firbank shifted
a lens from group to group so as to fix attention on no one
group but on their total relationships and, by association, on
the age-old values which they travesty. The characters, their
movement, and the implications of their circumstances are
fused for expressiveness. However restless and energetic in
movement these scenes may be (though lacking in the skeletal
action of fiction), they convey, as Pound said of an image,
"an intellectual and emotional complex in an instant of time."

This method had been fully developed by the time Firbank
wrote *Valmouth,* published in 1919. *Valmouth* also contains
the two main conventions of Firbank's literary maturity. The
ideal of his novels is his concept of the spirit of Christ; the
struggle in them is one between the world and the spirit. In
Valmouth, for the first time, Firbank evaluated the Church as
simply one more of man's delusions and relegated it to the
world. *The Flower Beneath the Foot* developed that state-

7. Pp. 26–39 and 115–29.

ment with thematic and technical brilliance. But in *Valmouth* Firbank suggested the conflict also in terms of the "civil-savage" and its resolution in the simple life. This was a thesis with which he had experimented as early as 1906 in "The Wavering Disciple" and which he brought to literary perfection in *Prancing Nigger*. With sure judgment Firbank chose the first and more profound of these conventions for *Concerning the Eccentricities of Cardinal Pirelli*.

The two views of the sacristy, giving, as Ford Madox Ford said of his own work, not facts but what Firbank saw to be "the spirit of an age, of a town, of a movement," provide a fitting environment for Cardinal Pirelli. He trembles on the threshold of tragedy in his self-knowledge and incapacity to serve God as man or priest. As he paces "a cloistered walk, laden with the odour of sun-tired flowers" in a twilight "planned for wooing, unbending, consent," Pirelli muses:

> Morality. Poise! For without temperance and equilibrium —— The Cardinal halted.
>
> But in the shifting underlight about him the flushed camellias and the sweet night-jasmines suggested none; neither did the shape of a garden-Eros pointing radiantly the dusk.
>
> "For unless we have balance—" the Cardinal murmured, distraught, admiring against the elusive nuances of the afterglow the cupid's voluptuous hams.
>
> It was against these, once, in a tempestuous mood that his mistress had smashed her fansticks.[8]

Pirelli is not deceived. He knows that moderation is a virtue, but it contradicts the lush beauty and temptation of the world, especially in the hot glory of summer. And the Church's authority is flawed, unreliable.

The tension in the character of the Cardinal is most clearly

8. Pp. 16–17.

disclosed by his own introspection. Repeatedly his thoughts stray from his hunger for God to his hunger for the world, and often he is incapable of distinguishing between the two. No sooner has he prayed for moral poise, "balance," than he begins to rationalize his eagerness to escape the cathedral close even though to do so he is "obliged to stoop to creep":

> With the Pirelli pride, with resourceful intimacy he communed with his heart: deception is a humiliation; but humiliation is a Virtue—a Cardinal, like myself, and one of the delicate violets of our Lady's crown. . . . Incontestably, too, . . . many a prod to a discourse, many a sapient thrust, delivered *ex cathedra,* amid the broken sobs of either sex, had been inspired, before now, by what prurient persons might term, perhaps, a "frolic."[9]

As he wanders about his garden toward the close of day and looks at the "blessed basilicas" visible in the distance, he asks himself, "All, was it vanity? Those pointing stars and spectral leaning towers, this mitre, this jewelled ring, these trembling hands, these sweet reflected colours, white of daffodil and golden rose. All, was it vanity?"[1] And again, as he sits at his dinner served by the boy Chicklet, Pirelli deliberates whether a "lad of such alertness might be entrusted to give him a henna shampoo." His thoughts go on:

> It was easy enough to remove the towels before it got too red. The difficulty was to apply the henna; evenly everywhere; fair play all round; no favouring the right side more than the left, but golden Justice for each grey hair. Impartiality: proportion! Fatal otherwise![2]

9. Pp. 21–2.
1. P. 103.
2. Pp. 108–9.

At times he enjoys undefiled worldliness, as when, after a young man has kissed his hand, he tells himself how delicate is the savor of "these kisses of young men, ravished from greedy Royalty."³ But usually his thoughts fuse and blend the spirit with the flesh, making no distinction between them. It is only after filling his glass seven or eight times that he sees the "radiant spirit" of Saint Theresa, who walks in search of a part of the manuscript of her *Way of Perfection*, and he entreats her with "wistful ecstasy," " 'Teach me, oh, teach me, dear Mother, the Way of Perfection.' "⁴ Even as he stands ready to rouse the sleeping Chicklet, that "age of bloom and fleeting folly," and thus set in motion the last mad chase in the cathedral, Pirelli prays, " 'Lead us not into temptation.' "⁵

The wild pursuit of the child again mingles contrary desires or, in Firbank's phrase, the concrete and the ideal—qualities, he said, "not inseldom found combined in fairy childhood."⁶ This longing for the simplicity and innocence of the child was a romantic aspect of the 1920's. On one level it showed itself in women's fashions (baby-doll shoes, boyish haircuts, and short skirts), Mary Pickford's golden curls, and popular songs with lyrics which simulated childish vocables, such as "Boop Oop a Doop." On another level it implied a reluctance to confront the knowledge of good and evil which the post-war, so-called lost generation had learned at a terrible cost. Long before the twenties, Firbank had glorified the innocence of childhood in *Odette* and repeated it in 1921 with *Santal*. The boy of *Cardinal Pirelli*, however, is remote from the youthful searcher for Allah in *Santal* and the little Odette, whose purity transcends evil and despair. Indeed, the boy of *Cardinal Pirelli* is a denial of the immaculate spirit in children; there is

3. P. 59.
4. P. 114.
5. P. 139.
6. P. 147.

an ambiguity in this child, Chicklet, and the pursuit of him which coincides with Pirelli's moral incompetence. The boy's flight from the Cardinal is more tantalizing than sincere, and his innocence is sadly imperfect. He hesitates once in his wild scamper to ask Pirelli:

> "You'd do the handsome by me, sir; you'd not be mean? . . . The Fathers only give us texts; you'd be surprised, your Greatness, at the stinginess of some! . . . You'd run to something better, sir: you'd give me something more substantial?"[7]

As for the Cardinal, his chasing the boy is contradictory on every side. He has come seeking Chicklet in the cathedral to lighten a punishment imposed, Pirelli suddenly realizes, in the cruelty of love. His pursuit of this child is the final impotence of morality. For all his prayers, Pirelli cannot turn from temptation; and his desire to capture and possess the doubtful purity of the boy has violation as its aim.

Literally, the chase ends at dawn, when Cardinal Pirelli, his heart "in painful riot," falls dead before a painting which exhibits "the splendour of Christ's martyrdom." Having shed his crimson mantle, he lies "dispossessed" of everything except his mitre, "nude and elementary . . . as Adam himself." Expressively, the chase ends when his flight from maturity, a transgression against order, brings Pirelli to his death. Then, freed from the world's systems of which the Church is one, he lies exposed, helpless, a man with God's hand—the mitre—on his brow.

7. P. 146.

y, de Max, Jean Pozzi, Landsberg, others—were either dead
engrossed with their own affairs; some had gone elsewhere.
[e had a more recent friend there, however, in Francis
leming-Jones. Her "malade," her "poor David Sears," had died
1923, and she lived alone at 9 rue Henri-Heine. After their
[r]st acquaintance at Versailles in 1921, she and Ronald had
aintained a desultory correspondence. Then, partly because
[sh]e was older than he, he had told her about his responsibili-
[tie]s and worries after his mother's death. In gratitude for the
[sy]mpathy with which she responded, he had chosen a rug
[fro]m his mother's effects and given it to her. Now he had a
[fe]w hours with Miss Fleming-Jones at 9 rue Henri-Heine, in-
[sp]ected the rug, and talked about his literary hopes and dis-
[ap]pointments. Of his health, he made light, saying only that
[a] doctor had advised a week's complete rest.[3] In Paris,
[ne]vertheless, the full impact of his physician's prognosis be-
[ca]me clear. Walking in the street in Montparnasse Firbank
[su]ddenly encountered Nancy Cunard and together they went
[to] the Dôme, where they had a "long and very peaceful talk."
[Na]ncy remembered it:

How consecutive he was. A new personality was revealed . . .
Thinking of it a little later, that talk seemed to me as good
[a]nd long and all-of-a piece as if we had been walking together in some fine, fresh place—perhaps over the great cliff
[s]cenery around Varengeville or Berneval in Normandy on
[e]ither side of Dieppe. . . . The effect of his conversation was
[a]s stimulating as the wind over the rough cliff-grass, with the
[s]pray at the rocks below and a few gulls on the wind. It
[s]howed me the vitality of his being beneath all the "fantasia-
[f]antasia."

[3]. Francis X. Fleming-Jones to RF, Bessinger-Cologny, Switzerland,
[Dece]mber 5, 1924; Paris, March 29, 1925, May 21, 1925 (MJB).

❧ XV ❧

Brentano's refusal of *Cardinal Pirelli* as
prognosis added urgency to Firbank's eff
English edition of his complete works.
Brentano's to bring out his books, revi
now *Cardinal Pirelli* was rejected, and
late May that Brentano's would not "go
He was very disappointed after "hustli
but he was also concerned about his
since Stuart Rose had left Brentano
Vechten, "Rose is a great loss to me, &
my old age on whom to depend!" H
bling"; because of it Van Vechten migh
ter Savage Landor,' or some old hack
theless, Firbank continued to talk abou
intention to try Chatto & Windus or H
of his works. In fact he approached G
gested an edition partly underwritten
tiations with Chapman had failed to
clusion by early August when Fir
Arcachon in the Gironde.

En route Firbank stopped a day
love among all cities (except perhaps
believe). There, as in London, his ol

1. RF to CVV, London, May 23, 1925.
2. Cf. Guy Chapman to RF, London, June
unknown).

Because Firbank was silent as usual about what concerned him most, Nancy was unable to account for what seemed to be the revelation of another personality. She wondered whether the "gratuitous-sounding link between him and the conversation-walk may have been inspired by wishful thinking." She knew, however, that "something concrete about his personality came into being that day: he could never be 'the legend' "[4] to her any more. Appropriately enough, in Paris, where he had so carefully created his artificial temperament, it was plain that at last he was stripped of it.

Going on to Arcachon, he took rooms at the Villa Primrose, boulevard de la Plage. In Arcachon he appeared to spend his days much as usual. Almost immediately after his arrival, at Richards's request, Firbank considered the proposal of the bookseller William Jackson that a large paper edition of 250 signed copies of *Cardinal Pirelli* be produced as well as the ordinary edition. Firbank was ready to agree on condition that Jackson and other booksellers guarantee to him £50 and ten free copies. "I cannot," Firbank declared, "go to the fatigue in August . . . of signing my name 250 times for Nothing."[5] The project was abandoned. At the end of the year he informed Jackson that it was too difficult "to arrange satisfactorily from abroad," and he offered to sign an ordinary copy when it appeared.[6] Some time in September, he planned once more for a translation of his novels into German. Francis Fleming-Jones, on a visit to Berlin, had interested Dr. Max Meyerfeld, translator of several English authors, including Oscar Wilde, George Moore, and John Galsworthy. Meyerfeld proposed to translate a number of Firbank's books, start-

4. Cunard: "Thoughts About Ronald Firbank," p. 5 (MJB).
5. RF to GR, Arcachon, August 15, 1925; cf. GR to RF, London, August 5 and 20, 1925.
6. RF to William Jackson, Cairo, December 27, 1925 (The Lilly Library, Indiana University).

ing with *Valmouth*. The idea was congenial to Firbank, and Miss Fleming-Jones was "pleased & flattered at having been the means of putting" the two men "in touch."[7] Meyerfeld's translation was never published.

Otherwise Firbank was occupied with completing and revising *The Artificial Princess*. He had found it, still called "Salomé Or 'Tis A Pity That She Would," with a number of his early pieces preserved by Baba when he had sorted her papers in June. He had reread these juvenile compositions, marking most of those unpublished but already typed "Not to be published RF."[8] Only two seemed to have possibilities. One was "Lady Appledore's Mésalliance," and on it he wrote "? Revise considerably in places—If—";[9] the other was *The Artificial Princess*. He wrote Van Vechten about all these works; beginning with "Lila" composed in 1896, Firbank listed fifteen titles, and for those few already published, their places of publication. He was "delighted," he said, with the "short novel (unfinished) The Artificial Princess" and assured Van Vechten that he, too, would like it "better than anything else" Firbank had done.[1] When he wrote that letter in London, he had already sent the manuscript to be typed, and by July he started to revise, lettering the new name on the typescript and making notes for the last chapter. He wrote part of it, and that too he revised and had typed and sent to him in Arcachon. There he finished *The Artificial Princess*, started in 1906 and tried again in 1910. His intention was to publish it; he promised Van Vechten a copy as soon as it appeared.[2]

7. Francis X. Fleming-Jones to RF, Berlin, September 30, 1925 (MJB). See above, p. 265.
8. Cf. MJB: *Bibliography of Ronald Firbank*, Ts 2, 3, *et passim*.
9. P. [i] of the typescript (MJB).
1. RF to CVV, London, June 22, 1925.
2. Cf. RF to CVV, Arcachon, September 11, 1925.

Firbank did little else at Arcachon. "Arcachon," he told Van Vechten, "is nice & restful, & I go gliding about the sea all day in a motor-launch, with my grey hair streaming."[3] He was even too indolent to respond with much enthusiasm to Nevinson's report that Stella Benson admired him.[4] His only activity besides the work on *The Artificial Princess* was to make a few notes for the "New York novel," which he planned to write next; some of these, phrases having to do with a character called Mrs. Rosemerchant, are scrawled across the pages of the unfinished foreword for *The Artificial Princess*. He also wrote to Heather assuring her: "Do remember always I am anxious for your success & happiness & to be of use."[5] Once more he suggested travel to Heather—Egypt, Switzerland, the Riviera, other places *"far* less expensive than England with the present excellent exchange." He talked of various journeys he himself might make, including one to New York. That city had almost replaced Vienna in his imagination. But his doctor had suggested Egypt or Davos in Switzerland for his lungs, and by the end of September, finding Arcachon "triste," he was anticipating his departure.[6]

In October he went by way of Marseille to Cairo. There, on November 1, 1925, as he wrote to Grant Richards, he "began a new novel—on New York!" Six weeks later he described his work in more detail to Carl Van Vechten, referring to some version of the book which never materialized:

I have just started my American novel with New York & Palm Beach for setting. I pitch a parasol, & a little French writing table (that opens & closes, the darling) every morning in the Libyan-desert, & sit & picture it all in the mirage

3. Ibid.
4. C. R. W. Nevinson to RF, London, September 17, 1925 (MJB).
5. RF to HF, Arcachon, August 25, 1925.
6. RF to HF, Arcachon, September 26, 1925.

—so beautiful & poetic it seems sometimes: I begin to love
it—especially Harlem. I am evolving a divine negress—Aunt
Andromeda & her friend—M[rs] Storykoff, married to a Pole
who runs a dope-den off Gramercy Park.[7]

Although he had caught a cold by that time, a real threat in
his precarious state of health, he was gay and happy in Egypt.
Helen Carew remarked on his having said so in November.
He wrote cheerful, nonsensical letters to Van Vechten:

It seems "queer," for a single soul like me, to be writing,
on a clear moonlit night, to an *inconnu* away in the far
Americas—I hope you will not find me fast?? I am a *spinster*
sir, & by God's grace, intend to stay so; I have just been
exploring the hotel-library (antiquated some) & left behind
(I should say) by Napoleon, after the battle of the Pyramids.[8]

At Christmas he had greetings from his friends, among them
Charles and Kathleen Nevinson in London and Miss Fleming-
Jones in Paris. As the winter months advanced, Firbank left
Shepheard's Hotel for the environs of Cairo, going first to the
Mena House, The Pyramids, and settling eventually at the
Grand Hotel in Helouan. In February he told Heather about
"being occupied as usual writing" and about having "spent
the whole of winter in the country villages in the desert
around Cairo which are rather attractive & so restful."[9] That
month he wrote to his London doctor, Furber, to inquire
about the efficacy of injections in his case;[1] but he felt well
enough, as he had not in the previous winter, to think of going

7. RF to CVV, Cairo, December 17, 1925.
8. Ibid.
9. RF to HF, Helouan, February 17, 1926.
1. Cf. Edward P. Furber to RF, London, February 19, 1926 (Fales).

"towards Easter to Sicily & probably before leaving Egypt, to Palestine, which is lovely with wild flowers in March." He had no immediate plans to go back to England until spring, but he offered to do so if Heather wanted him. He told her he would "return to it yet awhile for no other reason!"[2]

His tone now with Heather was gentle. The reconciliation in London had been sincere. "I hope," he wrote to her, "you are happy well & as unworried as one can be in the age we live."[3] Egypt's sunshine filled his letters, and he regarded both his sister and everything about him with the tenderness of a man about to lose what he valued.

There was even satisfaction in preparing for the inevitable loss. From Egypt, Firbank completed arrangements which assured a collected edition of his novels. By a deed of trust dated April 23, 1926, he empowered the Society of Authors to apply £1,000, which he paid to the Society, and the interest on that sum toward publication of a new edition of his works "in the event of the death of the author within five years" from the date of the agreement. The deed provided for investment of the £1,000 in British government securities. However macabre such an arrangement might be, it was a realistic action which to Firbank avenged his mortality. He was happy with what he had done.

The only real strain in this euphoric period was the fact that Grant Richards kept delaying the publication of *Concerning the Eccentricities of Cardinal Pirelli*. On November 1, 1925, Firbank inquired whether the book was out and his three copies on their way to him. The packers, porters, and binders associated with the book trade were on strike; thus the book trade had come to a halt. Firbank then decided that he preferred to hold the book until 1926 unless it "could come out *at once*

2. RF to HF, Helouan, February 17, 1926.
3. Ibid.

with a '26' impress."[4] When the strike was ended in December, Firbank suggested rushing five hundred copies to be "ready by New Year's day suitably dated."[5] Then he heard from Helen Carew that Richards personally, not his firm, was being put into bankruptcy, and Firbank concluded that his book would appear as soon as Richards could "snatch a calm hour from the Bailiffs to attend to the Cardinal."[6] But nothing happened. After repeated letters and telegrams, which elicited no word from Richards, Firbank threatened in March to put the matter in "other hands." Then Richards promised to have the book out in April; but he still allowed production to lag until it was made impossible once more by the General Strike, which began on May 3, 1926.[7] There the situation stood when Firbank went to Rome in mid-May.

Firbank's plan was to engage a flat before going to England. After a visit in London, he would then return to occupy the flat in Rome. Because he was there for a short stay, he took a room at the Hotel Quirinale. The despair and uncertainty which had haunted him the year before in Rome were not now apparent. He had faced his mother's death. His health was poorer and he coughed constantly, but he joked about it. He told Victor Cunard that he had invented a new disease for Pirelli, "Boheara," and then caught it himself. He was eager for companionship and readily went with Lord Berners on a motor excursion to Lake Nemi. Berners described him "ambling down the precipitous streets of Genzano followed by a crowd of children" shouting after him the name of an Italian comic film character, Ridolini. Firbank stopped

4. RF to GR, Cairo, November 22, 1925. Cf. GR to RF, London, November 12, 1925.
5. RF to GR, Cairo, December 10, 1925.
6. RF to CVV, Cairo, December 17, 1925. Cf. Helen Carew to RF, London, November 22, 1925 (Fales).
7. Cf. RF to GR, Helouan, January 16, 1926, February 20, 1926, March 26, 1926, April 22, 1926; GR to RF, London, April 6, 1926, May 12, 1926.

from time to time and scattered "handfuls of nickel coins," a proceeding which excited the children still more and enlarged their numbers.[8]

That was the last meeting between Berners and Firbank. Late one evening a few days after this outing, the Hotel Quirinale called Berners on the telephone to say that Firbank was very ill with pneumonia and wanted to see him. He promptly got in touch with the doctor in attendance, a Dr. Green, with offices at 20 Piazza di Spagna. The doctor was reassuring. Firbank had refused to go into a nursing home and had agreed to have a nurse only that day, but he was so much better that the nurse had been dismissed for the night. Berners decided to wait until morning before visiting Firbank. That was on Friday, May 21, 1926. Before midnight, Ronald Firbank was dead.

8. Lord Berners: "Ronald Firbank," in Ifan Kyrle Fletcher: *Ronald Firbank A Memoir* (London, 1930), p. 148. Cf. Nancy Cunard to MJB, London, January 3, 1954.

❧ *Afterword* ❧

I

Ronald Firbank lies in Campo Verano beneath a stone marked by a simple cross and this legend:

R I P

PRAY FOR THE SOUL OF

ARTHUR ANNESLEY RONALD

FIRBANK

WHO ENTERED INTO REST

ON 21ST MAY 1926

FAR AWAY FROM HIS COUNTRY

His way there, after his death, was marked by confusion and mistakes which no one would have laughed at more gleefully than Firbank himself.

His death occurred at the beginning of a Bank Holiday, that British institution which shuts every shop and office and sends a great part of the population into a weekend's merry-making or retirement or both. Notifying anyone—his solicitors or his sister—was uncertain and slow in those circumstances. There was more delay because Firbank's passport showed St. Julian's, Newport, Monmouthshire, as his place of permanent residence. Finally, late on Saturday, May 22, the solicitors Field Roscoe & Co. learned of the death by a telegram from the British consulate in Rome, and some time later in the evening they managed to talk on the telephone with Heather, who was in Hove, Sussex. Surprised at her brother's sudden death and forced into an immediate decision, Heather instructed only that Ronald be buried "suitably" in Rome. In sending that message to the British consulate, a message which was also delayed unaccountably for several days, Field Roscoe contributed the information that Firbank was "Church of England."[1]

No priest came forward to say that he had given Firbank the last rites or to claim him for the Church. Because Firbank had asked his hotel on the night of his death to summon Berners, Berners was asked to help the British consulate make arrangements for Firbank's funeral. He, too, assumed that Firbank was a member of the Church of England, a Protestant, and he decided that Firbank would be pleased to "lie in the shade of the Pyramid of Cestius, in the company of Keats and Shelley." And so, more than ten days after his death, on the morning of June 1, 1926, "an early summer morning under a cloudless Italian sky, amid the cypresses and roses and the singing of the nightingales," with the Reverend Lonsdale Ragg, Chaplain of All Saints Anglican Church in the via del Babuino, officiating, funeral services were held for Ronald Firbank at the Protestant cemetery at Testaccio.[2] Pending the purchase of a grave and in accordance with Italian regulations, Firbank's body in its "double shell casket" with silk lining,

---

1. Cf. Field Roscoe & Co. to HF, London, May 25, 1926 (Beinecke Rare Book and Manuscript Library, Yale University).
2. Lord Berners: "Ronald Firbank" in Fletcher: *Ronald Firbank A Memoir*, p. 149; Livio Jannattoni: "La Tomba di Arthur Annesley Ronald Firbank," *English Miscellany, III* (1952), 282; cf. Lord Berners to Jocelyn Brooke, Berkshire, November 19, 1948 (Berg).

brass handles, and hand-engraved plate was placed in a temporary vault.

The consulate, in a letter signed "B. Sullivan H. B. M. Consul," duly reported these facts to Field Roscoe the next day.[3] They in turn, through the solicitors Nicholl Manisty & Co., reported them to Heather, and she discovered what she considered an error in her brother's interment. It had taken place in a Protestant cemetery, and as a Catholic he belonged in a Catholic cemetery. With the help of her solicitors and the superintendent of Rome's foreign cemeteries, Marcello P. Piermattei, Heather arranged for Firbank's remains to be transferred to the Municipal Catholic Cemetery at Verano, near St. Laurent's "fuori le Mura." Unfortunately, even as late as mid-August, no graves for one person were available for purchase at Campo Verano. On that date Piermattei stated that a number of such niches would be ready for sale in a new section of the cemetery before the end of September and that he had applied for one. The new section was being opened by the Roman authorities at Piermattei's suggestion for the burial of foreign Catholics. Thus, in late September, with the assistance of the Rector of San Silvestro in Capite and the Cappucini of the cemetery, Ronald Firbank was at last laid to rest at Campo Verano and to his memory was placed the stone which is now defaced by weather and time.[4]

A more durable memorial to Ronald Firbank exists, after all, in an Anglican church, the parish church of St. Julian's Vicarage in Newport. Firbank had given the site of the church and provided for a "life-size" crucifix to be placed high on

3. (Beinecke Rare Book and Manuscript Library, Yale University).
4. Cf. Marcello P. Piermattei to Field Roscoe & Co., Rome, July 3, 1926; Marcello P. Piermattei to Nicholl Manisty & Co., Rome, July 3, 1926, August 13, 1926 (Beinecke Rare Book and Manuscript Library, Yale University); Jannattoni: "La Tomba di Arthur Annesley Ronald Firbank," pp. 282–3.

the outside east wall and below it a stone with an inscription commemorating the deaths of Sir Thomas and Lady Firbank. When the church was consecrated on September 23, 1926, the foundation stone also bore a memorial to Ronald Firbank, who is named as the "Donor of the site of this Church."[5]

Firbank had hardly been laid to rest and the stones set up in his memory when a rumor was circulated that he was not dead, that he was "wandering round and observing in remote countries."[6] Newspapers carried columns which tried to make a mystery of his death and succeeded only in being farcical. The New York *Evening Post*, for example, had a story signed by Milton Mackaye in its October 8, 1926, issue with headlines which read, "Firbank, Sophisticates' Idol, Dead? or Alive and Well? Evening Post Learns Proof of Writer's Death is Lacking—Manuscripts Missing, No Trace of Body, and Publishers are Baffled." The following day the *Post* pretended to have solved the mystery it had created with another thoroughly inaccurate story about Firbank's death and his unfinished work.

II

The *Evening Post's* reference, of course, is to the "New York novel." Called *The New Rythum,* it was the one unfinished work which Firbank left. There are, however, a number of his works, including what there is of *The New Rythum,* which have been published for the first time since his death. The most recent are "*The Wind & The Roses*" and *Far Away;*

5. Cf. J. A. Callestt to HF, Newport, Monmouthshire, June 5, 1926 (whereabouts unknown); A. J. Adams to MJB, Newport, Monmouthshire, June 8, 1967.
6. Sitwell: "Ronald Firbank," *Noble Essences,* p. 88.

these were brought out privately, one in 1965 and the other in 1966.[7] In 1962 "Lady Appledore's Mésalliance" appeared in the summer number of *Cornhill Magazine*.[8] It received book publication later that year, when it was included in the volume containing the fragment of *The New Rythum*, a reprint of *A Study in Temperament*, and extracts from most of his unpublished early pieces, under the title *The New Rythum and Other Pieces*.[9] Firbank might very likely have said of the contents of this book, as he did of *Prancing Nigger* when he found it filled with typographical errors, that it made "one shy."[1] *The Artificial Princess* appeared in 1934, sponsored by his old friend Coleridge Kennard. Firbank would have approved; he had prepared it for publication.[2] Indeed, it is one of the two posthumous publications which are fully warranted. The other is *Concerning the Eccentricities of Cardinal Pirelli*. Firbank had been dead almost six weeks when Grant Richards at last issued the book on June 29, 1926.

III

In these and in his other works is Firbank's most durable monument. Walter Lowenfels spoke from the knowledge of a lifetime devoted to the craft of writing when he said about Ronald Firbank, "What counts in a writer is what he made of his own life in his books. All the rest is humanity's endless story."[3]

7. See above, pp. 34, 53.
8. Pp. [329]–425.
9. Cf. MJB: *Bibliography of Ronald Firbank*, A19.
1. RF to Sewell Stokes, Rome, June 22, 1924.
2. See above, p. 288.
3. Walter Lowenfels to MJB, Peekskill, New York, June 21, 1967.

✲ Bibliography ✲

Appended here is a list in chronological order of Ronald Firbank's printed works. Full bibliographical description of all those which appeared before 1963 except "An Early Flemish Painter" is available in my book *A Bibliography of Ronald Firbank*, published in 1963 in the Soho series by Rupert Hart-Davis Ltd., London.

1898 c.	"The Fairies Wood"
1904	"La Princesse aux Soleils Romance Parlée"
1905	"Harmonie"
1905	*Odette D'Antrevernes and A Study in Temperament*
1905	"Souvenir d'Automne"
1906	" 'The Wavering Disciple.' A Fantasia"
1907	"An Early Flemish Painter"
1907	"A Study in Opal"
1915	*Vainglory*
1916	*Inclinations*
1916	*Odette A Fairy Tale for Weary People*
1917	*Caprice*
1919	"Fantasia for Orchestra in F Sharp Minor"
1919	*Valmouth*
1920	*The Princess Zoubaroff*
1921	*Santal*
1923	*The Flower Beneath the Foot*

1923   "A Broken Orchid (From Sorrow in Sunlight)"
1924   *Prancing Nigger*
1924   *Sorrow in Sunlight*
1926   *Concerning the Eccentricities of Cardinal Pirelli*
1934   *The Artificial Princess*
1934   *A Letter from Arthur Ronald Firbank to Madame Albani . . .*
1962   "Lady Appledore's Mésalliance"
1962   *The New Rythum and Other Pieces*
1965   *"The Wind & The Roses"*
1966   *Far Away*

Of the original editions of Ronald Firbank's works, only *The New Rythum and Other Pieces*, published in Great Britain by Gerald Duckworth & Co. Ltd. and in the United States by New Directions, is still in print. A number of his works have been republished and are currently available. In Great Britain, Duckworth has issued an illustrated edition of *Valmouth* (1956) and *The Complete Ronald Firbank* (1961), which lacks the juvenilia. Penguin Book No. 1570 (1961) is a reprint of *Valmouth, Prancing Nigger,* and *Concerning the Eccentricities of Cardinal Pirelli.* In the United States, New Directions has in print two volumes of Firbank's novels. One is *Three Novels* (1951), called *Three More Novels* on the dust jacket and in advertisements; it contains reissues of *Vainglory, Inclinations,* and *Caprice.* The other is *Two Novels* (1962), New Directions Paperbook 128, which contains reissues of *The Flower Beneath the Foot* and *Prancing Nigger.*

❧ Index ❧

A Note About the Author

Miriam J. Benkovitz is Professor of English Literature at Skidmore College, Saratoga Springs, New York. She was born in Chattanooga, Tennessee, in 1911, received a B.A. degree at Vanderbilt University, an M.A. at George Peabody College, and both an M.A. and a Ph.D. at Yale University. Editor of Fanny Burney's *Edwy and Elgiva* (Hamden, Connecticut, 1957), she has contributed essays to various journals and to *Nancy Cunard: Brave Poet, Indomitable Rebel* (Philadelphia, 1968). She wrote the "Chronology" in *Two Novels* by Ronald Firbank (New York, 1962) and is the author, also, of *The Bibliography of Ronald Firbank* (London, 1963).

A Note on the Type

The text of this book was set on the Linotype in Fairfield, a type face designed by the distinguished American artist and engraver Rudolph Ruzicka. This type displays the sober and sane qualities of a master craftsman whose talent has long been dedicated to clarity. Rudolph Ruzicka was born in Bohemia in 1883 and came to America in 1894. He has designed and illustrated many books and has created a considerable list of individual prints in a variety of techniques.

Composed, printed and bound by
The Haddon Craftsmen, Inc.,
Scranton, Pennsylvania
Typography and binding by Golda Fishbein